Equine welfare

Equine welfare

Marthe Kiley-Worthington

J. A. Allen
London

British Library cataloguing in publication data
A catalogue record for this book is available from
the British Library

ISBN 0 85131 704 9

Published in Great Britain in 1997 by
J. A. Allen & Company Limited
1, Lower Grosvenor Place
London, SW1W 0EL

Typeset by Textype Typesetters, Cambridge
Printed in Hong Kong by Duh Hua Printing Press Co. Ltd

Edited by Susan Beer
Designed by Nancy Lawrence

To Carif, son of Crysthannah Royal and Calif
1979–96

Contents

Acknowledgements

I must thank first the equines, some of whom have been my mentors, my friends and companions, my work partners and my stimulants for writing this book. Over the years they have pointed out to me their problems, and what might be done about at least some of them.

My partner, Chris Rendle, has constantly encouraged me to continue working and thinking, and taken on the everyday work to allow me time. He has been a sounding block for ideas, putting up with my difficulties and frustrations at every stage, and an enduring source of help; even though he did go to sleep over the final reading of the manuscript!

Thank you to Rosie Brindley for her help in editing and typing. Many people have critically read different parts, including Mike Mews, Theresa Wright, Kate Rawls, Debs Anstey, Delith Jones, to all of whom I am grateful. The remaining inaccuracies and mistakes have to be mine.

The finance for the research and writing of this book was provided by Little Ash Eco-Farm and Animal Behaviour Consultants, and the animals of the farm, to whom I am very grateful.

Introduction

It was a cold half dawn as the alarm rang and I extracted my late teenage body from warm coverlets in the landlady-run grooms' quarters where I had to pay for the privilege of mucking out and grooming horses at a British Horse Society approved stable. One glance out of the window displayed the never-ending-wonder shapes and sun-glitter of the early morning frost on the empty paddocks across the road. I looked forward to another early morning mucking out stables and concrete-sweeping before a huge greasy delicious breakfast of fried bread and eggs liberally plastered with tomato ketchup. At this ceremony, not only the 'girls' (the working pupils were always female) would be at breakfast, but sometimes the large fierce (female) 'stable manager' and even the ex-Spanish Riding School Instructor, Mr Hall, who would occasionally put in an appearance to banter in his quaint Germanesque English (a carefully cultivated accent to indicate such a distinguished background). His brief appearance was always accompanied by a respectful hush in stable talk.

This was over thirty years ago at the stables owned by, at that time, one of the only exponents of the Spanish Riding School teaching in Britain. I wonder occasionally as I walk around similar yards now, if things have changed much, or at all on the human front; I know they have not on the horse front because that is what I have been studying.

All six horses whom it was my job to 'look after' were confined to stables made on Victorian lines with bricks, mortar and solid walls isolating one horse from another, stable clocks, 'anti-weaving' bars over the doors and plush covers for saddles. The yards were run along military lines as a result of the fact

1

A typical stable yard

that horses were originally kept in stables by princes, kings and, in particular, the army.

We would spend around ten hours a day doing jobs, most of which seemed to have little or no reason or utility for either horse or human. The original function of most of these pastimes developed in the stable yard was to keep the privates busy and off the streets; to ensure they were under the officers' disciplinary control the majority of the time and so had little time for drinking and whoring. It would seem unreasonable in 1960, never mind 1997, to continue to run stable yards the same way when there are no privates to be kept off the streets but only enthusiastic horse-loving girls who could do with more time to read, study and learn to sort out the important from the unimportant tasks. At the yard where I was, and at every 'approved' yard today, each horse has to be mucked out each morning. This means searching through all the straw (piling it to the sides) to find any mucky or wet bits, which are removed. The floor is then swept before the straw is replaced. The 'correct way' to construct a horse's bed, is to pile more straw around the walls than in the middle, and to plait the new straw at the door. Serious damage would be done to your ear drums, and your day's enjoyment, by the 'yard manager' if this were not done as required! I don't think we suffered particularly from this treatment; perhaps it was all part of growing up, but one thing we were taught, just like the Light Brigade, was 'not to question why'. . . in fact you failed your examinations if you did.

It only took a few weeks before (even at the age of seventeen) I, like a host of youngsters before and since, began to ask myself why it was done this way. At the end of the day was it really true that both the horses and the grooms were enjoying this life and did all this *really* enhance the horses' welfare? Even if this was believed to be the case, was this *in fact* correct from the horses' point of view? Did anyone know? To what extent were these horses benefiting from being kept spotlessly clean, in single isolated boxes, competing in world-class events and never larking together in the frosty fields? Were emotional concerns of importance to the horses (as they clearly were to the grooms), and were they able to demonstrate any affection, enjoyment, delight, fun in their association with humans, or only aggression, dislike, annoyance and frustration? Was it all a question of domination of the horse by humans, followed by a constant enforcement of one's own will over the horses who will, as almost every horse owner will tell you, 'try to outdo you, and get away with it'?

Horses as a rule appeared to be used for the advancement of the humans, either socially or economically. Yet, the talk in the tack room where the working students, grooms and stable managers met, gossiped and drank instant coffee out of rather sticky mugs, was always about the individual personalities of their charges, about their likes and dislikes, their mannerisms, their emotions, their beauty and awfulness. It was almost identical to the talk in the cloakrooms of a girls' boarding school, only some of the time the grooms were talking about horses not other girls or teachers. Surely the humans were there not just for their own personal advancement, socially or economically, but primarily because of their emotional attachment: fondness for horses. The question which remained, however, was whether the way things were done enhanced the *horses'* enjoyment and quality of life, or not. If not, then things must change.

Horses attract so many people. This is often believed to be because of the status and money traditionally associated with them, the fame and fortune, the possibilities of winning competitions, the historic views of them as being the playthings of princes and kings. Another reason often given is the thrill and risk of galloping around leaping over jumps, the attraction of humans to danger; the adrenalin surge. Or is it the beauty of their silky shimmering skins, the proportions of their bodies, the glories of their movement and the elegance of their heads that attracts many of us into lifelong servitude? But, does it have to be a servitude? Even if it does, is it a servitude that is of benefit to the horse, or is it the result of traditional human beliefs, and sometimes detrimental to the welfare of the horse? Surely, we should live with horses so that both human and horse benefit, and neither is indebted to the other, in a symbiotic association characterised by cooperation.

These were the questions that began to trouble me on that first two-month exposure to the establishment horse-management and training practices at Robert Hall's up-market training centre near Slough in the south of Britain. I had come from Africa, and although the British Cavalry influence had been there, it somehow had been diluted by the African sun and culture.

This book attempts to answer some of these questions and raises many others. It is the result of my research over the last thirty years or so. It is meant to make the horse owner, the animal liberationist, the trainer, the groom, the racegoer, the farrier, the veterinarian, the fox-hunting enthusiast or picketer, or any thoughtful human, examine their beliefs and behaviour, and to help us all progress in our understanding of, and relationship with the horse.

Although it is sometimes difficult to re-examine what we have been taught and practised, particularly if we have been doing this for years, nevertheless, now is the time. This book will attempt to be an exercise in rational thinking; to examine carefully how we keep, relate to, teach horses, and what we do with them. Are we *sure* we have got it right from the equine's point of view? What evidence have we either way, and what can be done about it if we are not treating our horses as well as we might?

We have been conducting practical experiments and tests on different ways of keeping and teaching equines on our experimental farm and stud over the last thirty years. We will examine some of the successes, and some of the failures, to help develop ideas for improved associations with horses, and suggest where the limits should be drawn from the horses' point of view. The book is critical of current establishment horse husbandry and training practices, but also I hope, seriously constructive. It is to help us all face the future with our horses with compromise, thoughtfulness, a lack of hypocrisy and concern for the flourishing of both ourselves and our horses; to help us build, in Aristotelian terms, a more 'virtuous life together'.

It is not the first time that many of the arguments about what is cruel, and what constitutes 'good welfare' have been brought together from a number of disciplines. It is, however, the first time these arguments have been assessed and applied to one species group and its management and training, in this case: equines. Because of this, I am hoping that it will be of interest not only to those caught up with equines, but also to those involved in any way with debates about animal welfare.

Part 1

Equine welfare and how we measure it

1

A brief history of ideas

There is no doubt that equine welfare is a complex subject, and needs careful thought. A brief review of the history of ideas on animal welfare will show where the thinking has arrived now, and how we might progress.

Horses have been in association with humans for between 5 and 8,000 years; some of their bones have been found near early human settlements and farms in the 'fertile crescent', the area between the Tigris and Euphrates rivers now in present-day Syria and Iraq. These early humans not only hunted horses, but raised and kept them to ride and do draught work. The horse was first domesticated, came into contact with, and became familiar with humans probably as a result of being hunted and killed by these early humans. Some of the mares killed had foals, and these might have been raised by the humans, perhaps initially for fun, but later they had their uses for transport, draught and recreation (see Kiley-Worthington 1987 for a fuller account).

Raising young animals in the home generally results in emotional bonds being formed between the humans and the animals . . . they become familiar with and often fond of one another. When humans were raising foals, perhaps some might even have suckled them if they were very young; people certainly suckled piglets and in some parts of New Guinea they still do.

As a result these early hominids would have been aware of the foal's 'sentience', that is his ability to experience pain and pleasure and have other feelings. In the process of raising and associating with these young animals emotional attachment would have developed at least sometimes between the human and the foal, and vice versa. Once emotional attachments arise

9

between individual humans (or humans and other creatures), then a concern for the other's welfare also arises. Anyone who is fond of the foal, cares what happens to him, and begins to consider what s/he and other humans should or should not do in relation to equines. . . begins to consider equine welfare. We can safely assume, then, that a concern for equine welfare by humans began with the initial contact between them, that is domestication. Because no books were written, we can only guess at the attitude to equine welfare at this time. There is, however, a considerable oral tradition still extant among various human cultures concerning their attitudes to equines and their moral beliefs about how to behave towards them. One of the best known of these, at present, is the West's growing understanding of the culture of certain groups of American Indians which was founded on respect for other sentient (feeling) beings (and even objects) in the environment. Once this respect arises, a moral code develops concerning what should and should not be done or allowed to happen. This, in turn, leads to the development of environmental ethics and concerns about animal welfare.

A concern with animal welfare is not therefore something that is new; every culture which has had to do with animals must have had a series of beliefs about this, although they have varied greatly. The ancient Greeks for example not only considered that the horse and other equines must be physically and emotionally comfortable, but that the horse must also 'understand' what the rider/trainer is asking of him (Xenophon 350 BC). In fact Aristotle (320 BC) considered a 'virtuous life' (a good and fulfilling life) to be a life that ensured that the being was able to fulfil the *telos* of his species, the horseness of the horse or the donkeyness of the donkey. Aristotle applied the *telos* notion quite generally.

The next important step in the thinking about animal welfare came perhaps with the development of Christianity. Christianity put forward the idea that God created humans in his image and that they had certain unique characteristics, one of which was a soul that other animals did not have. This was one factor that seems to have been very important in the rise of the belief in the differences between humans and other animals. Modern scholars debate whether this was what the Bible and Christ actually said, or the way it has been interpreted. Some argue that even if there is such a difference, it is the Christian's duty to be a 'good steward' and look after other living beings well (Attfield 1983).

The next well-known and important landmark which followed on from this was the work of Descartes (1596–1650) who, because he believed that the only thing he could be sure of was his own mental existence 'cogito ergo sum' – 'I think therefore I am' – maintained that what appeared to be feelings in other animals were illusion; they were just physiological responses. In fact, he argued that one could not be sure that anything at all existed until we had much more convincing evidence than just that of our senses, because the interpretation of what we perceive is coloured by our personal interpretation, and therefore may be illusion. This sceptical questioning idea was taken up widely and became the foundation of the 'scientific revolution' and what has been called the 'scientific method'. This maintains that we cannot be sure of anything, however commonplace and apparently obvious, until it has been proved to be the case by experimental tests, with empirical results. Thus it was (and still is in some places) maintained that until there was more concrete evidence of pain (and other feelings) in animals than just what their behaviour denoted, we cannot be sure that they really *feel* pain or any other emotion.

Descartes also argued strongly for a division between the mind and the body. Humans, he argued, had bodies like other animals, but they also had 'minds' because they had souls. Other animals did not have minds or souls. He was prepared to assume that other humans had feelings but, according to his own thesis, even this is difficult to justify. It has generated the 'problem of other minds' . . . how can we have knowledge about the mental states of others? What goes on in 'other minds' even if they are human and, even more difficult, what goes on in other species' minds, equines' for example?

It was possible, according to Descartes, to consider that other humans had feelings, because they had souls, could think rationally and had language. During Descartes's time, and for a long time afterwards (in fact the same attitudes are held today by some scientists, e.g. Iggo 1984), this belief helped to legitimise almost anything being done to animals, often in the name of science; dogs were dissected alive and conscious to show how the blood system worked, and so on. Since they could not feel, there was no moral obligation not to cause pain or suffering. However not all were convinced of these arguments, for example, Voltaire (1764). Indeed, the wife of one of Descartes's colleagues is said to have left him to fund the first anti-vivisection society, after she found him vivisecting the family dog!

The rapid spread of Descartes's ideas in relation to the treatment of animals does seem curious since Europe at that time was predominantly agricultural; most humans were familiar with and had daily to do with a variety of animals and must have had some 'common sense' awareness that animals did appear to have feelings and suffer, just like our 'common sense' understanding of when other humans feel pain. The spread of the Cartesian (as Descartes's position is known) view of animals is particularly surprising since it was in France that, previously, animals had not only been recognised as having feelings, but had been granted moral responsibility! Pigs were tried for killing babies and sentenced. Thus, animals were considered not only capable of feeling things but were also held to be responsible for their actions and could be punished if they did not behave morally (Adams 1960).

Perhaps the Cartesian position was widely adopted because it was often convenient: it is sometimes easier not to recognise the animal in pain as it is killed, or the animal suffering from lack of food, water or shelter (Rollin 1989). The rapid and wide adoption of this attitude also helped to make the distinction between animals and humans greater. This position is vital as it allows humans to behave towards other animals in ways which would be morally unacceptable if applied to themselves, for example, to raise animals to be killed and eaten, and to exploit and to use animals in many different ways which is not to their advantage. In order to justify this there has to be a clear distinction made between animals and humans. This Cartesian/Judeo-Christian attitude to animals has been the predominant one in Western cultures since (see Singer 1976, chapter 5, for further discussion of this).

Since Descartes, there have been many thinkers and scholars who have written on the issue of animals and their welfare. It has not always been maintained that animals don't feel, even in Western culture. However, the belief in the *difference* between humans and all other animals has been generally maintained, and even grown with the urbanisation of humans and their increasing lack of exposure to other animals.

This is particularly surprising since Darwin's (1809–82) theory of evolution, which has been adopted by scientists (and many theologians), is founded on the idea of continuation between species; that is that the same general rules apply to all living things. Scientists have been (and some of them still are) the chief exponents of 'Cartesian logic' as it has been called, sometimes holding irrational views as a result. They, like all of us, reflect their cultural heritage.

One example is the rationale given by scientists for using animals for physiological experimentation. They argue that by so doing, because of the *similarities* physiologically between humans and other animals, they will learn more about the way the human works without having to cause pain and thus learn more about the curing of human diseases. Few pause to ask if they are so similar, then why is it acceptable to experiment on animals when demonstrably causing pain, suffering and death, when it is not acceptable to do this on humans? The response from the 'scientists' may be that, although animals are *physiologically* similar, *behaviourally* they are not; they cannot feel or have mental functions like us humans so even if they suffer or feel pain, it is not the same sort of thing (Iggo 1984). This argument of course represents Descartes's belief in the split between Body and Mind. Yet scientists working on behaviour and 'the mind' have also used animals as experimental subjects to learn more about the human mind. In the search to discover how learning works for example, rats, mice and pigeons have been used, suffered and sometimes killed by the thousands, just as they have for experimental work on physiology, genetics and pathology. Of course, there is little doubt that there has been much discovered about behaviour from this research which has been of benefit to humans, and possibly here and there to some animals. Yet it does illustrate the scientists' inconsistent approach. On the one hand the scientist has generally reckoned that the animals were similar to human animals, on the other (where it was less convenient to hold this view), they are held to be different. An inconsistency that is not compatible with the rational approach is supposed to be the basis of the scientific method! (See Rollin 1989).

Philosophers, since ethics and morals are part of their business, have been rather more critical of almost every position taken on these issues. One interest of philosophers is also the philosophy of science and in whether, and how, claims to knowledge can be justified. One of the early philosophers who was widely read and had much influence in beginning to alter the general public's attitude to animals and their welfare was Salt (1851–1939, book 1980). Perhaps the benchmark book on equine welfare was *Black Beauty* (Sewell 1877), written by a young woman who had become extremely concerned about the current ethics of equine welfare in the nineteenth century, when horses were used by humans for a great variety of activities including being the major source of energy for agriculture, transport and fighting wars, as well as being associated with human status and recreation (e.g. fox-hunting and racing). This well-written, tear-jerking story became a best seller, and the fact that it is still sold, read and feature and television films are made of it, indicates its continued impact. There were many people who felt like Anna Sewell at that time. The result was to spark off a rethink about equine and other animal welfare issues which in turn started the formulation of laws concerning animal welfare in Britain.

After the second world war there was a shortage of food in Europe and Britain in particular. Large sums of government money were deployed to encourage increases in food production by providing government agricultural services and economic incentives to individual farmers. The expense and excessive use of resources was considered of little consequence at that time since the priority was to produce more food and a more varied diet for the people of Britain. Large-scale use of energy, fertilisers, and other inputs were actively encouraged and aided by grants to individual food producers. One of the major effects of this was the development and construction of methods of husbandry and buildings to house much greater numbers of animals in a smaller area for human food than had ever been raised before.

In part, as a result of science having been interpreted in a Cartesian way and scientists having been educated into that way of thinking (that is, that even higher mammals did not feel pain or suffer in a way we could relate to) intensive animal husbandry developed and took off as a profitable 'modern and progressive' way of keeping animals and making money in agriculture. This, even though the food so produced is often economic only because of grant aid, is very wasteful of resources and in real terms inefficient (see Kiley-Worthington

1993). The strength of this belief was evident when veterinarians, who swear to relieve animal suffering in their hippocratic oath on graduation, went along with these developments without question. It was a London housewife, Ruth Harrison, who alerted the public to what was happening in her very important book *Animal machines* (1964). Ruth Harrison's book generated so much public concern that the government in Britain was forced to appoint a committee to investigate the allegations. The result was the Brambell report (1965).

A few years later, these investigations were followed by Peter Singer's *Animal liberation* (1976) in which he argued that sentient (feeling) beings suffered often for what he called 'trivial reasons' (for money or to produce food for humans that was necessary for survival or good living) and that this was unethical. He also pointed out that if the basis for making a distinction between animals and humans in the way they were treated was made on grounds of the humans' greater sense of self-awareness and greater intellectual/cognitive abilities, and their use of language, then what about the mentally handicapped humans and infants who are not able to do maths or talk? If language and the ability to do advanced cognitive exercises with the mind differentiated humans from other mammals, then surely it would be justified to assume the handicapped cannot suffer either. This book, and several others published in Britain and the United States about the same time (e.g. Clarke 1978, Rollin 1981, Reagan 1982, Midgley 1983), alerted public thinking and enlivened the debates.

These debates continue in government. Further legislation on grounds of animal welfare has resulted, and continues now in the EEC. One piece of legislation which has recently hit the headlines and resulted in much public action was the banning of the raising of calves in individual pens or crates in Britain (although it continues in other parts of the EEC) without outlawing the export of calves for this to happen to them elsewhere. Another relevant debate is the outlawing of the export of live equines under a certain price in order to avoid equines being exported to be killed for meat in other European countries. This legislation the horse-interested public have managed to force through parliament. The acceptance of this 'special status' of equines, at least in the public's mind, is well illustrated by this law. Why is it acceptable to eat cattle, sheep, pigs and so on and export them live to kill when it is not for horses? Is there a fundamental difference between equines and these other higher mammals which ensures that they must be considered differently? If so what is this? In case the reader believes that Britain is more concerned about animal welfare, it must be pointed out that laws are being passed in Switzerland and various other European countries which go further than those in Britain at present, for example laws to outlaw battery cages for hens, or the keeping of sows in sow stalls.

The animal welfare debates are now so commonplace that it is difficult for anyone who has anything at all to do with animals to escape them. One might believe that one looks after the animals one has well and correctly, yet whoever you are, sooner or later you will be exposed to people who think otherwise about your animal management. It is time that the equine interested public as well as farmers, pet keepers, zoos, circuses, and laboratory animal keepers thought seriously about what they do, why, how and whether it could be improved.

There is an emerging 'political correctness' concerning one's attitude to animals and what should happen to them. For example it is 'politically incorrect' at present in much of Britain, and the United States, to consider that performing animals in aquaria or circuses, are acceptable, however they are trained or kept and for whatever reason. Instead of the animal being considered a robot-like creature with no feelings, he is now considered to be almost exactly like a human who can suffer and even 'lose dignity', and on the other hand, something so alien that he must not be involved with humans at all but live out there in the 'wild yonder', the lovely, 'perfect' natural world, despite the recognition that it is, in fact, bloody in tooth and claw. It is politically correct to be devoted to the preservation of species, and often to have as little as possible to do with animals, particularly wild animals.

Part of the dogma is that it is becoming more widely assumed that, like works of art, the 'natural world' is precious and marvellous, but any interference by man will inevitably be destructive. This view loses sight of the fact that humans are part of the living world too. It is what I have called *animal apartheid* and is becoming increasingly widely held. It is applied mainly to wild animals (those that have not lived in association with humans and had their breeding controlled by humans) equines such as zebras, onagers, wild asses. More and more the same arguments are also being applied to domestic animals, by, for example, those opposed to dogs in towns, to the use of horses by the police, to hunting, to racing, to cats or any other animal/human association.

To date, it is those who have to do with laboratory animals and intensively raised farm animals to whom most of the attention has been addressed by the public, but pet owners are not exempt. Horse owners in the developed countries have, to date, had relatively little public attention directed at their husbandry. In developing countries, however, where equines are still one of the major sources of energy for transport and work, equine welfare has, with the help of donations from developed countries, taken a higher profile than for example that of dogs, or other farm animals. There are now international conferences and aid programmes directed at discussing measures to improve the lot of the working equine (Fielding and Pearson 1991, and Proceedings of the Conference on Working Equines, Rabat, Morocco 1994).

As a result of public pressure, money has been made available for scientific research on animal welfare. Some of this has led to further understanding, and we do now have some agreement that animals can and do feel pain, and on how to measure suffering (see chapter 3). However, there has, as yet, been relatively little financed research directed to developing *optimal environments* for equines, or any other species.

Since this book is about equine welfare, our object is to develop detailed guidelines for the establishment of the best 'equine-friendly' environments based on the knowledge we have at present, and rational discussion of many relevant ideas.

Apart from my real concern for equines and how they live, they are in this book also being used as a 'test case' to look at what goes on in the husbandry, training and use of one group of higher mammals who are used and kept for a great variety of purposes by humans, and some of whom also still exist in the wild. Equines are of particular interest because they are often considered to be playthings and not maintained 'just for money'. The result is that the relatively low economic importance, indeed even economic cost of horses, aids many people sincerely to believe that they are looking after and working their equines with great concern for their welfare. But have they got it right, as far as the equine is concerned?

Although some of the discussions here will relate exclusively to equines, nevertheless, the debates concerning many of the practices in the husbandry, training and use of them are also relevant to other mammals be they cattle, pigs, sheep, dogs, lions or elephants. Equines are therefore being used as a test case for the development of guidelines to improve well-being and quality of life of all creatures and that of the humans associated with them, now and in the future: to develop a symbiotic association which is of advantage to both. One current idea gaining much ground amongst sections of the urban public in particular, is that *we really should not have animals at all because inevitably they will suffer when coming in contact with humans,* and in addition they will have to behave *unnaturally* which in itself is considered by the exponents of this view to cause suffering (Reagan 1982). *Animal apartheid* has resulted in extreme positions being taken on both sides. In relation to equines this applies to opposition to fox- and stag-hunting, circuses and zoos and so on, with violence being committed by humans on both sides of the fence, resulting in little except further entrenchment of views.

The majority of readers of this book who are interested in equines will find animal apartheid a very unpalatable idea, as I do myself. My reasons are:

(a) I do not believe that contact with humans *inevitably* has to cause prolonged suffering to equines, or other animals for that matter.

(b) It does of course depend how the equines are looked after, managed and trained. Done well (however this is), this contact can be an enriching experience: it can improve *the quality of life of the humans* certainly, and possibly of the equines too.

(c) Is doing unnatural things necessarily bad and going to reduce the quality of life for human or animal? After all humans learn to read and write and we all agree that they should do. This is not *natural* but it is considered to enrich life. Correctly done, so that there is no suffering, learning different and new things could presumably also enrich the life of equines . . . unless of course they do not have a mind and cannot learn things.

On the other hand we must take some of the arguments for animal apartheid seriously, or we may find that legislation will

The author lecturing her friend, Oberlik, who has a suitable reaction!

Talking with Oberlik.

further control our ability to keep and work with horses. We must seriously assess whether or not our animals are suffering in the environments in which they are living, and whether or not the things they are taught *do* increase or decrease the quality of their lives.

First, we will examine the current attitudes to, and ways of treating equines.

(1) *Parasitism* This is where one partner benefits (usually the human) at the cost of the other (the equine), where the animals are suffering for prolonged periods as a result of the way they are kept or worked. Then the human is parasitic on the horse and if equines are considered 'sentient', this is not an acceptable relationship and an 'animal apartheid' approach might be better. Is this the case in modern equine management? I argue in the following chapters that it very often is; that much of the establishment teaching on how to look after horses is misguided and actually induces suffering, and consequently results in a parasitic relationship between humans and horses. However, does this need to be the case, can things change so that it is not, and if so in what direction? They can, and we discuss how in this chapter.

Equally, sometimes the human is disadvantaged by the horse; not only is she bucked off and bruised or even killed, but also she may allow herself to work long hours when she does not want to; to rush back and forth doing this or that, to keep and protect the horse when this does not result in the enrichment of her life. For example she may be neglecting her children or spouse – all of whom she is fond of. The difference is that usually the human has a choice and can extract herself from the situation (although this is not always achieved). As a result of her cultural background and education in matters equine, she may not realise she does have a choice and so continues to live a life of drudgery, believing that the equine needs her diligence and sacrifice and because she 'loves' the horses so. A very Northern European Calvinistic but common approach – Calvin believed that humans were put on this earth to suffer and only through suffering would pleasure (and a place in heaven) be earned.

Just as common is the situation where even though the human does have a life of drudgery, financial hardship and physical strain, looking after her horses the way she does –

nevertheless this is willingly endured for other benefits.

Slavery is often considered one type of parasitism; one living to the disadvantage of the other. In the case of slaves, they were housed and fed, often not very well, and in return had to work but received no other benefit from their owners. In particular they were not free to come and go as they wished, should they wish, and thus it was argued, suffered.

Is this the relationship we have with our equines? It is perhaps the most common one. The equines are certainly not often free to come and go as they wish, or even free to perform all the behaviour in their repertoire. Although they may not show obvious signs of suffering (wounds and illnesses, or being hit, and so on), it would often be difficult to argue that the quality of their life was *better* than if they were not with humans. But is this inevitable?

Slavery also has another side. Some slaves, after being released from their enforced attachment and association with their masters, did not rush off, but preferred to stay with their existing status (that is working for board and lodging and not money). What they gained from this association was security, and some of them had, it seems, become fond of their masters and did not want to quit; they felt they needed to stay and to help. Is this an unhealthy, unnatural choice, does it just reflect the outrageousness of slavery, or are there other considerations here? In other words is 'slavery' always bad for the slave? Again, this is something to consider for our equines and other animals we have living with us.

(2) *Commensalism* is another type of relationship between species which is found in living systems. This is where the two species get along more or less but where the relationship is not to either's advantage. Again, this is a common relationship between equines and humans. Neither benefits much, and any benefits there are, are offset by the disadvantages. For example, the horses cost a lot to keep, they are sometimes fun to ride, but sometimes a nuisance and the whole thing dangerous or unpleasant. From the horses' point of view they are regularly fed and watered, but have to live in restricted dull conditions with occasional trips, sometimes unpleasant experiences, and heavy-handed human treatment. The equine may not show evidence of distress, but he may not show much evidence of pleasure either (see chapter 6).

Symbiosis

(3) *Symbiosis* This is the relationship that we would all like, one where both partners benefit and have enriched lives in one way or another. The majority of people who have horses (even when they ring me up to consult me concerning a behavioural problem of their horse!) will seriously believe that this is the relationship *they* have with their horses. It is not always easy to say 'Are you sure from the horse's point of view that he is benefiting and happy?'

One way of knowing when this has *not* been achieved is if the equines show evidence of 'stress' or 'distress' (see chapter 4). They should *also* show some signs of positively 'enjoying themselves' (see 'pleasure', chapter 6), and so should the human, which is not always the case for either in some stable yards or competitions.

Inevitably as with any relationship, the horse/human relationship may swing between parasitism, commensalism and symbiosis, but we would all like it to be settled more towards 3 than 1. Does this happen, how can we measure it, and how could it happen more? In particular how do we know when it has happened, when do we have a *symbiotic relationship* with our horses?

The first criteria that should be met are those dictated by

evolution. The equine is a large mammal who has evolved to cope with a certain physical and social life. Exactly what this is was the subject of my last book (Kiley-Worthington 1987). The equine also has evolved a brain and a mind and consequently has some intellectual/cognitive needs. Superimposed on basic evolutionary needs are *the lifetime experiences* of the individual equine. Different individuals will find different types of lifestyle/management and training more or less acceptable because of these.

These are the main considerations we must make in trying to achieve a symbiotic relationship with our equines. There are also of course individual genetic make ups, and perhaps breed differences which will allow for more or less adaptation to different conditions. But we must be careful here not to use a breed or genetic difference to excuse our husbandry or training which may not be in line with the other evolutionary or past experience needs of a particular horse. This is very often done: 'Oh, what do you expect, he is an Arab' or 'You can't teach a thoroughbred to work on the land.' Every living thing is the result of both its genes and its environment, but it is not very helpful to put things that go wrong down to the animal's breeding.

It is curious that, although recognising that humans and other animals have similar biochemistry, and are controlled by the same genetic rules, nevertheless we now *do not* use such arguments to attribute causes to human behaviour – these would be racist or sexist arguments. It is no longer generally accepted that because someone is black, or yellow, female or what you will that he/she will be stupid, erratic, unreliable, emotional etc. It is generally understood that the problems that the human might have, whether behavioural, psychological or even physical may be the result of 'nurture'; the result of upbringing, the environment in which he has had to live: his home, his school, his neighbourhood, and are not just because he is of a certain race or sex. Yet it is still quite acceptable to say that 'arab horses are scatty', 'all so and so's offspring are aggressive' and so on, however they have been brought up, or whatever they may have learnt from humans or each other.

Equines do not have unvarying lifetime experiences any more than humans do. The preconceived notions people may have concerning the behaviour of a particular breed, sex or type of horse often ensure that they behave in ways which will make certain that these notions become true. The human has certain expectations, behaves in certain ways and conveys messages to the horse, often through body language and visual cues, which cause the equine to behave in the expected way. For example, if you are told before you approach a horse's box 'be careful he bites', you approach the box more cautiously, tense and ready to react in whatever way you have decided. The horse sees you coming, reads these signs, and interprets this, in a way which results in him trying to bite you. He may, for example, react to slight tenseness and fear with fear and defensive threat, which may involve biting you. In addition he has learnt that it works, if he bites, people go away and take their anxiety elsewhere.

Pre-conceived notions or ideas are those that have been decided on before an individual is encountered. They may have been established as a result of being taught something as 'fact' and therefore not actually examining the truth. They may have become part of the traditional folklore – and unquestionably accepted as correct – just the way it has always been done. They may also arise as a result of the experience of the human during his/her lifetime – and not thereafter, examined. Interestingly enough although it is the horses who often suffer as a result of human 'preconceived notions' – equines also develop them. One bad experience with a trailer will give the animal the 'preconceived notion' that all trailers are dangerous and to be avoided. Even the preconceived notion of one horse can infect others – just as in humans! One sees another refusing to load, and refuses himself.

We do know when we have got it *wrong* and the equine is *not* in a symbiotic relationship with humans. We can for example measure how long he lives (one index of an increasing standard and quality of life used for humans). We can now also measure prolonged stress and distress, and we can assess the frequency of disease and the use of surgery, drugs and so on to attempt to overcome these problems – all evidence for all not being well (part I). We can look at what goes on in the way the animals are kept, the way they are trained and the uses they are put to to assess when and where there is distress or pleasure, and make suggestions of how to change things to increase the chances of symbiosis with equines (parts II and III) and finally we can draw up some guidelines on how the 'optimal equine friendly environment' would be, and try it out (part III).

2

Should we use equines?

The immediate question that may occur to those who think about these issues is that if equines are sentient, feeling beings, who have emotions and desires and needs, even if these are not identical with those of humans, should they not be given equal consideration to humans (see Singer 1976 and De Grazia 1996 for further discussion of this). Since current evidence suggests that we are much more similar to equines, even cognitively than we thought (see chapter 7), should we then be using them at all for our own ends? The riding of them, the using of them to transport things, to cultivate and grow food for us or even for themselves, might not be acceptable if they are to be awarded equal status with humans.

The first consideration here, as it would be for humans, is whether these activities cause the animals to suffer, cause them *pain* and/or *distress?* If this is the case, and it is a characteristic of the activity – for example, the riding of them will *of its nature* cause prolonged suffering (e.g. injury to the back or the legs, over-tiredness and shorter lives), then we can argue that it certainly is wrong – morally incorrect – to do this. This is an argument that must be faced, not swept away by the horse-owning/using public. It involves looking at the various ways in which equines are ridden, driven and used, in order to assess whether it is necessarily the case that this using of them (never mind the keeping of equines), is morally acceptable. We examine this in the following chapters (chapters 3 and 4).

Here we are considering all equines, not just domestic horses and donkeys, and this brings in the issue of 'domestication'. Because the effect of domestication on the morphology (body) of many animals is very obvious (body size differences, coat colour changes etc.), it is widely believed that there are fundamental genetic behavioural differences between even closely related wild and domestic animals. This has been discussed in my previous book (Kiley-Worthington 1987 chapter 1; 1990b chapter 7). There is growing evidence that the effects of domestication have not been to change genetically fundamental behaviours, for example, social organisation, maternal behaviour, communication, sexual behaviour, eating habits and habitat preferences, and, as far as we know to date, the basic cognition of the animal. However, as already pointed out, lifetime experiences are *crucial* to how the equine (or any other mammal) adapts to different situations, how he behaves towards humans, what he learns and almost every aspect of his behaviour.

Since this is the case, making distinctions between our treatment of animals that are traditionally 'wild', even though they may have been born in captivity, as opposed to 'domestic' on grounds of their genetic behavioural differences is illogical. The different lifetime experiences will control the majority of their fundamental behavioural differences. Thus there is no evidence that statements such as 'zebras are very difficult to train' or 'horses must be kept in stables because they are domestic' are anything but widely held beliefs which are not supported by any evidence.

However, despite the lack of evidence for the belief that we should treat wild animals differently from domestic ones (even if the 'wild' animal was born in central London and the 'domestic' animal born in the outback of Australia) nevertheless it remains part of our 'cultural belief system'. We may like it better that way, and consider that an infringement of his natural being and behaviour is worse for the former than the latter, but this does, in fact, depend on the conditions under which each is kept. It does not depend on whether or not such an animal is usually wild or has had 5,000 years of domestication. Thus there appears to be no reason to make assumptions concerning what we should or should not do with different members of the equine group. If we can justify training and riding one type, then, provided we are not causing suffering and are keeping the animals (whether domestic or 'wild') under conditions that are both ecologically and ethologically sound (see chapters 19 and 20), then it is acceptable for any member of the tribe; but the question here is can we justify using any of them at all?

There may be a case for recreating a 'natural world' for some of them as is being attempted for the Przevalsky horses in Russia and France. The efforts made to conserve the Exmoor and Dartmoor ponies in Britain is another example. But is this the only way all equines should live?

Should we interfere with another sentient being (human or non-human, wild or domestic), teach or educate him, even if we do it well and in a way which he finds pleasurable? Because, this is, after all, an infringement of his natural being and behaviour. Is it therefore undesirable and an imposition?

If we adopt this attitude for humans in our everyday lives it would mean ensuring that the 'natural' personality and behaviour of each individual would not be encouraged to adapt and fit in with the existing conditions and society, even for pleasurable experiences and long-term benefits. In other words, 'cultural' experiences and education would not exist. It would not seem to be a desirable approach to foster the development of a 'fulfilling' life for a human. Why then is it considered the only acceptable way for equines (or other species) to live?

It might be argued that since the young human is of the same species as those teaching, manipulating and culturally indoctrinating her, this is acceptable, but if it were an equine, a wolf, a whale or a dolphin doing this, this would not be acceptable. Yet, provided each species also has contact with his own, it is clear that there are many humans who certainly have had their lives enriched by being with, having emotional contacts with and having animals help them in many ways. Take for example those who are blind and have a guide dog who guides them around so that they have much more independence; or those old folk who live alone and have a cat who keeps them company and exchanges emotional experiences and attachments with them; or those who work horses or donkeys each day on the fields and develop not only deep emotional relationships with them, and would hate to be parted from them, but also are able to stay alive as a result.

If being in association with other species is desirable for humans, why should it not be for another social species – equines? Surely learning and education, from their own and other species, development of themselves as members of their own culture and to be fulfilled social sentient cognitive beings, could be as enriching for equines as for humans. It may be achieved (as with humans) by exposure to different species and different cultures as well as their own, different situations, different work and experiences.

If one is going to assume, as some argue (e.g. Wittgenstein 1953, Nagel 1974), that these animals have almost nothing in common with humans, it might be argued for no mixing with them. Even if this were the case, there seems to be little reason why we should not associate with equines, and they with us, provided that it does not necessitate suffering, with the possible outcome that our lives would be enriched and perhaps theirs too.

The problem arises in how to distinguish between what is 'interference', and what is 'education'. This is a problem not only with equines but with humans too. A teenager often argues that what the parents are insisting is 'education' (and of long-term benefit to him), is just 'interference and infringement of freedoms'.

Life itself is full of risks, problems and experiences not all of which are, or need to be enjoyable all the time. Is it better than death, even though there may be some suffering here and there? Then again, without suffering how would we recognise pleasure? Life is indeed magical, mysterious and infinitely marvellous, but to be so it must have its good and bad. It is a question of where we draw the line of what is too much, but to argue that risks, problems and unpleasant experiences must be omitted destroys what life is about.

Equines and humans, canines and dolphins, cattle, oryx and sheep, for example, have evolved to be social animals and cope with all the give and take that this involves, because in the long run it was of advantage to the survival of you, me, equines, bovines and bees. If this is the case, then why should our socialisation be restricted *only* to members of our own species? We evolved in an environment where we shared the world with other species, use and are used by other individuals (e.g. infants being looked after by mothers) and other species, even in the wild. For example, equines, a prey species, spend much of their time with other species, and gain from them in terms of finding food and water and spotting and avoiding predators, as in the case of the Burchells zebras mixing and living with gnu, Thompson gazelles and impala on the East African plains.

The limits of where interspecies *use* becomes *abuse* must be drawn, clearly. But why cannot the relationship *between*, as well

*The relationship between human and equine can be
of mutual benefit*

as *within*, species be one of mutual benefit? There are enough
examples of this in the natural world to make one realise that
this is no invention of humans, no 'unnatural' act!

Thus, I see no reason to outlaw as 'immoral acts' riding,
driving, working, or using equines in any way *provided it results
in a relationship of mutual benefit*, and no prolonged stress or
distress. Why should this not be achieved? Whether it is, or is
not, at present is another matter. Even if we are not doing very
well at this at the moment it does not mean that it cannot and
should not happen.

3

Cruelty, pain, suffering and physical stress

The first question pertinent to equine welfare, and that which has to date received the most attention (Stamp-Dawkins 1980, Rollin 1989), can be phrased: if we consider that equines are 'sentient' (feel and can suffer) *when* are they suffering? Most of us will consider this is often not too difficult a question. Indeed some readers, whom I will try to convince are wrong, will consider that this is *never* a difficult question; they *know* when equines are in pain or suffering, either because they 'know horses so well, and have had them all their lives' or because 'it is obvious, isn't it?'

Those of us who are slightly more modest and consider we can sometimes make a judgement will usually only be quite sure when these judgements are made with physical evidence: the horse has broken his leg, the donkey has been standing in mud for the last six weeks and has swollen and inflamed legs, or the pony's ribs are all sticking out, he has no flesh on his quarters and is too weak to move towards food.

We may even be cautious about whether or not the equine is definitely in pain. When he limps it is clear there must be some pain; when he has a slight digestive upset and now and then looks at his flank or kicks it, it is not quite so clear.

Pain

At a recent British Veterinary Association workshop on pain a paper was given by Chambers (1993) who admitted that for the veterinarian the recognition of pain in horses is 'almost entirely subjective'. The physiological measures of pain (e.g. increase in heart rate, release of adrenalin etc., see below) may be the result of other stimuli rather than pain (e.g. emotional states such as fear or aggression).

Equines show a large variation in the way they respond to pain, some becoming more excited, others more stoic and immobile. Chambers divides the behaviours associated with pain into mild acute, severe acute and chronic but points out what many of us know, that it is difficult to equate a particular behaviour with a particular stimulus even in a clinical situation with clinical cues. If in a clinical situation it is difficult to assess whether or not the animal is in pain (that is when he is already sick, or will be operated on) then it is more difficult at other times without these cues!

But if the equine is not feeling pain, does this mean his welfare is good? Of course not; freedom from physical pain is certainly not the only requirement any higher mammal has. Life can be very unpleasant even if there is no immediate physical pain and there is no reason to doubt this may be true for non-human mammals too. For example the starving pony who is too weak to stand up and walk out of the mud may not be in immediate pain, but she is certainly suffering. It is not uncommon to find that individuals in this type of situation appear to give up trying to survive, as if they have taken the decision that 'life is just not worth living'.

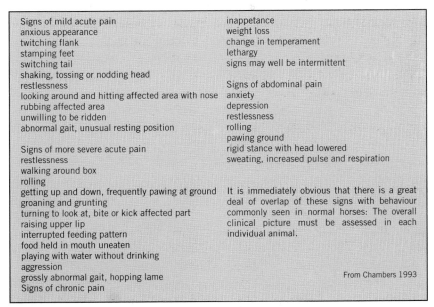

Signs of mild acute pain	inappetance
anxious appearance	weight loss
twitching flank	change in temperament
stamping feet	lethargy
switching tail	signs may well be intermittent
shaking, tossing or nodding head	
restlessness	Signs of abdominal pain
looking around and hitting affected area with nose	anxiety
rubbing affected area	depression
unwilling to be ridden	restlessness
abnormal gait, unusual resting position	rolling
	pawing ground
Signs of more severe acute pain	rigid stance with head lowered
restlessness	sweating, increased pulse and respiration
walking around box	
rolling	
getting up and down, frequently pawing at ground	It is immediately obvious that there is a great
groaning and grunting	deal of overlap of these signs with behaviour
turning to look at, bite or kick affected part	commonly seen in normal horses: The overall
raising upper lip	clinical picture must be assessed in each
interrupted feeding pattern	individual animal.
food held in mouth uneaten	
playing with water without drinking	
aggression	
grossly abnormal gait, hopping lame	From Chambers 1993
Signs of chronic pain	

Figure 3.1 Pain and distress in horses

The conditions may not be that bad, the horse may just be isolated alone in a wet field without shelter, companionship and with little food. Is he suffering? It might be mentioned that such a horse is suffering from 'stress'. . . but is it a helpful word to use? The first thing perhaps is to look at what we mean (or what we should mean if we are going to understand each other) when we say 'stress'.

Stress

The term 'stress' is very widely used in popular language and often with very confusing results. It is very frequently used to explain why the equine is behaving in a particular way: 'ah well, he is under "stress"'. Everyone nods and goes away satisfied: 'Oh, her horse was stressed, that is why it did not win'. What does that tell anyone other than that the horse did not win the competition? Stress is not an explanation, it is not even a cause, it is an *effect*.

There is no doubt that all horses in all types of environments may suffer from physiological stress. This is when there are measurable physiological changes. These were identified first by a man called Selye in 1950. They include things such as an increase in heart rate and respiration rate; various hormonal changes including raised levels of adrenalin and cortico-steroids. Selye found that many of these body changes worked together and called this set of responses which were sparked off by sudden and sometimes potentially life-threatening environmental changes (for example a sudden noise, a very hot or very cold stimulus, something very frightening appearing) the *General Adaptive Syndrome*. The idea of the GAS he suggested, and this has generally been adopted since, is that such responses were suitable responses in order to change the body so that it is able to *survive* and *cope* with such problems. The effects of physiological stress therefore are primarily to help survival and the body to adapt to difficult conditions (e.g. run away faster, circulate the blood faster and reduce the effect of a burn or a freeze; ensure increasing oxygen to allow the muscles to operate quicker and for longer).

The problem with 'stress' only comes when the kind of conditions that give rise to these responses continue for prolonged periods of time, resulting in these physiological responses continuing. These responses become life-threatening rather than life-enhancing. For example, one of the effects of prolonged stress is a reduction of the body's abilities to fight disease through its immune system, an obvious life-threatening effect. Another is changes in the excretion of various hormones that can affect the body in many ways and also dramatically affect behaviour. Another is the excretion of hydrochloric acid in the stomach giving rise to ulcers. These 'stress' effects are undesirable but they are not a cause they are an *effect*. The problem remains in identifying what in the environment is *causing* these responses, and then reduce them.

Stress is not therefore always bad news. As far as the welfare of horses or humans is concerned, what we must look for is whether there is any sign that the type of life they are leading, socially, physically, or intellectually – that is also emotionally – is causing *long-term stress*. If so then it would be sensible, in order to prolong a life of quality and improving welfare, to redesign the environment for the equine. Thus it is the long-term effect of 'stress' that has a derogatory effect, and which gives 'stress' a bad name. An ability to exhibit physiological stress effects in response to the environment is, in the short term, a life-enhancing requirement.

One of the most obvious longer-term negative effects of stress can be the frequent occurrence of disease of one sort or another. It is clear that if an animal, or human is frequently ill, there is something wrong either with the environment which is affecting the physiology, or there may be a persistent mal-function of the body. The chances of this happening are more likely when the animal has been physiologically stressed for some time. There are also, of course, genetic influences on this. Some individuals may be more or less genetically prone to the evil effects of stress.

If we are interested in equine welfare the question we must ask ourselves is 'does the environment in which I keep my equines result in them being physiologically stressed for prolonged periods?' If it does, then it would be appropriate to try and change the environment. Because of genetic differ-ences and sometimes individual past experiences, horses may react differently; thus what appears to be satisfactory for one individual may not be so for another. However we are interested in equine welfare, and must give the benefit of any doubt to the equine. Although there may be individuals who will be able to adapt to extremes of environment, the type of environment we are trying to work out for equines is that which is likely to be 'optimal for the majority'. Are there some guidelines that we can use to start with; 'General Rules' to reduce prolonged stress, and how are we going to be able to tell if our equines are suffering prolonged physiological stress?

Physical effects

Some effects are quite obvious. If the animal is in pain or suffering as a result of the types of conditions we have mentioned above (e.g. malnourished, kept short of clean water, given inappropriate food for his physiological needs and persistently in poor condition) he is more likely to succumb to disease; less likely to be able to combat normal parasitic infections, such as worms for example. Worms are the commonest and most important problem in many tropical equines who belong to poor people and are often badly nourished and overworked (Svendsen 1986). On the other hand, should the equine always be fat? Over-weight can be a major health problem to equines and humans alike. In many developed countries diseases from over-feeding, over-protection and behavioural stress are very common (see part II).

An obvious cause of prolonged stress is when the animal constantly has *wounds* and *bruises*; he may be in pain, have disease or lameness that has not been treated. Neglect of the feet so the horse is incapable of moving easily is commonly used by welfare societies to bring charges of cruelty. These types of conditions are rather extreme and as a rule there are Animal Welfare organisations whose job it is to spot and report severe cases of this nature. However there are other ways of identifying prolonged stress which may not be as obvious and may be a great deal more common even among the equines that are considered 'well kept'. In fact these may be the result of modern husbandry practices, and teaching, and not easily identified except by the thinking owner or caretaker.

One of these is *obesity* which is encouraged in show horses. There is nowadays a traditional belief in Britain and Europe that if the equine is not fat with no ribs showing at any time of the year, it is not good enough, and the horse is not 'well cared for'. There will be mutterings around the club, and the owner will lose status. Yet, the natural conditions under which horses evolved to live were not those that would keep him constantly very fat. He carried extra weight at the end of the growing season (the autumn, or wet season in the tropics) to carry him through the winter or dry season. As a result, come the spring, or the next rains, he would be relatively thin often with his ribs showing. Allowing him to be very fat throughout the year may well not be an improvement to his health and his longevity any more than overweight is for human beings, rather, in humans it is now recognised as one of the most important diseases of an over-indulgent world. It is obesity that must be guarded against much more stringently, in horses, too, if we are really interested in equine welfare. Giving prizes to grossly over-weight animals who probably never have any other exercise than trotting around the show ring must surely be wrong. . . as far as horse welfare is concerned (see chapter 13).

Another indication of 'stress' is to look at the frequency of infection. One example of this which is of much concern to stable managers are coughs and equine flu; another extremely common occurrence is lameness. Ill health and lameness are not 'just bad luck'; there are frequently identifiable causes. One of these causes may well be persistent physiological stress which has reduced the equine's ability to fight infection. This may be the case in persistent outbreaks of coughing in stabled horses. The problem then is to correct the physical, possibly social and/or intellectual environment (see below) so that the animals are no longer under prolonged stress. The person to be consulted in the first instance, is of course the veterinarian. He will be able to identify the disease and suggest improvements in the physical husbandry system so that it has less chance of occurring again. This is very unlikely to be a full assessment of the cause although it may help temporarily. The vet may also prescribe drugs to control the disease. Some caretakers may leave it at that. . . control the disease with drugs rather than try and wipe out the cause.

This brings us to another way of assessing stress in equines. How often do *drugs* have to be used and which drugs? Do the animals in one particular stable need to have as many drugs administered as another? We must also consider how much drug use is acceptable and of what type.

The purist will say that ideally, no drugs should be used, and therefore any drugs used to help cure disease or control pain are a sign of an inappropriate 'stressed' environment. Vaccines, carefully controlled treatments and inoculations to help the immune system cope with unfamiliar infections (such as the inoculation of horses against African Horse sickness in Spain in 1989) may be acceptable. But what about the inoculation of animals for equine influenza; is that a necessary and acceptable use of drugs? Or does the need for its use as a result of the constant outbreaks of coughing and equine influenza in stables indicate that the animals are physiologically stressed? This is debatable. One possibility is that the present prevalence of equine influenza is the result of a reduced activity of the immune system as a result of prolonged stress. Should then one redesign the environment or just inoculate?

The first approach is to try and control the disease. Take a common example – coughing in stabled horses. The animals are given cough medicines, sometimes antibiotics to control secondary infection. They may previously also have been vaccinated against some strains of equine influenza. However, there are also environmental causes. It is generally recognised that horses cough because they often live for twenty hours at least out of every twenty four in an enclosed stable where dust from the bed, the hay and the grooming is constantly around and where the viruses breathed out by one infected horse may well be breathed in by a neighbour who then contracts the disease. As a result, to cut down infection in the first place the animal may be even more isolated from others than he was before. But the most usual procedure is to stop feeding dry hay, feed it soaked or feed 'haylage' (silage in small bags sold very expensively). Alternatively, the horse may not be given any hay at all, but just wet feeds. The straw bed may be replaced by shavings, peat or shredded newspapers; all rather dubious solutions for a variety of reasons ecological as well as ethical. These procedures do sometimes reduce the coughing, but rarely get rid of it.

The question is not often asked if it is necessary or desirable to keep the horses in single dusty stables at all. They have not evolved to live in them and such environments may cause prolonged physiological stress to some, perhaps the majority, for physical, social and intellectual reasons. This is confirmed by the general consensus which is that horses that live outside in groups, even throughout the winter, have fewer coughs. Perhaps there is a way of reducing the 'stress' inherent in the single stabled equine as a result of his physical and psychological needs not being met. Surely this would be in the interests not only of the equines, but of the owners too.

The animals in their natural well-aired home range, eating the foods they have evolved to eat, grass and dried standing grass, are very unlikely to become infected. It is animals in stables in a dusty, maybe draughty environment, often fed foods they have not evolved to be able to cope with easily, and often isolated from their conspecific, who are most likely to contract equine influenza. These animals usually are physiologically and behaviourally distressed.

Then there are other drugs frequently used during breeding of equines: hormones, steroids, analgesics, tranquillisers, excitants and others. Are each and every one of them necessary to reduce pain and suffering, or do some of them actually cause it? Are they used to try and combat physiological stress that has been induced by inappropriate management?

What drugs are used and how frequently they are necessary, must be considered if we are going seriously to try and assess when horses are suffering the effects of physiological stress. Central to this understanding is the recognition that disease, and often accident, are not just chance random effects, but rather the result of previous treatment and the animal's present environment. Just as in humans; for example consider the plague that raged around Southern England in the fifteenth century and decimated the population. Even with this contagious deadly disease, not everyone caught it. Some survived, because of their physical, social, environmental or genetic circumstances. Now we do not have the plague and have controlled polio and whooping cough by vaccination, and wiped out small pox. . . but humans still get 'flu, colds, and many other diseases depending on these factors.

It is perfectly true that we could keep horses and humans in a zombified state of apparent nirvana with the use of appropriate drugs; why don't we do this, it would indeed obscure any stress. But is this acceptable, and if it is not why not? In the case of the equines many might argue that they don't do this because it is expensive and would grossly affect their performance at the task we keep them for. In the case of humans there are serious medical as well as ethical considerations relating to the widespread use of tranquillisers, antidepressants and the like which will not easily be resolved – but are these debates not also relevant to equines? If not, why not?

4

Behavioural stress and distress

We have discussed evidence for pain and physiological stress in equines, two possible measures of suffering which are routinely used even if there are problems associated with them. There is however another way in which suffering can be measured which is of particular importance to the majority of stabled horses. This is the possible existence, and measurement of, 'behavioural distress'. This may have its origins in either physical, emotional or intellectual inadequacies of the environment. When talking about humans, 'depression', 'sad', 'neurotic', 'pathological' are some of the words used.

It is recognised that humans can be suffering even though they may be well fed, warm, clean and not in pain, that is in a condition in which all their physical needs are catered for. However there is still the opportunity for suffering under such conditions in that there may exist emotional problems: perhaps they are isolated from companions or friends, or have to live closely with others they dislike; their babies may be taken away from them, or they are prevented from having sex, to name some possible deprivations; thus it is recognised in humans that emotional difficulties can give rise to suffering.

Humans can also suffer from mental/intellectual inadequacies in the environment. For example insufficient stimulation of the mind: boredom, or over-stimulation, or an inability to understand situations, or problems resulting in mental and emotional confusion. It appears that in order to avoid such suffering there needs to be a certain level of stimulation of the mind; too little or too much, or a high level of unpredictability in the environment leads to emotional or mental confusion. There appears to be an 'optimal level of environmental stimulation' (Welsh 1964).

There are, therefore, three areas which can give rise to suffering in humans: (1) physical, (2) emotional and (3) intellectual. These are not however necessarily separated. Either some or all of these factors can contribute to the suffering, partly because of the inter-relatedness of body and mind.

It is only in the last couple of decades that scientists have seriously begun to understand that other higher mammals, which of course include equines, as well as humans, suffer from emotional problems as well as physical ones (e.g. Kiley-Worthington 1977, Stamp-Dawkins 1980). Some philosophers have argued for animal welfare and rights on the grounds of their 'sentience' (ability to feel) for a century (e.g. Salt 1980, Reagan 1982 and Singer 1976). If higher mammals have emotions, even if these are rather different from ours, then it will surely follow that they are liable to emotional difficulties; everything will not go right all the time. Others deny animals 'rights' whilst yet admitting that they can suffer and do have emotions (Frey 1983, Leahy 1991).

More controversial at present is whether equines can have 'intellectual needs' which if not satisfied may lead to suffering. In order to have these, it must first be agreed that they have a mind (see chapter 7). I have argued that this is the case: equines have minds although these may be rather different from human, dog, whale or chimp minds. This may remain controversial for some years to come, nevertheless if we are *seriously* concerned with equine welfare, then it is necessary to give the benefit of the doubt to the equines: in other words, *if there is any chance of them having a mind, then we should assume that they have for the present.*

Those readers who have to do with horses, particularly training them, will agree that horses *have* minds. If they did not have minds, we would not be able to teach them the things we do, and they would behave the way they do with us or without. That is not to say that their minds are just like yours, or mine for that matter. Equines do often behave unpredictably when we are teaching them, and we sometimes find what they do very strange and different from the way we would have behaved in similar circumstances . . . but then having said that, most people find some other humans may behave in ways that they find extremely odd and unpredictable but do not therefore deny them a mind. We just have to admit that the ways of equines are different from yours or mine.

If the needs of their emotions and 'mind' are not fulfilled, then equines may be able to show behavioural distress. But how are we going to know, and measure this? In the last few years there has been a growing interest shown by applied ethologists (those who study animal behaviour) in assessing this, mainly as a result of the public's growing concern with animal welfare, particularly that of farm animals. How do we know if cattle in intensive stock yards or chickens in batteries are suffering when they have most of their physical needs catered for? If there is evidence that they suffer in certain husbandry conditions, then there is an argument to outlaw such systems. For example, the keeping of veal calves in crates and laying hens in batteries has now been outlawed in some European countries, and codes of practice which will become law in the future have been produced for all farm livestock (equines are not considered 'farm livestock' in Britain so there is no 'code' for them as yet) (MAFF Codes of Practice for farm livestock 1990).

The ways that are and have been used to assess behavioural distress are given in figure 4.1. We will discuss them one by one. The central point here is that if an equine shows one or several of these behaviours, he may be considered to be showing evidence of behavioural distress and this is the result of some inadequacy in his environment, it is not just an 'act of God'. The inadequacy may be physical, emotional, intellectual or all of these, but however it is looked at there is 'something not right' for that particular equine. If we are seriously interested in his welfare, it is important to try and understand what this might be and put it right. Unfortunately, it turns out that evidence for behavioural distress in stabled horses in some of the years that are considered 'the best' is extremely high (Kiley-Worthington 1990 and McGreevy 1994). I conducted a survey over three years and was very surprised to find the figures so high. This is one reason that has prompted me to write this book in the hopes that those with equines will begin to think more about what they are doing and whether it is the best possible way from the *horses'* point of view; although it may be the traditional way, or the way that has been taught.

So let us look at how behavioural distress can be recognised.

- Evidence of physical ill-health (including poor nutrition, wounds etc.)

- Evidence of frequent occupational diseases

- Need for the use of drugs and/or surgery to maintain the system of husbandry

- Behavourial changes:
  (a) performance of abnormal behaviours (that are not normally in the animals' repertoire, and which appear to be of little benefit to the animal: e.g. running at bars, pacing)
  (b) stereotypies i.e. the performance of repeated behaviour fixed in all details and apparently purposeless (e.g. crib-biting, wind-sucking, weaving, head twisting)
  (c) substantial increase in inter- or intra-specific aggression compared to the wild or feral state
  (d) large differences in time budgets from the wild or feral animal
  (e) substantial increases in behaviour related to frustration or conflict (e.g. often behaviour relating to locomotion and/or cutaneous stimulation)
  (f) substantial ontogenic behavioural changes (animals performing behaviour characteristics of a very different time in their development e.g. calves of 16 weeks walking as if they were a day or so old)

- Behavioural restrictions – this is the inability to perform all the behaviour in the animals' natural repertoire which does not cause severe or prolonged suffering to others.

Figure 4.1 Possible indicators of distress in animals

(1) The performance of abnormal behaviours

These are behaviours that are not normally in the species repertoire and appear to be of little benefit to the animal directly. For example, pacing of lions in cages. In stabled horses behaviour such as stable walking and persistent wood eating are in this category. Persistent head throwing or tossing is another very common problem in the stabled or ridden horse. Self-mutilation is occasional, where the horse bites himself again and again in the same or a similar place. Destroying his rug by pulling and biting it is another. There are many other behaviours that equines perform in this category, and new ones are often being brought to my attention.

(2) The performance of stereotypies

Stereotypies are behaviours that are 'repeated, constant in form, and appear to be of no particular purpose'. They occur in many species; the first research done on them was done on human children who particularly when living in institutions develop them (Hutt and Hutt 1965). Stereotypies, because they are very obvious, have now been studied in many species including equines, primates, elephants, and rodents (Kiley-Worthington 1977, '83, '87, Mason 1979).

Most usual stereotypies (apparently purposeless behaviour, repeated in all details)

Crib-biting	Head twisting
Wind sucking	Head nodding
Weaving	

Abnormal behaviours (repeated very frequently, not in the normal repertoire, but not always fixed in all details)

Box walking/pacing	Rearing, bucking
Box kicking with hind leg, with front leg	Tongue protruding
Self mutilation (biting or persistent rubbing)	Wood chewing
Tail swishing	Lip licking
Rug pulling and destroying	Persistent pawing
Head shaking, nodding or twisting	Chewing

Aggressing self, other horses, or humans (biting, kicking, lunging at, trampling)
Persistent ear flattening to other equines or humans.

Neuroses

Inability to stand still at any time	Shivering with fear
Leaping away from handling	Nipping and stamping when groomed
Over reacting to environmental change	Over excitement
Rushing away from familiar objects	Bolting
Excessive calling	Refusal to enter lorry or trailer
Refusal to be led, rearing, rushing away etc.	Fear of traffic

Inability to lift or have leg held up for hoof cleaning or shoeing
Spooking and refusal to enter familiar places, narrow places, or gateways
Rushing around when left in familiar place, over-excitement and fear

Depression
Standing immobile for prolonged periods, often separated from companions, or isolated from other horses. Showing no interest in surroundings
Head and tail low, ears sideways, often resting leg, 'switching out' from unacceptable environment for prolonged periods at atypical times
Refusal to eat, drink, lie down, or react to social partner
Lying down for prolonged periods with no physical reason, often after separation

Figure 4.2 Some frequent signs of behavioural distress in equines

We now know a considerable amount about them, and indeed in equines, we know enough about their cause to be able to ensure that they *do not occur in the next generation of young horses*. At present it is unlikely that the performance of stereotypies will be eliminated but at least they are now being recognised and remedies discussed. Figure 4.2 gives a list of the most usual stereotypies that occur in horses.

One of the difficult things about stereotypies and one of the reasons why there is now generously funded research on them (at present there are three research projects spending around £250,000 on them in British veterinary schools!) is that they are *highly habit forming*. Thus once the equine starts to perform a stereotypy if the conditions that have sparked it off are not changed, it will rapidly become a habit which within a few months will begin to occur in many different situations regardless of the original cause. Performing the behaviour itself becomes rewarding to the horse and thus it becomes more common and of a higher and higher 'habit strength'. The result in a year or two is that the stereotypy has generalised to occur in almost every situation and changing the environment for the horse will not stop it (Kiley-Worthington 1977 and 1983).

It is not always understood that there are two phases in the development of stereotypies:

(a) *Establishing stereotypies*, during which it is still possible to cure, in the young horse up to around four or five years old, depending on how much he has performed a stereotypy, and
(b) *Established stereotypies* which are of very high habit strength, and are almost impossible to cure completely even if all apparent causes are removed, although with careful management they can be dramatically reduced. Such established stereotypies tend to 'generalise' and occur in many situations: when the animal is bored, over-excited, frustrated, hungry, expectant, frightened, before and after eating and so on.

It is widely believed that the chances of a horse developing a stereotypy (like most other undesirable behaviour) is genetic. The truth of it is, that like almost all behaviour, there may be a genetic tendency to develop a stereotypy in a horse from a line of stereotypy performers, but with thought, appropriate management and an understanding of how and why horses perform them, the horse will not necessarily develop one. My own stud illustrates this point well. It was established in 1959 with the purchase of an established crib-biting thoroughbred mare who was eight years old. Kathiawar gave me first-hand experience of this, and set me thinking why she did it. This resulted in a series of observations, experiments and surveys. Her grandson had a chequered youth (his mother was killed and he was mishandled in my absence, finally being put in a single stable for five months while I was in Africa and was not informed). When I returned, he was a weaver. However he never became a generalised weaver as we managed to change the conditions under which he was kept and handled in time. For the rest of his seventeen years thereafter, he occasionally weaved and it was always predictable, but it never generalised nor became of high habit. He clearly had the genetic tendency to develop stereotypies, and had as a youth been kept in the condition that give rise to them (single stables, under-exercised, and inappropriately handled with insufficient environmental and intellectual stimulation), but with care this never generalised to occur for prolonged periods or in many situations. We have now bred the sixth generation from the foundation mare, and even though there remains some genetic tendency to develop such behaviour (as well as the potential to show other signs of behaviour distress) we have not had any other horses that have developed either (fifty-four animals born and raised to date over thirty-six years). I am very aware, however that it would be very easy to develop these behaviours by changing the husbandry, but they are kept somewhat differently from most horses of their calibre (part IV).

Another belief is that 'blood horses' (thoroughbreds, arabs and so on) may develop stereotypies but that ponies and donkeys do not. Both ponies and donkeys can develop stereotypies but it is true that they develop them less frequently. However is this the result of the way they are kept and their lifetime experiences, or is it genetic? Ponies and donkeys are rarely kept in the restrictive, isolated and manipulated way in which blood horses usually are; and are consequently less likely to suffer behavioural distress. Some show ponies, even of moorland breeds, do develop stereotypies if kept in inappropriate stabling. This tends to support the hypothesis that whether or not animals develop stereotypies depends to a great extent on their lifetime experiences although the genes may increase or decrease the threshold for the development of them.

	Racing stables		Teaching stables*	
No. of establishments	5		12	
No. of horses	76		150	
	number	%	number	%
No. on phenylbutazone	5	6.5	43	28
Denervated	20	26.5	6	4
TOTAL	25	33	49	32
Wood chewing	70	92	50	33
Crib-biting or wind sucking	6	7.8	9	6
Weaving or stable walking	12	15.7	10	6.6
Head throwing or tossing	10	13.1	20	13.3
Stable kicking	8	10.7	15	10
High aggression levels	30	39.4	35	23.3
Stable neurosis	26	34	47	31.3
TOTAL	162	212.7	186	123.5

* = BHS approved

Figure 4.3 The use of analgesic drugs, surgery (denervation) and the occurrence of behavioural problems in a sample of stabled horses

(3) High levels of aggression either intra (within) or inter (between) species

In humans who have inappropriate living conditions, and are distressed, aggression often increases. For example violence in high-rise flats, or higher levels of aggression and violence in poor communities deprived of some of the facilities that are normal in that society. Is this true of equines?

Are horses fundamentally aggressive animals (as many television wildlife films would have us believe; the world is highly competitive and aggression is necessary for survival) or not? Is aggression towards one's own or another species going to foster survival and is it always going to be the case that societies organise themselves competitively? We have for several years been recording the behaviour in detail of horses to other horses when they are allowed to live together in family groups. We have found that aggression is really not common either towards other horses or other species including humans. None of our experimental horses have kicked or bitten a human for example. Others have found similar low levels of aggression in feral horses (e.g. Duncan 1980).

We also looked at 'affiliation' between horses and found that behaviour related to cohesion of the group was much more common than that related to splitting it, that is aggression. It was also not necessary to postulate the idea of 'dominance hierarchy' which presupposes that there will inevitably be aggression between individuals. What is important and necessary to know in order to make sure the husbandry is as good as possible for all, is that individual horses, like humans, have different roles in the society and different personalities. Not that one is 'boss' and the rest compete to be next boss and so on (see Kiley-Worthington 1987).

The normal levels of any type of aggression in feral horses, or horses in groups, in large fields is 0.6/horse/hour (Kiley-Worthington in press). This included even slight annoyance, like turning quarters towards another.

Often, of course, horses are not allowed any free contact with each other on grounds that they will be aggressive anyway: 'he cannot go out with the group, they kick him or he kicks them. . .' In other words they are behaving pathologically. This is the result of their past experiences just as it is for humans. If a horse (other than a stallion or gelding with another stallion and mares) cannot be placed with a group on grounds that he may kick or be kicked and injured, then there is evidence for behavioural distress and the way the animals are kept and trained must be seriously assessed to find out where the problem lies. It is *not* the fault of the horse, it is the fault of the management and should be changed . . . if we are *serious* about our interest in horse welfare.

If then a particular stable yard, or a particular horse, shows high levels of aggression it would be right to assume that *all is not well for that horse/or in that yard*. One of the things that continually impresses me about horses, is how non-aggressive they are. It never ceases to amaze me how even when they are kept in totally inappropriate conditions, socially, physically, emotionally and intellectually, and often thoughtlessly handled, or handled as if they were a machine or a particularly dangerous venomous snake, how extraordinarily tolerant and non-aggressive and pleasant they are – this is often not the case with humans kept under similar conditions. Even when humans and other animals are aggressive towards them, they are often extremely tolerant and non-aggressive.

The interesting question is *why* are they so non-aggressive to each other and other species, so cooperative, and so tolerant? They are not at all like primates, or various predators such as canines and felines in this respect. Perhaps we have more to learn from horses than we think.

(4) Large changes in time budgets

Time budgets are the way time is budgeted out for different activities. If one is a horse, a large herbivore, there is a certain amount of time that is necessary for eating, for sleeping, for moving about, for riding, for socialising, for playing and so on. Studies on feral horses show us how time is normally budgeted by horses at different times of the year. (See fig. 4.4.) So far feral donkeys have not been studied in this way as far as I am aware. Studies for twenty-four hour periods on how horses spend their time in pastures, in stables, in groups and so on have been recorded. One of the interesting results is that it is surprising how little these time budgets do in fact vary; horses, even when food is very plentiful or very scarce will only vary the time they spend grazing by around two hours a day, and they normally spend around sixteen hours grazing. Now if the horse is kept in a single stable and fed a low fibre diet because it is believed, for example, that he should eat more carbohydrate and protein to make him grow bigger or run faster, then he is able to finish all the food he has to eat in around two or three hours a day. This means that he has around fourteen hours free. He may be well nourished, but *what is he going to do with the fourteen hours?* If he is in a stable his options are very few, one of them frequently becomes the performance of abnormal behaviour, and/or stereotypies, in order to stimulate himself and fill up the time. Another possibility (which is often used by solitary prisoners or sows tethered in stalls), is that he sleeps much more.

So if we see that there are gross changes from the norm in the equines' time budgets, we can assume that all may not be well for that equine. Clearly the odd day travelling, or where the routine is disturbed or changed may cause a change in time budgets and during this time one could argue that he was stressed and distressed perhaps. But, remember the General Adaptive Syndrome that helps the body and mind to adapt to such stress; it is not the odd days that will do him much harm if he is normally healthy, just as with most healthy humans who can do without a night's sleep every now and then. It is when it happens *every day* for perhaps months or years that serious trouble will be caused, both physically and psychologically, often resulting in signs of profound behavioural distress.

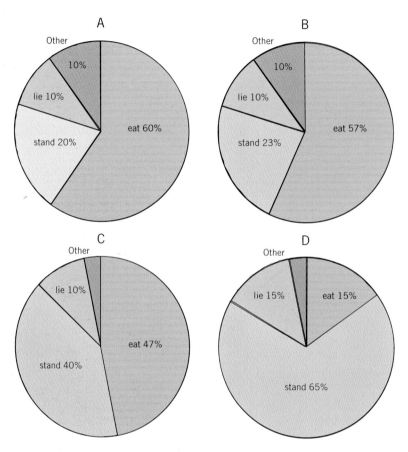

A The average time budgets for Camargue horses throughout the year. (After Duncan 1980.)

B Time budgets for a group of eight horses in a yard with *ad libitum* hay and straw.

C The time budgets for three horses in individual stables fed *ad libitum* hay and straw and able to see and touch each other.

D Time budgets for horses in stables where they cannot touch each other and only see each other over stable doors; they were fed restricted fibre (about 3kg/day, horses of 15.2 – 16hh).

Figure 4.4 Time budgets of horses in different environments

(5) Frequent behaviour indicative of frustration or conflict

Behaviour that is indicative of frustration or a conflict of some sort (e.g. a desire to approach, but also slight fear and desire to avoid) is often related to cutaneous (skin) stimulation irritation (skin itches; scratching or licking the body, head throwing, tossing or shaking, ear twitching, tail wagging, skin twitching) or manipulation of things in the environment (e.g. for horses biting and chewing, pawing) or irritation in the nose (sneezing and snorting), restless behaviour (e.g. frequent walking and stopping, or getting up and lying down). These are of course normal behaviours, but when they occur much more frequently than is usual, then it is possible to say that the equine is *frustrated, irritated or in an environment which causes conflict.* Many of these types of behaviour are the types of behaviour which are called 'displacement behaviours', apparently irrelevant behaviours that occur when the behaviour the individual would like to perform is not possible, either because it is blocked (e.g. the animal wants to eat but cannot reach the food), or the individual has an approach/avoidance conflict (he wants to approach nearer, but he knows he will be attacked and so also wants to run away).

These types of behaviour can again be measured, and if they are much more frequent than in the normal feral animal, the equine may be distressed. Again this is not the type of behaviour one worries about if it occurs now and then, indeed some frustration and conflict may not be a particularly bad thing. It is only if there is very much more than usual over a period of time – such as when head throwing or shaking, or excessive pawing become common that it can be safe to assume that the equine is distressed.

These are behaviours which relate to behavioural distress. However, the occurrence of one or several of these does not mean that all is not well and we must completely change how we keep the equine. Just like physiological 'stress', a little behavioural 'stress' does no harm. In fact without distress, how are we or our equines to appreciate joy and happiness?

The very frequent or prolonged occurrence of any one of these behaviours does however indicate that all is not well for the animal and may well result in symptoms of physiological stress; physical illness for example. This is certainly not in the equine's interest nor in the interests of his human keepers who will have more work, more worry and more expense while continuing to keep the equine in inappropriate environments.

It is possible to recognise and measure behavioural stress as well as physiological stress in equines, and it is often much easier because the behaviour is there to be seen by all, rather than having to take blood samples or pulse rates to assess 'physiological stress'. The very high levels of behavioural stress/distress recorded in stables at the top end of the equine establishment in Britain (Kiley-Worthington 1990b) and which also occur throughout Europe and USA, indicate clearly that all is not well with horse management as practised by the conventional equine establishment. Some current recommended practices can be seen to be *not* in the best interests of the equine himself. They may be inappropriate and misguided rather than deliberately cruel but nevertheless demonstrably wrong from the equine's point of view (see part II).

If we cannot improve on these standards, then like sow stalls or battery chicken cages, horse stables must and will be legislated against by welfare lobbies. If these levels of behavioural distress will not do for sows in stalls, veal calves in crates, chickens in battery cages, or dairy cows in their housing systems, then why should they be acceptable for horses? This does not mean of course that horses must no longer be kept and worked for recreation, racing or any other purpose but it does mean that things will have to change.

The people who keep horses in these ways, including the managers, workers and proprietors of the stables I visited are not cruel or evil people; they are doing what they think is best for the horses under their care and they have learnt the techniques from others at the top of the tree. They are ignorant perhaps, and sometimes thoughtless. Now we do have much of the knowledge necessary to make improvements in horse husbandry – from the horses' point of view. We may always be able to improve this further and try out other ideas, but the first step is to recognise that changes must be made – and make them.

This is happening and will continue to happen more and more as more concerned people have horses or wish to have to do with them, and start asking questions and thinking critically about what they are told and taught. Let us seriously debate the issues, not just sweep them away with the huffs, puffs and sniffs so characteristic of the pompous, threatened and ill-informed in any sphere. I for one am very happy to debate any of the statements I have made here, so start by attacking this position but do so critically and logically, not with arguments founded on emotion and human convenience. There are many who stand to lose money and status by such an approach but is that an argument for continuing as we are? Does and should the 'horse industry' as it is so unappealingly called exist to generate jobs and money for humans to the detriment of the horse (and the environment)? Are jobs and money for humans more important than what happens to horses? The majority would probably say NO in answer to these questions, but they do not always, or even often, act accordingly.

Figure 4.5 (Set on the following pages)Personality profiles of 1 stallion and 3 mares

The top histograms show the amount of aggression, withdrawing, affiliation and ignoring that each horse performs and receives from others.

The 2nd set of histograms show the amount of social involvement – whether individuals are more often performers or receivers of others' actions. For example, the stallion Baksheesh is predominantly a performer, not a receiver, and very socially involved. Omeya, who is also very socially involved, is more often a receiver. Shereen and Shiraz, who are full sisters, show more or less the same pattern here.

The 3rd set of histograms show the various hierarchies that can be calculated. Note that the individuals tend to use behaviour which strengthens the bonds between them. They show high scores for deflating situations, by ignoring acts which might cause the group to be disturbed.

The point of this figure is to show that the 'dominance hierarchy' theory is one-dimensional and can be misleading. Equines have complex and cooperative relationships.

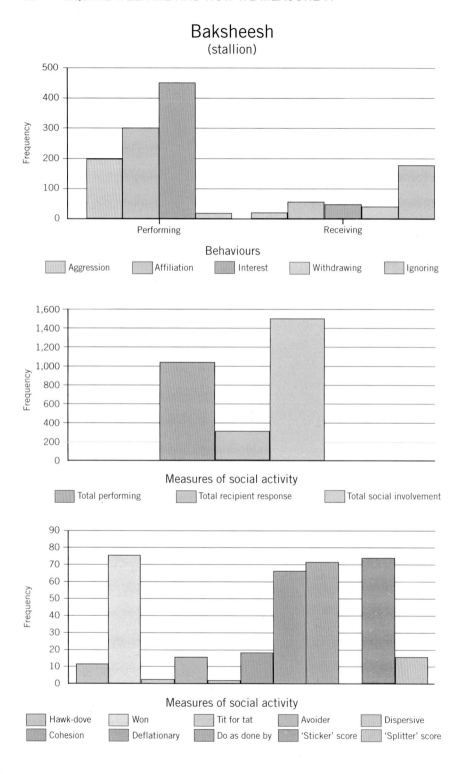

Baksheesh
(stallion)

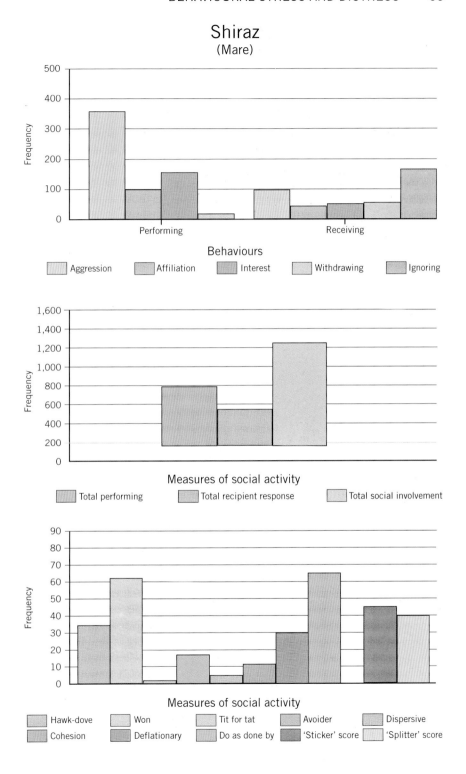

Shiraz
(Mare)

Baksheesh (left) and Shiraz (right)

Shereen

Shereen with her foal

Omeya

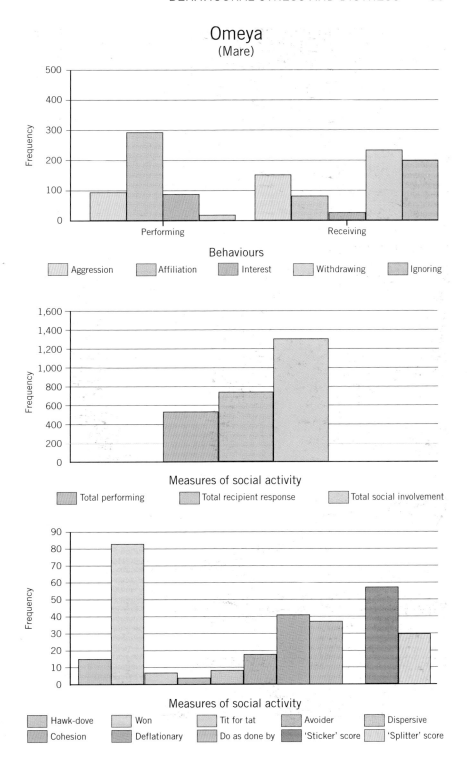

Omeya
(Mare)

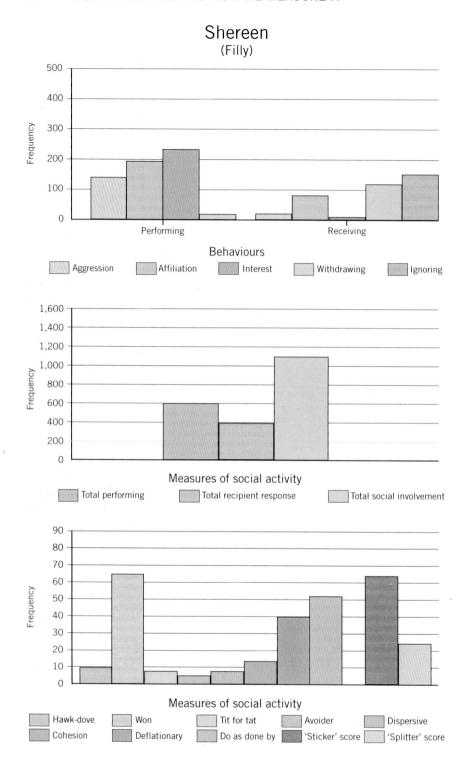

Shereen
(Filly)

5

Behavioural restriction and deprivation

When, in 1965, the British government began to accept that animal welfare was something they would have to consider seriously, a man called Brambell was asked to chair a committee to discuss the issue. The result was the Brambell Report on Animal Welfare (1965). One of the contributors was William Thorpe, an ethologist (studied animal behaviour) at Cambridge who had recently published a book entitled *Learning and instinct in animals* (1956). He made a significant contribution to the Brambell Report in that he argued that the animal should be allowed to perform his natural behaviours, although only a few of these were considered *really* necessary (he should be able to lie down and get up with ease, move a little and scratch himself). This was considered by the scientific establishment at the time to be radical stuff: after all it was not recognised generally by scientists that animals were sentient and had feelings. For the next two decades the scientists interested in animal welfare (although by then admitting that the animals probably could feel and suffer), considered that until a series of experiments had been conducted where the animal was given a choice we could not conclude that he *needed* to do anything; thus it was argued that it would not be necessary to provide facilities for him to perform many behaviours until it was tested that he chose to (see Stamp-Dawkins 1980).

This argument seemed faulty since, if one accepted evolutionary theory, all behavioural tendencies (just like features of the body) have a function, which is to increase survival and reproductive success. Preventing an animal from performing any behaviour might cause him to suffer. The starting point, therefore, should rationally be *to allow him to perform all the behaviours in his repertoire which did not cause suffering to others* (as others also have the right not to suffer) – if we are seriously interested in his welfare.

If we consider that we need to restrict his behaviour in one way or another for our own convenience, then we must make good arguments for this on the grounds that it will not increase either his suffering or that of others: we must prove that its deprivation *does not cause suffering*, rather than prove that the animal suffers if deprived. The 'normal' behaviour of the animal is of importance to him, or it would not be performed, so to prevent it will be likely to cause the animal (or human) problems. This is called 'shifting the burden of proof'.

We might argue that he really does not need sex for example, but since we do not know if sex is more or less important to him than, say, it is to humans, we are not in a position to be able to make judgements on *which* behaviours he should be able to perform and which could legitimately be restricted. It might after all be that, for example, sex is *more* important to horses than it is to humans, so to deny it to them would make them suffer *more* than humans do when it is denied. It is generally considered an infringement of human rights to prevent sex or castrate male humans. On what grounds do we then castrate horses?

This means that if we are to make a rational scientific decision on what an animal should be allowed to do and what not, we must know how important it is to the animal. However this importance will change from time to time as all behavioural priorities do. It may also change as a result of his life-time experiences, but *until we have evidence to the contrary* we must conclude that the animal should be able to perform all the behaviours in his repertoire because they have evolved and are part of what he is, even if we do not understand why.

Take one simple example: it is widely believed and published in innumerable text books on 'stud management' that stallions will be likely to hurt or kill foals. Therefore they must not run with the mare during breeding. If this were the case throughout evolution how come equines did not rapidly become extinct? There may be a genetic abnormality or life-time experience that has resulted in pathological behaviour such as one horse killing another – but this would not be selected for unless it was advantageous to the individual and consequently the society. So the questions are (1) Is this true?

(2) If it is, have we selected for such pathological behaviour in our domestic horse? (3) Is it the result of individual pathologies of stallions because of their lifetime experiences? The third alternative is most likely in the majority of cases, and there is proof of this.

Thus we must conclude, if we are rational, that the animal (or human) *should be able to perform all the behaviour in his repertoire which does not cause suffering to others* as a general rule. Any behaviour we prevent him doing is likely to cause him to suffer, although it might benefit us, the 'caretakers'. If without other evidence it is suggested it will be to the equine's benefit, this is a 'belief of convenience'. There are many examples of this in horse husbandry, for example keeping horses in single stables isolated from free contact with others so that (a) they are clean when brought out to ride and (b) they cannot kick each other. It is often stated that the horse is then 'better off' than out in the field with others even though as a result of this husbandry the horse behaves pathologically and is consequently more likely to injure others or be injured by them.

Another example of a 'belief of convenience' in horse husbandry is that it is quite acceptable to prevent mares having courtship and mating naturally, indeed it is often argued, that it is of benefit to them as 'they might get kicked'. It is not considered that as a result, the mares *will* miss out on the excitement and joy of sex. Nor is it often pointed out that they certainly do not seem to enjoy the covering strategies currently encouraged and considered 'good horse welfare and husbandry' (see Morel 1993). When the mare is to be 'covered' by a stallion she is often immobilised by being hobbled and twitched: very considerable behavioural restrictions (see chapter 11 for further discussion).

Even if hobbling and twitching does not 'hurt' nevertheless the fact that it is necessary before the mare will stand is like saying to a woman as she is tied down before being raped 'don't worry this won't hurt and is good for you'. Yet rape is a criminal offence – a serious infringement of an individual's behavioural liberty and in some cultures punished by death. Since the mare is being copulated against her desire (because she has to be restricted and restrained), it is rational to consider such practices 'equine rape'. The argument that is often used against the use of the emotive term 'rape' is that the mare either 'does not know what she is doing, (or what is happening), or that 'she is just acting by instinct'. Such statements deny that the mare is a sentient being; in this case she is considered like a motor car. This is another 'belief of convenience'. The real reason for such practices is human convenience, sometimes including economic gain and status enhancement. What it definitely does *not* do is 'improve horse

The following pictures show social interactions in a group of horses.

Messages are being sent and received all the time. For example, here every individual is aware of what everyone else is doing, although the mare and foal have their backs to the others and appear to be staring over the gate, and the chestnut mare on the left appears to be dozing. The grey mare on the left has noticed the possible approach of the stallion (with ears pricked at the camera), but does not want the grey pony to come closer (she is swishing her tail). They grey pony has taken this message on, but might approach her anyway, and is only too aware of the stallion behind her.

Here the stallion greets the grey pony, while the young chestnut gelding watches with intense interest, but not wanting to get too close (indicated by his high head and tail carriage, slightly tense posture and direction of gaze).

welfare'. If all horses are pathological in respect to breeding and likely to cause each other suffering we should ask ourselves why this is. After all feral and wild horses manage it rather well.

It may of course be possible to argue in certain conditions a degree of behavioural restraint is necessary and ethically

The chestnut mare is saying to the grey filly 'Move off, you annoy me.' The grey mare on the left has already started to move away, while the yearling gelding, son of the chestnut, watches together with others. Aggressive acts attract human attention, and give rise to the oversimplified idea of 'dominance hierarchy' (see figure 4.5).

The stallion (grey looking left) is staring over the hedge, thus telling the grey filly who is walking past him and would like his attention, that he is not interested. The chestnut mare's head is up, and her ears are directed to focus attention on him. At the same time, she is slightly irritated that the grey filly has interrupted her and the stallion.

acceptable. The important thing is that behavioural restraint must be recognised as being likely to *cause* suffering and therefore wrong, rather than generally right and likely to *reduce* suffering. Even when it is argued for in one particular case, as for humans, it must be recognised that it is something we must try and change for the future. Behavioural freedom is highly prized in humans (although not all humans necessarily take advantage of it); why should it not be of great importance to other higher mammals; equines for example? Let me give an example of a problem that such 'beliefs of convenience' can cause when one is trying to reduce behavioural restrictions for equines.

One year we had five young arab and arab cross colts who were of high quality, and with their background and abilities there was no reason why they should not have done exceedingly well in performance and conformation competitions as well as being sweet gentle companions who had been raised in a group and free of stress or distress (which we had monitored). We advertised them, and had various people come to see them and try them. They were so delightful, we had no trouble at all in finding several suitable people who wished to buy each of them for the price we asked. But first, the buyers had to consult with their husband, stable manager, livery owner, and so on. Despite the enthusiasm of the buyers and our acceptance of them as suitable people to have the horses, each rang back in tears to say there were unable to have the horse they wanted as they had been advised 'not to have a stallion', the livery owner 'would not have the horse in the yard', or the husband 'would not allow his wife to have a stallion' (even in 1994!), and so on.

This went on for a total of around ten people and we ended up having to have the colts castrated. We realised that if they were sold as stallions their life in the present British horse-owning climate, would generally be of a lower quality than as geldings. They would be kept isolated, boxed up most of the time, not given either the physical, emotional, or intellectual stimulation they needed and probably end up as horses with major problems: behaviourally pathological. We were effectively forced by the current belief system to castrate the horses 'for their own good', although we already knew that stallions will only become 'difficult' if treated inappropriately. Yet in other parts of the world, stallions are the usual riding horse. Perhaps in another decade or two this will not be so necessary at least for horses of some quality sold to knowledgable homes (see chapter 11 for further discussion of breeding practices).

Most people intuitively or culturally do agree with this position on behavioural restraint. When we make intuitive judgements concerning the welfare of canines or equines the first thing that is usually of concern to people is physical pain and suffering, the second is the degree of behavioural restriction. For example, if a horse has been shut up in his stable for six months, even though he is well fed and apparently physically well, it will be considered 'cruel' because he has been behaviourally restricted for a long time. I should mention that in the last year, I have had three horses presented to me with major behavioural problems who have been shut up in their stables for periods of 3 months to 1 year (they were all arabs too); it is not that unusual!

So we do recognise to a degree that behavioural restraint is not good for equines, but can we have a way of measuring it so we can see which types of environments really are more restrictive than others, and how the degree of restriction compares? Inevitably all animals including humans will have some behavioural restraint in part of their lives, but how much, when, where and how?

I have made an effort over the years to quantify the degree of behavioural restraint in different types of equine husbandry. What we should be able to do, is to ensure that the animals in our care have at least the same amount of behavioural freedoms and choices as they do in feral or wild situations. The wild or feral equines do not have unrestricted lives, in fact it is often argued that they have more suffering than domestic animals. There will be times when they cannot eat or drink because of drought or snow, when they are hunted or killed, when they have no shelter, and when they are cold or very wet, when sick or ill and they will not be treated and so on. However, it is clear that the current establishment practices of keeping horses in single stables can be very behaviourally restrictive. It is possible to keep horses, even horses competing and winning, with at least as little behavioural restriction as in the wild. It might perhaps in the future be possible to improve on this, just as we believe it is possible for humans. Although many of us find present urban life difficult and stressful we do not go off and live as hunter gatherers. Why? Because it will be physically uncomfortable, we may starve and we will not have access to drugs when we need them. We may also not have the same level of intellectual stimulation that we have by learning things from others, by reading books or watching television.

Of course neither horses nor humans will necessarily be allowed to behave exactly as they like all the time. There are times when children have to sit still and listen, times when horses may have to be ridden or, pull ploughs, donkeys cart water, mules pull sleighs; times when they may have to be alone for a while, or tied up, transported in a vehicle and so on. Provided they are educated to be able to put up with all these and many other things, and they do not continue for so long that they show evidence of prolonged physiological stress or behavioural distress, there is no reason why there should not be some restraint some of the time. It is when it becomes the way the equine has to live *the majority* of the time and when he shows evidence of suffering that it is indicated that all is not acceptable and must be changed.

Equines are extremely adaptable and fast learners and there is no reason to believe that they should *only* perform the behaviour in their natural repertoire any more than humans should. We do not naturally read and write, it has to be taught to us, but by so doing it is believed that we, as individuals, benefit. Can we not have the same approach for equines? They can after all learn to do many different things not in their behavioural repertoire and by so doing their lives may be enriched. They may go to different places, experience different things, have different relationships and so on. Even if we have no evidence that their lives are enriched and that they are any happier, at least they must not suffer as a result.

Have we got it right so far? First we must come to grips with turning the assumption around: we start by designing the environment for our equine so that he can *perform all his natural behaviours which do not cause suffering to others*, rather than by trying to over-protect and control him. If it is necessary to over-protect or control him, then the environment is unacceptable to him and we must rethink it. A popular image of how the 'natural world' works is that it is red in tooth and claw, life is competitive and bloody. Equines, it is believed, like all other animals, given half a chance will be uncontrollable aggressive monsters trying to 'out do' us and 'get away with it'. This may be the way human primates see the world – but is it the way equines do? Humans can certainly alter the way equines behave, and the quality of their lifetime experience, for the better and for the worse.

6

Pleasure and joy: how to measure it

If we can measure distress in equines then surely we should be able to measure happiness or joy. If they can feel unhappy and distressed, then it would be logical to assume that they can equally feel happy and joyful. Most horse owners (even those who are consulting me because they are aware that all is not well with their horse's life) will, when starting to talk about horse behaviour state that 'my horse is happy'.

How do we make these judgements, and are there any grounds for them? Often one does have to admit, if one is honest, that one makes these judgements on the grounds that we feel the way we are keeping that particular horse is the best possible way, and therefore he is happy. It is a statement of concern, but not necessarily of knowledge concerning how to understand whether or not the horse is happy. We do care about our equines and how they feel, but how can we measure if they are happy – indeed can we?

There are some suggestions that we can make here. First there must be no 'distress' and little behavioural restriction. In addition there should be behavioural evidence of some positive emotion; 'happiness or joy'. A starting point in measuring this might be to make a comparison, by using concepts of conditional anthropomorphism. How do we know if other humans are happy? Playing games, laughing, joking, smiling and generally doing things we like doing is one way. Unfortunately horses do not laugh in an identifiable way so one option is not open. On the other hand horses do play. Playing is considered to be an activity (physical or mental) that exists apparently for its own sake, of having as its main aim 'pleasure' by yielding detachment from 'serious aims and ends'.

Galloping and leaping round for fun.

Play in animals has not often been thought of as an emotional response but rather as a purposeful functional learning situation in order to ensure that the animal will have the skills to perform particular acts – like catching mice for cats. Horses play fight, play sex, play chase, play leap about, play spook and so on. In particular they appear to gallop or leap about in play; for the 'joy of movement'. This fits in well with their evolutionary background and one might assume that play involving movement will be particularly important to equines since they have evolved to be skilled specialists in speed and endurance of movement. Doubt about the existence of a positive emotion – pleasure – and its cause is no more justified than doubt about the equine feeling 'terror', 'fear' or 'pain' – although we may have more trouble recognising it from the animal's behaviour.

Another group of activities that give pleasure to humans and are often chosen for horses and humans to perform are affiliative behaviours; touching or nuzzling other known or liked individuals, mutual grooming, standing near or over others, nickering to other particular individuals in greeting, choosing the company of certain individuals and developing friendships. Our research and others (e.g. Fraser 1968) shows that horses do show marked preferences for individuals, they show likes and dislikes of others. Some individuals are popular and some are not.

Pleasure may also be given to equines (in much the same way as to humans). For example when they are approved of

Affiliative behaviour of equines has often been overlooked. Here three youngsters choose to doze close to each other, but conscious of the others' presence (note positions of the ears).

either by other equines or humans. It is also possible that equines take pleasure in training or performing with humans. It has quite often been reported that experienced performing horses (like experienced performing humans) respond to audience applause and even increase their efforts in performance when they hear or see the responses of an appreciative audience. This is not too surprising as the atmosphere created by the approval or disapproval of large numbers of others even of another species would not be difficult for horses to pick up given their highly developed ability to respond to subliminal visual cues, whether from humans or other species. Even with inexperienced horses, if the audience is primed to show approval, not necessarily clapping initially, but murmuring and gasping and laughing and smiling, young horses will adapt and accept strange and often scary new environments and objects more quickly and relax more noticeably. The next phase is to perform with greater energy and exaggeration – is this a positive response indicating joy and pleasure?

Our recent research indicates that not only dogs' but horses', heifers' and lamas' reward for performing an activity can simply be verbal praise. Learning a task can be speeded up by using positive reinforcements – provided the horse, llama or whatever animal, is already familiar with the vocabulary used; verbal and gesticular. This would seem to indicate that the horse or other animal finds it 'pleasurable' being told he/she is good and has performed well – otherwise why would he/she do it? Possible behaviour associated with feelings of pleasure in equines is included as a result of using 'conditional anthropomorphism', observations of behaviour and its consequences (see Kiley-Worthington, 1990a).

Some of these behaviours appear to be especially characteristic of equines; particularly those related to locomotion (running, leaping, bucking, rearing, etc.) Horses after being restricted in stables or yards will characteristically gallop around in a social group after release, and play is most often related to moving in groups, and exaggerated rapid movements of one sort and another. Other social play involves leaping and cavorting, nuzzling and touching. Affiliative behaviour also presumably gives some pleasure (otherwise why would they perform it?). There must be an immediate reason as well as an evolutionary (long-term) one. Just to argue that affiliation helps groups stay together and aids individual survival is not enough as, although this may be a long-term reason why it is performed, there must also be an immediate reason. After all the equine has many options at any one time – why does he nuzzle others – presumably because he likes them; he has an 'emotional motivation'. In social groups where the horses have few behavioural restrictions imposed on them from outside equines engage in much 'affiliative behaviour'.

As with humans, affiliative behaviour encourages affiliative responses ('make love not war'). This seems to indicate that experiencing pleasure might be the reason why groups stay together – in other words that the emotion of 'pleasure' is very important in the cohesion of the group and because staying as a group has been selected for by evolution both the *feeling* and the *demonstration* of pleasure have also been selected for as they benefit the individual and his reproductive potential.

Swimming with the horses after a training ride when hot and sweaty on a summer's day; what better way to be refreshed?

If we are interested in equine welfare and consider it our moral obligation to ensure that horses have good lives, not only must they not show evidence of distress and/or behavioural restriction but there must also be evidence of pleasure in their behaviour; demonstrating that life is fun. If they do not show evidence of pleasure in their life then we have not got it quite right for them.

But how much pleasure is enough? When do we consider our equines to be 'really happy'? This is a very difficult question, in just the same way as it is for humans. Both equines and humans can have severe emotional problems when they clearly are *not* happy in conditions which physically might appear ideal. Then one must consider whether their emotional/social/intellectual lives have gaps in them. Even feral or wild horses may not be happy and show pleasure all the time (e.g. in winter when hungry, sick or cold). Perhaps the starting place is to say that our equines must show *at least* as much evidence for pleasure as their feral cousins but we should hope to find more since we, the humans, are providing a 'better life' – and at best enriching their lives.

To do this we must measure how many times they show pleasurable interactions between each other. The important thing is that we start thinking about how much pleasure our equines display in their daily lives – how happy are they *really*?

Other possible indications of 'happiness'/pleasure/joy can also be displayed in their interactions with humans. They show lack of pleasure clearly, 'resisting' doing what we ask (e.g. by stopping and refusing to do something, by becoming fearful, frustrated, panicked and even aggressive towards the human). They demonstrate their pleasure for example by coming when called, seeking out human company when they have a choice, by greeting and calling to humans, by being relaxed when with them or asked to do various actions. By directing any of their affiliative behaviours to humans; nuzzling, smelling, touching, and by choosing to stay nearby when they have a choice, following and being part of the human social group – and not just for food reward. Compared to dogs it is remarkable how little this is allowed by humans. This could be because we humans have not thought of it as an option, and/or is it because equines are generally kept more remote from humans most of the time – out of the house with only horse company? It is probably both – but the test is to see if by developing a very positive working relationship with the equine, he will choose human company and association with at least his human social partners even though he may have access to his best equine friend too. There is evidence from people who have gone on long treks with a horse or horses that this happens. It is one of the questions we are researching (see Kiley-Worthington and Randle in prep.).

Equines are far less demonstrative in their affection and pleasure than dogs for example but is this just that we are not so switched on to their visual cues? It may be we are just too crass to notice the signs of delight and pleasure, or even disgust and dislike that they are giving loud and clear to each other – even if they shout out loud we may not hear or understand!

One interesting experiment we have done is to see if our cognitive subject Shemal would stay with us when out on walks in strange places. Does she charge off as we mostly believe equines do (so we keep them on a lead all the time or tie them up) or does she (and our other cognitive subjects of different species) stay around? Shemal goes off for little forays. Perhaps because horses cover land quickly and see far distances, their idea of 'being with the group' is much farther apart than for humans or llamas – but she comes back. We even played 'hide and seek' with her once in a wood – hiding when she had gone ahead – she soon stopped grazing, looked about and then galloped back towards where she had last seen us, calling – and then, when she saw us hiding behind some trees, relaxed and approached us like a foal returning to its mother.

It is sometimes believed that because equines are not as demonstrative in their affections as most canines for example, that they don't have any emotional bonds with humans (see Whitmore 1990, a spokesperson for the British Horse Society). If this is in fact the case, then since they do form emotional bonds with other species, even if they don't with humans, there must be a reason. The way in which humans relate to them and their husbandry conditions must surely be carefully examined to see if they might not be at fault.

7

The equine mind

So far this book has suggested that we do have some answers on how to improve the environments for our equines (chapters 2–5); we do know quite a lot about how equine physiology works (how their bodies work), and what they need to make them work (although even here it is easy to make mistakes in our assumptions). We know quite a bit about the equines' social life and its evolution, and we know a little about their emotional life... on these grounds we can now make an 'informed guesstimate' as to how to design environments that should fit well with equines' physical, emotional and social needs. It may not be what we are doing at present, but if we think about it, we *do know the direction in which we should go*, to give the animals the benefit of any doubt.

The working of the equine mind, 'cognition', is the subject we know least about. This has only in the last decade or two become of serious interest to philosophers and scientists in relation to animal welfare. The crucial questions which remain at the heart of welfare issues are:

(1) What *is* his mind? Does he have one, and if so how similar and how different is it to yours or mine, to that of the dog, the cow, the whale, the dolphin, or the ape?

(2) How does his mind work?

(3) What human mental capacities does he lack?

(4) Is he aware of others having minds or of his own – self aware?

A brief history of the development and the first steps towards trying to understand these questions and how to begin to answer them will help to set the stage before we discuss what we think we know about these questions so far, in relation to equines. Such a review can also help you the reader to identify where you stand on this issue as *you do* have an opinion and *you will* take up a position in these arguments. My task here is simply to try to make you question your position, whatever it is, to emphasise that if you are so sure you do know, then evidence must be produced to back your case. I hope it will help you to think about the questions which to my mind are by far the most interesting and lie at the heart of the current debates on equine welfare.

A brief history of ideas on animal minds

We have already mentioned the ancient Greeks in relation to the development of thinking about animal welfare, and in some respects the history of ideas on animal minds parallels and even controls the development of thinking about animal welfare. Aristotle (350 BC) seems to have assumed that animals had minds (at least higher mammals anyway, and these are the ones we are going to restrict this discussion to), and that individual animals had individual characters. He talked about the *telos* of an animal, the horseness of the horse, the donkeyness of the donkey – meaning in each case the fully developed potential of the animal which it possessed as a member of its particular species.

The development of Cartesian thinking in the seventeenth century put a stop to the consideration that animals had minds (see chapter 1). Animals were just robotic structures who had no minds and no emotions; at least this was considered the rational stance until it could be *proved* otherwise. The justification for this belief was twofold. In the first instance it was related to the dominant faith, Christianity, which had been understood, at least since Descartes, to make distinctions between animals and humans on the grounds of humans possessing souls and having been made in the image of God; thus other humans mattered to Christians – other animals much less so. The Judeo-Christian position is a 'speciesist' position (Singer 1976) which has dominated the thinking of the western world, making distinctions with regard to the moral status of beings, dependent on their species – human or animal.

The second argument for making distinctions between humans and other animals rests on human development and the use of language. Because of language it has repeatedly been argued, only humans could think, could reason, and could perform a whole number of complex operations that without language would be impossible (Frey 1983, Leahy 1991, Kennedy 1992).

This belief became a central concept of our culture, and many other cultures, although not all (e.g. Buddhism, Hinduism). Because the western culture spread widely and became associated in the minds of the colonisers (and gradually as a result of 'education' or 'development' of their subjects), with 'development' and 'civilisation' such a concept continued and spread often unquestioned throughout the world.

One of the most influential moral philosophers of recent centuries (Kant 1724–1804) argued that the reason why we must be nice to animals was, not that it mattered how they were treated for themselves, since they could rarely suffer because they did not have minds and could not think rationally, but that if humans were nasty to animals, then this might increase the chances of these humans being inconsiderate and nasty to other humans which was morally wrong, since other humans can think rationally and can suffer. He did not explain how, if animals were so different and inferior to humans, why it was that humans seeing other human beings being nasty to animals would copy this behaviour towards other humans. After all we don't worry when someone sees someone else hitting a brick that they will then go off and hit humans! It would seem then, that even Kant recognised some similarities between humans and animals otherwise he would not have made this argument.

One of the recent developments in thinking about animal welfare in which the key figures were (to our shame as scientists) all philosophers (see Singer 1976, Midgley 1979, Rollin 1989) was not based on questioning our beliefs about the mental abilities of animals so much as questioning their emotionality, and consequently their ability to *suffer*, and therefore the need for us to have moral concern for them.

Because of the importance language had (and often still has) in defining species differences, various psychologists decided to see if they could teach chimpanzees, who were after all our close relatives, to talk. The Kelloggs were the first of these and they raised a young chimpanzee with their own child for five years. They tried and tried to teach the chimp to talk, but at the end of thousands of hours, she was only, with difficulty, able to pronounce two or three words: 'cup' and 'Mum', while their own human child was speaking well and constructing sentences. It was consequently thought that perhaps the belief was right, that animals can't use language and this then can be used as the main distinction between us. But then another couple of psychologists, the Gardiners in Nevada had the idea of not trying to teach a young female chimp to talk *human* language, but rather to use gestures, since perhaps the structure of the throat, larynx and mouth and their nerve supply was different in the chimpanzee, so making speech very difficult or even impossible; not necessarily because their mind could not handle the concepts or complexity of language but because their muscles could not.

They decided to teach their chimp, Washoe, American sign language (AMSLAN) which is used by the deaf and dumb. After a few years of only exposing the chimp to Amslan, and raising her in a complex and interesting environment with minders and her own private play room and caravan to live in, Washoe had a vocabulary of around 150 words that she could and would sign. Not only this, but she was able to construct sentences and use words in new combinations and ways. For example when asked what a duck was (whom she had never seen before), she described it as 'a water bird'.

This put the cat among the pigeons so to speak, and there was an immediate outcry: perhaps we were not so different from other animals after all, perhaps they could learn and use at least a simple language. If they could learn even a simple language and use it, then the door was wide open to let at least chimps enter the world of 'the human race' and one of the major differences between the mind of the animals and humans would have disappeared. This would in turn require major changes in humans' attitudes to animals, their husbandry and their welfare: perhaps even a Bill of Rights for animals.

But no, the cultural belief system being as strong as it was, there was immediate and severe criticism of this work on all sorts of grounds, some spurious and some relatively sensible. The criticism that hit hardest was that the chimp was not actually making up the signs herself, she was responding to signs made by the human interrogator who was almost sub-consciously making the signs, or making gestural suggestions as to what the signs should be. This was called the 'Clever Hans Effect' and the interesting thing here was that it all began with a horse!

The horse was a horse called Hans who belonged to a German called von Osten in Berlin in 1904. He could do simple mathematical sums: 5 + 3 = 8, and tapped out the answer with his front foot. He could go to and touch an object according to its colour, when asked such a question as 'find a red object'; and he could answer 'yes' and 'no' sensibly to questions in German by nodding and shaking his head. Indeed, he would answer questions and do these things for other people not just his owner. This again challenged the beliefs of the time. Could horses do maths, and learn to make complex distinctions, answer questions and so on? Surely not – yet it did not seem to be a trick. A commission of doctors and scientists was sent to see Hans and von Osten to find out what was going on. The commission was aware that there might be some trickery and investigated possibilities of this, they also sent von Osten away so he could not give any cues, but the horse continued to be able to answer the questions! Finally they had to conclude that 'Clever Hans was himself providing answers to questions involving counting, music and locating nearby objects; that this was done without trickery on the part of human beings, and, yet, that it was not yet possible to assess Hans's degree of cleverness of intelligence' (Candland 1993).

However there was a member of the commission who had been studying suggestion and hypnosis, and he put one of his students to study Clever Hans carefully. What the student finally found was that Clever Hans was responding to very slight 'sub-liminal' (i.e. unobserved or unobservable cues) being given without intention by certain individuals in the audience. In other words Clever Hans was being cued how to respond without the people knowing they were cuing him. As he approached the correct answer, the audience would tense up, and then perhaps slightly relax when he reached the right number, direct their gaze at the required object or whatever was relevant to the question. The really interesting thing was, I believe, that Clever Hans was indeed very clever. He had taught himself to read all these signs which to him being a horse with a very acute and perhaps sophisticated visual awareness was presumably relatively easy, but for humans because of their reliance on language, not easy at all.

Anyway, the fact remained that although Hans was solving the problem, he was not using the methods humans would use to solve it: viz: language or the understanding of symbols and concepts of number, and therefore what he had done was dismissed – it did not really count. Yet Clever Hans was indeed remarkable. A friend of von Osten (who was unjustly discredited when this was exposed), thought so too and took Hans on and with two other horses continued to develop their skills. Unfortunately very little of this information is available as the papers seem to have been destroyed in the first world war, and since 'the Hans Affair' had been 'solved' no one bothered to recognise the importance and interest of this work. The dismissal of this work underlines the controlling influence current opinion and cultural beliefs have on the thinking and research of the scientist; that is his *inevitable* lack of objectivity.

Here we had an animal who was solving the problems, but in quite a different way from the way we 'normal' humans would. Yet rather than it sparking off further interest and excitement in trying to understand how the equine mind might work in different ways and have strengths as well as weaknesses which humans do not have, it was used by the scientists of the early and now late twentieth century as a derogatory discovery: low and behold, chimps were *only* using the Clever Hans effect (Tembrock 1968). Such was the power of this criticism and the belief of the scientific establishment in the *status quo* and the necessary 'objectivity' of science and scientists, that when Washoe and another chimp Nim were shown to be responding to subliminal cues given by the humans they were 'talking to', this had the same effect as around a hundred years earlier with Clever Hans: not excitement leading to further examination and understanding of a different mind, but rather, a dramatic cessation of funding for work on animal minds at all, and dismissal of the questions.

However, there were one or two exceptions – people who had by chance begun such investigations and who continued. One of them was Sue Savage-Rumbaugh who had just begun a well-financed research programme teaching language via a computer to two chimps, and subsequently several more. My own application for finance to work on this problem in equines which I submitted in 1980 after visiting the Gardiners in Nevada and (unfortunately while these criticisms were being made) was met with sneers and derision by my colleagues. It may not have been very well thought out, but it did raise many questions which need answers, rather than sweeping them under the carpet.

Things have changed now however, not because the cultural attitude to animals has dramatically altered, but rather because of the growing interest of the general public in animal welfare and environmental conservation. Apes, whales and dolphins are threatened species and the public are very interested in them, particularly since some research has now been conducted on their behaviour and communication and it is evident that they are doing interesting things with their minds that we did not suspect they could.

Another very important impetus to re-opening questions concerning the minds of animals arises oddly enough from the growing interest in artificial intelligence under its umbrella 'cognitive science'. This is because the development of computers raised questions about the possibility of designing machines to be able to make intelligent decisions and even talk. Science fiction is full of the accounts of what happens in such cases, and the ideas have grown as the possibility has grown. It turned out to be rather more difficult to do this than was initially suspected. One approach to trying to build intelligent machines has been to try and understand in greater depth how the cognitive/mental abilities of animals as well as humans work on the grounds that animals might be a simpler model of what is needed to approach a human-type cognitively functional machine. Cognitive science has to have a multi-disciplinary approach including mathematicians, computer programmers, biologists, psychologists, ethologists, neuro-physiologists, philosophers and so on to put their two-pennyworth in, to help towards greater understanding of 'the mind', in this case any mind; machine, man, or mouse.

This has given rise to the questioning of many previously widely held beliefs concerning relevant topics; it has also encouraged research in relevant areas. Perhaps one of its most important effects has been to bring human specialists together to communicate in some common language in order for each to understand the other and be able to extract useful information from other academic disciplines.

At the same time, the experimental psychologist whose main concern has been, until recently, to try to understand learning and how it works (usually with rats and pigeons), has come to the conclusion that learning does not just work by conditioning in a relaxed type way. Rather, animals as well as humans learn things without a conditioning process: from the colour of a motor car, to the way across the moor. We all know that the horse manages to remember routes and particularly the way home. The feral equine *knows* about his home area and where he is in it and much about this has not been conditioned learning; it has been the absorption of information without conditioning. This has been called 'silent learning'. The experimental psychologists who themselves have been central exponents of the scientific method and 'behaviourism' (the belief in materialism and the idea that the mind and the brain are one) have themselves invented the study of animal minds: *animal cognition* (Pearce 1987, Dickinson 1980).

Enough of the history; the consequences today are that there are, as a result, many more questions than answers. In the rest of this chapter I shall start by giving a quick resumé of what we mean when we talk about 'the mind', 'intelligence' and so on, and then outline a little of the way all this applies to equines and how their minds appear to be similar to, or different from ours.

Much of the later part of this chapter is supposition and guesstimate, but I have been concerned with, and interested in these questions for many years and have been accumulating ideas and information from my own research and that of others, which is both interesting and relevant.

Without these beginnings of an understanding of the equine mind, we cannot really go further with understanding and improving his/her welfare; this is one reason why it is so exciting and interesting, so complex and so frustrating. The equine mind is one of the main reasons why most of us keep and associate with horses: we don't love them only because they are 'black and beautiful'. If that were the case we would have a motor car or a beautiful painting instead. We love them because they have *a mind*, and to predict and understand their behaviour, to communicate even if only in flashes with the mind of another species is an ever-growing excitement and challenge.

The equine mind

At present the positions held on the question of the horse's mind can be roughly divided into two groups:

(1) Firstly there are those who hold a materialist view and they include almost all scientists involved with horses in any way at the moment (veterinarians, nutritionists, agriculturalists, many ethologists and psychologists, including behavioural consultants coming from a scientific background). Their view is that the brain and the mind (of horses at least if not of humans) is one, and that 'the mind' will eventually be explained by understanding more about fundamental physiology; nerve nets, the brain itself, hormones and other chemical and electrical functionings of the brain. Such people are called *materialists* and there is a long tradition of them in philosophy too.

(2) Secondly there is the Cartesian view that the brain and mind are entirely separate; that what the mind does is not and never will be explained by understanding more biochemistry and physiology because the mind is independent of the body, and higher mammals (including of course equines) are like humans in this respect. These people are called traditionally, *dualists*. Again there are many of them in the history of philosophy. Today they include many involved with alternative healing.

A few in the latter group will take their attitude to and understanding of equines further and consider that they not only have minds and bodies but also, like humans, spirits, souls, or astral beings. These they believe, usually work together to create the equine (or human), but they can also exist independently of each other.

(3) Thirdly there are those who try to make bridges between these two camps, who are not sure of either position and may wish to try to clarify what it all means. I am in this camp and my intention is to try to point out some of the questions that we need to research and a little of what we know about the horse's mind.

The situation is further confused however by those who take an anthropomorphic stance, and those who take a species-specific stance. Those who take the anthropomorphic stance may belong to either (1) or (2) above, but they hold the belief that equines are very similar to humans and that what we know about humans can apply to them. Then there are those speciesists who take the view that equines are so different from humans because they have evolved to live in different places in different ways that we must consider each species quite independently of each other, and in fact we may not be able to make any generalities, or even understand another species because their mind and brain will work so differently from ours. Again such people may belong to either of the above camps – so confusion gradually grows! Yet another contrast can be drawn, between people – usually scientists – who take the position that the equine, although able to do relatively simple things with his mind (such as learn and remember simple sequences), is not able to do many of the more sophisticated things with his mind that humans can do (such as plan, use rational thought, deception, empathy, be conscious of themselves and so on). The equines they believe are largely pre-programmed in their behaviour and how their mind operates by 'instinct'. The equine mind is thus relatively limited, and with application, we will be able to understand a great deal about it.

On the other side of the coin are the groups of people who dismiss science as they see it, and develop their own, such as studying the astral plains and supra-natural characteristics of equines utilising radionics, faith healing, laying on of hands, and many alternative medicines (see Tellington-Jones 1992).

The development here, to date, has particularly concentrated on treating unhealthy equines, including sometimes behavioural ill-health, rather than establishing their approach with the normal healthy animal.

There are inconsistencies and problems with both of the approaches just mentioned. For example the 'scientist' will be trained not to think about whether or not the equine is able to do complex mental athletics, and is similar to humans. He already *knows* that equines do not have language, do not think, do not have self-awareness, and consciousness of themselves. The questions are not asked. Similarly the alternative healers, although rejecting the current belief systems of science concerning the equine mind and how it operates, rapidly develop their own science and dogma which also reduces the number of questions they ask. For example many of them will consider that they can communicate with equines, and in their communication with them (which is then translated into English to be told to the onlookers), they use only homocentric concepts without a qualm. If these animals' minds are different from ours then can they not tell us something about this difference if they are so able to communicate, rather than remaining fixed in the normal 'western', rational, mind set? Alternatively, if equines are believed to have a very similar mind to humans and are able to use such concepts as lying, mathematics and so on, then why should they not learn language and communicate in this way? Why can only a few people communicate with them, and why do these people rapidly develop a particular dogma by which they teach each other? (e.g. T-team, radionics).

Surely the alternative therapies themselves fall into the same trap that gave them the rationale to develop their own alternative approach: they succeed in cutting off areas of potential enquiry and understanding just as those they criticise, the conventional scientist.

It would seem that both of these approaches have some nuggets of useful material in helping us understand the mind of the horse, but equally both are restrictive. In the following account, I shall try briefly to summarise what has emerged concerning *the evidence* for a current understanding of the mind of the horse wherever it comes from and particularly where it is relevant to welfare. However, it must be emphasised that this is an area where at present we are just scratching the surface; for every question not only are there a thousand answers, but also ten thousand more questions! The exciting thing is that we have begun to ask the questions, and to open our own minds to different ways of considering and thinking about these issues.

Equine intelligence

The first question that is usually asked of somone interested is 'are horses/donkeys/zebras and other equines intelligent?' Before that can be answered, we have to consider what intelligence is. Over the last century it has been defined in many different ways. Now with the rise of psychometrics the measurement of intelligence in humans has become its own science. The proponents consider that the IQ tests are so well designed that they are not just measuring the ability of the individual to do IQ tests, but also demonstrating general assessments concerning the individual's ability (whatever his culture or background), to perform in situations involving a particular type of problem solving, or rational thinking (see Kline 1991). Psychometrics for equines has yet to be developed, as in its present form it is only relevant to literate humans, although its approach might be useful when applied to other animals. Others, coming from a rather contorted evolutionary position, consider that intelligence involves behaviour which results in the individual being able to manipulate or profit from others' behaviour – Machiavellian intelligence (Bryne 1995). This comes from the proposal that social living was the reason why cognitive complex minds developed. Each individual must be aware of others and their behaviour by becoming a 'natural psychologist' (Humphrey 1984, Jolly 1966).

Individuals in order to survive and leave offspring must also accumulate knowledge about the physical environment. This may be just as important a catalyst for advanced cognitive development – 'intelligence'. Different species may emphasise different paths in their 'intelligence' which humans find difficult to understand.

In recent years there has been a break away from simple interpretations of intelligence with the advent of cognitive science which as we have seen, involves the input of many disciplines. There is a growing realisation that intelligence is complex, and that there are different types (although this is still heavily disputed, see MacPhail 1987).

What we may be doing when we make judgements such as 'my horse is so intelligent' is simply indicating that your horse has grasped some of the ways in which you react. . . and wants to please you. This brings one to the next question: where does emotion come into intelligence or does it? As a rule it has been considered that emotions do not and should not get tangled up with 'intelligence'. Yet it has recently been pointed out by many psychologists that learning, problem solving, in fact all behaviour is inevitably mixed up with emotions. In the first place, there has to be motivation. Emotions in one form or another (pleasure, fear, anxiety, terror, joy, etc.) motivate individuals to learn and 'understand'. Thus the intelligence debate is further fogged by its involvement with emotions, which does not mean that emotional individuals are more intelligent than others. It is just another variable that must be taken into account.

Then there is the difficulty of assessing intelligence as a result of information received from outside. If you have not heard what the teacher has asked you to do, you will score low marks, but this does not indicate low 'intelligence'. When dealing particularly with different species, sensory receptors are different and what to us would appear almost impossible, to equines may be very easy because they have received different messages. One example here is the equines' abilities to pick up visual cues which we humans are bad at, and similarly the humans' abilities to pick up verbal cues which horses are not so good at. Both might be able to learn to improve at the other skill and thus understand each other better. But this is more difficult than doing what we normally or naturally do.

There may as we have suggested, be different types of 'intelligence'. In humans, some people appear to have intelligence in learning and playing music, while others will be mathematicians. Others will be very able at using their mind to work out quick and efficient ways of doing simple tasks while those who may score highly in another way, academically for example, may be unable either to develop or use such intelligence. When does 'talent' become intelligence? The more one thinks about such things, the more difficult a definition becomes even with humans, never mind with another species which may be better than we are at certain mental tasks and worse at others.

In conclusion then, it appears that there are a multitude of ways in which 'intelligence' can be defined and measured. Perhaps when it comes to comparing species with species it is not a very useful concept; perhaps, in effect, it is not very useful when used even within one species. There may be a way in which a 'multi-dimensional understanding' of mental abilities could be useful to compare individuals and species in the future, but that is a long way off.

Communication and language

Communication and *what* is communicated is one way of trying to understand more about an animal's mind. After all, if he/she could *tell* us, how much easier it would be to understand more about the animal's mind.

Almost all horse owners believe that they can communicate with their horse and he with them and they will tell you innumerable stories and anecdotes if you demonstrate an interest in this topic. The problem of anecdotes is how much they are the result of that individual human's pre-conceived notions and beliefs – and how much is useful example. Anecdotes told and researched by trained personnel may be very valuable and reliable sources of information but there is no way that the frequent 'horse story' one hears really helps us to understand more about the horse's mind – but it often tells us something about the human who is telling it!

A more satisfactory way of learning more about animal minds and communication is to study them communicating with each other (Griffin 1992). It is not denied by almost anyone now that animals can communicate; but what they communicate, and how, remain areas of controversy. Since Darwin (1868) scientists have been studying animal communication. Lorenz and Tinbergen in the 1940s and fifties maintained that animals communicate using many sensory modalities: touch, sight, smell, hearing, taste. They perform certain behaviours and they believed that the signal and its message is 'instinctive': animals are pre-programmed and are sparked off by what are called 'innate releasing mechanisms'. Thus horses have a series of postures and facial expressions which have innate meanings and are performed instinctively.

In this way animals were believed to communicate information about the communicator's emotional state: whether he/she was feeling sexy, aggressive or fearful for example. The information was transferred by signals which began in the species' evolutionary past as typical behaviour relevant to that situation, but had then become exaggerated, and sometimes emancipated from the original cause and context to become important as a signal. This latter process involving exaggerations, stylisation perhaps and emancipation (from

*The yearling colt 'champs' by opening and closing his mouth with
the corners of the lips drawn back when greeting an older mare.
This implies 'I'm a rather young and hopeless chap and I just want
to be friends, and won't be any problem to you!' It may be
accompanied by squatting and even urinating when a young colt is
greeting the older stallion.*

what had caused the behaviour) was called 'ritualisation' (see
Huxley 1969). The ear-flattening of equines in aggressive
situations is a typical example. Here initially ear withdrawal
occurred when the animal was threatened around the head as a
protective response (to stop the ears being damaged). This ear
withdrawal was therefore characteristic of aggressive or
threatening situations. As a result it was a good candidate to
become a signal and convey information concerning aggresive
or defensive emotions to another. In the process it became
exaggerated, so that it was easy to see and clearly different from
ear withdrawal for other reasons (e.g. paying attention behind),
and it also became removed from its original cause: it became
characteristic of the aggressor and has a particular meaning:
'get out of the way or I will bite you, and I am serious' (see
Kiley-Worthington 1987 for further discussion of this). In this
way it is a ritualised display ('display' is a behaviour performed

to convey a message to others). Many of the ideas on the evolution of communication and how it worked in animal societies came from research on gulls and stickleback fish, but these ideas were then used generally to explain how communication worked in any species. This has been helpful up to a point but one problem, particularly with equines, is that they do not have many obvious ritualised displays, the ear flattening is one of the few they have. Does this mean that they are just not communicating or does communication work in other ways for them?

If there are more subtle signs that are conveying messages, then how are we to know this and separate the movements and postures performed for communication from those done for other reasons? For example when a horse pricks his ears and looks over the hedge, another horse (or a human) sees this and picks up the message that there is something interesting over there. Is the horse pricking his ears in order to communicate a message or is he *only* doing it because he has seen something interesting? One way of testing this is to find out if he would do this when he wanted to direct the attention of others over the hedge even though he was not particularly interested in what was over there himself. These questions are tricky, and what most ethologists (those who study animal behaviour and communication) did (and still do) is to avoid considering behaviour that is not performed *primarily* for communication as communication at all.

One of the areas where there is little dispute in this respect is that of vocalisation. There is generally no reason for making a vocalisation through the larynx for any other reason than to communicate. This ensured that animal noises became one of the central areas for the study of animal communication, including in particular, birdsong. There have been some very interesting and exciting discoveries as a result, but in equines, vocalisations are not very sophisticated and are related to giving information about the general state of arousal or excitement of the individual, rather than particular messages about a specific thing around (Kiley-Worthington 1976).

In some respects this was comforting because it meant that one of the central arguments for the difference between humans and other higher mammals remained intact; animals did *not* have language. If they have no language then it has been argued, as we have seen, there are many other mental exercises that will be unavailable to them. It was not until the Gardiners started teaching Washoe, the chimp, sign language and she, and now several other chimps, have learnt what one might call a language, that this particular idea was seriously questioned by academics. Yet, at the same time people who lived with animals, and particularly those who train them to do quite complex tasks, rely on the belief that the animal 'understands' the gestural or verbal language used, otherwise they would not be able to train them the way they do.

At this stage what exactly language was began to be discussed and defined. A man called Hockett (1958) drew up criteria for defining language and, when assessed, the chimps who had learnt a human-structured language seemed to fulfil all but one of these criteria. At our research centre we looked at the detailed communication between horses and found that even equines conformed to six of the eight criteria. Is language then, by definition, only that which humans use? Or are there other ways of looking at this?

It may well be that relatively complex ideas and thoughts may be put across from one equine to another, as yet we do not know. They may learn to use language in a similar way to us: understanding and using word order to convey different meanings and so on. They certainly can learn to comprehend language, but again we don't yet know how far this can go. Few experimental psychologists (who are centrally involved with learning) will consider that equines would *not* be able to learn the *meaning* of specific phrases, and not just the expression put into the words.

Can equines think about the future and the past? We do not yet know the answer and there remain many years of work to do. Yet what we do know is that they are skilled visual communicators, absorbing information concerning other individuals even of different species by picking up visual cues and interpreting them. They apparently have different areas of expertise when it comes to language than we do, but whether we will ever be able to understand enough about their way of communicating, or they about ours, to be able to iron out all the difficulties, and incomprehensions is difficult to say. Wittgenstein thought not; he may even have thought it would not be worth trying: 'if a lion could talk we could not understand him' (Wittgenstein 1953). More recently Nagel (1974) argued in a famous paper entitled 'What is it like to be a bat?' that each species was so different from us mentally that there would be no way in which we could understand what it was like to be them, suggesting that attempts to communicate with them could have only a limited hope of success. Others don't think he was right and research in the last ten years supports this. We may not have all the answers but we have more now as a result of looking, learning, recording and studying what and how animals communicate, than we had. We may never have the whole story, but we certainly are understanding more about 'what it is like to be a horse' than we did.

In conclusion, communication and language are important for understanding how equine minds might work and where their limits might be. But the more we find out, the less we find there are easy or rigid distinctions to be drawn between humans and equines in these respects. Equines are, however, sophisticated visual communicators (and may use other sensory modalities too, such as olfaction and tactile communication to a much greater extent than we do). We humans, by contrast are verbal auditory communicators.

It is rash at this stage to assume that no equines will ever be able to do many of the advanced cognitive processes that most humans can do with language. It may be so, but the more we learn about these animals' communicative abilities and escape from our preconceived notions of what they are able to do, the more they seem to be able to do! So far, unlike apes, dolphins and whales for example, equines have had almost no serious research attention in this respect. Perhaps, therefore, until there is more proof to the contrary we should assume *similarities* rather than differences of mind and communicative ability between horse and human.

Consciousness and self-awareness

This is another teasing difficult problem on which scholars have thought and written for a couple of thousand years. Only recently however, in the last two decades, have we seriously been considering whether our equines, dogs, cats, and bees are conscious, and if so, conscious of what?

It is generally understood now that there are various levels of consciousness.

(1) Not 'unconscious', and therefore able to respond to sensory sensations of various sorts: visual, tactile, olfactory and so on. Almost no one nowadays denies that equines can do this, they are conscious and able to perceive and react to things and objects: they are sentient.

(2) The next level is given various names, but involves a more analytical consciousness: being able to learn, to remember, have purpose, goals and beliefs; being able to think (however this is done without human type language) and act rationally, form concepts and use symbols in simple ways. There is no space to outline this argument in detail, but now, not only among the animal lovers, but also among the cognitive psychologists and ethologists, it is generally considered that equines as higher mammals will be able to do all of these things that dogs, pigeons, parrots, and rats have been shown to do, so that equines are conscious at this level also.

(3) The third level of consciousness is that concerned with awareness of one's own and others' minds – consciousness of self. Can a donkey think to itself in some form 'here I am, and I am getting thin and miserable'? Is s/he aware that other donkeys may have minds and be thinking about him, and can s/he predict what they might be thinking and act accordingly? Does s/he have an idea of the future and can s/he plan for it and plan to change it? Finally even if he could demonstrate at least some simple ability in this regard could the donkey or horse ever have the concept of something as advanced and homo-centric as a bank manager?

Some tests with chimps with mirrors have indicated that chimps may have an awareness of self, or at least learn this (Gallup et al. 1977). Similar tests with elephants however indicated that they would use the mirror to manipulate objects they could not see, but who knows if they were recognising themselves? (Povenelli et al. 1990). Nobody to date has reported such tests with any equine, although we are beginning to construct similar ones.

If it is difficult to test whether or not an animal has an idea of himself – the next best thing might be to see if he has an idea of other minds or other agents. Does he act as if he were aware that others have minds and can decide to do various things: does he ever deceive others? Again there are endless anecdotes about how horses or dogs deceive their owners. The problem with these is that they may just be the interpretation that the owner puts on the action. We cannot consider such stories as reliable evidence. But now that we are looking for answers we can construct tests to see what equines might do. This has been done with various primates which have been shown to use deception. It may be that equines are in any case not particularly interested in deception and lying, but more interested in 'honesty as a good policy' in social relationships (Kiley-Worthington in press). Do they show any evidence for compassion and empathy? This would indicate an awareness that others have feelings too, and therefore an awareness, not just of another body, but of his being: his mind. Again no research has so far been reported on this, although there are plenty of anecdotes.

Another approach is to consider *imitation*. Can equines imitate actions and learn by imitation? This would indicate an awareness of others and of their minds. There is increasing evidence that equines (and other higher mammals) can do this and even pass on information between generations in this way, e.g. elephants (Moss 1988, Kiley-Worthington and Randle 1995). One of the problems with equines is that unlike primates they do not manipulate things much of the time. Does this mean that they can't, won't, or just don't want or need to? Does this mean that they are not in the same ball park cognitively as primates, or are they just different and may perhaps be doing things of similar complexity, but different? Who knows? These questions have not to date been very seriously approached for many species; research and thinking along these lines is just beginning, but again perhaps it is wise, and rational, at this stage to leave the door open and consider that equines might indeed be performing these cognitive games too.

What do we know about the mind of equines?

Those of us who have much to do with equines, and particularly those of us who teach them, will agree on the whole that equines have physical, emotional and even intellectual/cognitive lives; that they have a mind. We know that they learn, and have desires. We consider that they have beliefs and have purpose and goal direction, that they can make decisions and 'think' and solve even quite complex problems rationally. In other words they show a range of complex cognitive/mental behaviour and do not just act in some pre-programmed 'instinctive' way although they do indeed, like the rest of us, show instinctive tendencies (a human one is to behave sexually at certain times to certain stimuli, another to walk bipedally). But how we, or equines, do these things, depends on our experiences and learning during our lifetime.

We know that equines are sophisticated visual communicators and have elaborate and complex social systems and relationships; that individuals even of one sex or age class vary greatly; and it is even becoming possible to outline the 'personality profile' of individuals (Kiley-Worthington 1987, p. 141).

We know that horses are movement specialists and when allowed to develop the skills are able to move at speed over rough ground, and even that they apparently take pleasure in moving 'for fun'. We also are learning to recognise in equines a complex communication system similar to language, but much is yet to be researched.

We know that they can learn rapidly (sometimes in one trial), that they remember well, that they form habits easily and tend to stick to them, that they can relearn and unlearn, and can learn complex sequences of acts (Kiley-Worthington 1987, chapter 9).

We know that they are conscious of the world, and react to it. This is called by some consciousness level (1). We also know that they are often at consciousness level (2), which involves accumulating cognitive knowledge about the world, showing purpose, goal directed behaviour, having beliefs, being able to 'think' and solve problems rationally.

We know that they can learn symbols and comprehend at least simple human language they have been taught. We think they can be taught to form concepts and may use them in their own lives, since although they have not been tested, other species usually considered less mentally able than equines have done this. This can be called consciousness level (3).

Finally we don't know if they are self-aware – consciousness level (4) – but they do show some evidence of awareness of others and other minds or agents, since they imitate each other and indeed can learn to imitate members of other species, thus learning from each other and that they are conscious of other minds and bodies (Kiley-Worthington and Randle in press). If they are aware of others' minds, beliefs and desires, then they may *also* be aware of their own (Griffin 1992).

At present we have to conclude that equines (at least the horses on which most of the research has been done, and there is no reason to believe that the other equines will be very different in their fundamental cognitive abilities) are able to do many things with their minds that most of us did not think they could. In other words their minds work much like ours in many ways, and where we have doubt we have decided it would at this stage be more rational to back *similarity* rather than *difference*. However they are after all horses, and different from us in many ways. Some things are more important to them than to us and vice-versa. We know little about this and once we have discovered the *similarities* of our cognitive abilities and workings we can better understand the *differences*.

Then how should we treat our horses? Is it just a question of being nice to them because, although they are unaware of many things and cannot plan, predict or be self-aware, they are quaint and we have moral obligations to be nice to them because at least they feel? Or is it a little more complex than this, and since they are rather more cognitively similar to us than we thought, should we not treat them with something of the same respect we show other humans? We have some indications of our similiarities with equines, and some of our differences but there remains a host of questions needing answers as to where the lines between similarities and differences should be drawn.

If we are to give the benefit of any doubt to the equines on these questions we can draw up *some* guidelines, but particularly in the area of cognition (mental life), these must remain speculative. However we have quite a good idea of the equine's physical and social needs. (Kiley-Worthington 1987, Rees 1984.)

8

Learning, handling and teaching

Equines, like all species including humans, have their behaviour controlled not only by physiological criteria, but also by their genetic make up . . . they have instinctive (preprogrammed) tendencies to behave in certain ways in certain situations, but they can also learn, and even these 'instinctive tendencies' can sometimes be changed as a result. Learning is defined in the English dictionary as 'getting knowledge of a subject, or a skill in something'. In the dictionary of psychology it is however defined as 'a modification of a response following upon, and resulting from experience of results'. Putting these together, perhaps we could define learning as something like: 'the acquiring of knowledge and changing of behaviour as a result of experience during the individual's lifetime'.

As we have mentioned (chapter 7), until the last decades, learning for animals was confined to 'conditioning' (Pavlovian and Operant or Instrumental conditioning see Fiske 1979, and Kiley-Worthington 1987, chapter 9, for a discussion of how horses learn). There are many scientists and others who still believe that animals only learn by conditioning and 'early learning' often called 'imprinting' which are semi-automatic responses which the animal has little control over, and thus quite different from humans mentally since, it is often believed, animals cannot think, or learn by other means: they are instinctive learning robots (see chapter 7).

In the last decade there has been a minor revolution concerning what and how animals learn based on laboratory experimentations conducted by those who have been studying learning: experimental psychologists. The result is that there is a general agreement among those who spend their life studying this problem, that higher mammals at least, of which of course

95

Using clear visual clues with a young horse that had never previously been in the ring/school. To send him away, I stand up straight and even raise my hand behind him, with shoulders back and an upright posture, looking him in the eye.

To get him to come towards me, I collapse my body and present my hand to him to follow to the centre, thus reducing any caution and rather encouraging his interest.

Shemal, one of our cognitive subjects, whom we have been working with for 3 years now, kicks the ball when asked, as one of us does the teaching, the other records the horse's response. The girth around her waist carries a pulse monitor to record her general level of excitement, which will give us some indication of her emotional state while she does this.

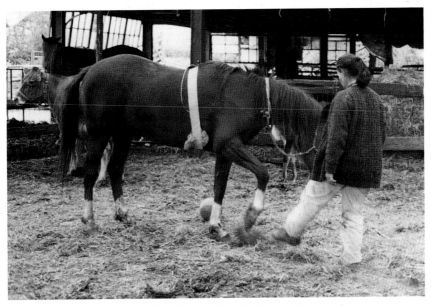

Shemal paws the ground when told to imitate the teacher.

Shemal stands on the pedestal and, after rotating around her front legs, she is given some food reward and told how brilliant she is; positive reinforcement. This has proved to be a very important motivation for the subjects, who learn very fast.

equines are one group, not only learn by conditioning but also are able to acquire knowledge about their surroundings and their behaviour by absorbing information which is not related to conditioning; it is if you like 'conditioning neutral'. There is also a general belief now among such scientists that many species are capable of learning more complex things than we previously thought possible, of remembering well, and so on.

As horse keepers and trainers many of us will have intuitively felt that equines are able to learn many things and some quite complex, because after all they are primarily kept to perform complex tasks which have to be learnt (e.g. carrying people on their backs, pulling vehicles, jumping jumps, learning dressage movements and so on). On the other hand there are some beliefs held among both scientists (who don't deal with equines), and those who teach about equines, that are the result of a general attitude: a reflection of our present cultural understanding. Some of these ideas are handed down one to another and have not been examined carefully. One example is that horses have to be taught everything on both sides because their brain does not have a *corpus callosum*, which is the piece of the brain that allows information to cross from the left to the right hemisphere and vice versa. This was an idea put forward by a scientist (see Heird et al. 1986) and is just not true; horses do have a *corpus callosum* . . . he must have dissected a queer brain! Another curious belief was that the retina of the horse's eye is 'ramped' not semi-circular, and thus the light rays fall on the retina at different distances from the lens, depending on the angle at which they strike the lens. Again this is faulty: the originator of this belief (which is still taught in many veterinary schools and equine studies courses) must have dissected a squashed eye. Research at Cornell in the seventies indicated that this widely taught theory was wrong.

Similarly certain trainers believe that 'horses learn very slowly' and so things have to be repeated frequently. They may believe that equines cannot learn much at all; they are stupid. Some of those interested in telepathy have insisted that they have talked in English (French, German what you will) to the equine, and s/he responded, not only in the same language but with all the normal human concepts, such as age and time (course on Animal Communication 1994, Gloucestershire). In other words equines can learn (or some people would consider just 'know') the same things as humans and in just the same way. There may be wisps of ideas in both of these approaches, but how do we sort out what may really be going on?

It is clear that there are different types of learning. In the first instance, as soon as the foal is born he begins to learn not only about where he is, but how to get up and use his body, and who his mother is. This is usually called 'imprinting' or 'early learning'. The idea here is that the foal in order to survive must recognise his mother, and if you like, have an 'imprint' made in his brain so that he can recognise her thereafter, so that he does not try and follow and suckle from the wrong mare. The general idea of 'imprinting' for which the models used were gulls and stickle back fish, was that this type of learning was irreversible. Once the youngster had learnt that this individual was Mum, that was it, nothing could shake this belief. Indeed trials with chicks 'imprinting' them on to model railway trains, or goslings onto Lorenz's hat have become classics. In mammals however, even this early learning appears to be much more complex. For example most youngsters are opportunists; they will try and suckle from another mother that lets them, and follow any likely source of food even forgetting who their own mother is if better meals are to be had elsewhere. Pigs, wild dogs, and many other species even look after and suckle each other's young communally.

Foals in the first few hours of their life have not only to recognise their mother, or at least an object worth trying to suckle from, but, more importantly, they have to get up and stand, walk, find the teat and suckle. All of which are complex behaviours which they have genetic tendencies to perform; but how and when they are performed is learnt and extremely varied between foals. Some may be up and suckling within ten minutes of birth, others may fall twenty times as they try to get up; they may not suckle for five hours or even more after birth. In addition there are no guarantees that the foal will follow his mother even after suckling; some will, some will not, some will follow another foal or gelding. So even imprinting is not hard, fast, irreversible learning in equines; it takes a good few days for the foal to recognise mum and stay with her, just as in human infants.

One of the very interesting things about foals is that they are born precocial: that is very well developed and immediately (unlike babies, who just lie around being helpless for months), they have to start learning fast: both the body and the mind are well developed at birth. Not only do they have to learn how to get up, suckle etc. – all complicated manoeuvres that humans take months to learn to do – but they must also be able to absorb infomation from the physical and social environment: who is who in their equine community, who will be nice and who to avoid, who is a member of the group and who is not. They also have to absorb information about the physical environment, where is the bog, how to cross the stream, not to walk through fences, what to eat once they start eating at around ten days old. Much of this is learnt by watching and imitating mum, and other older horses.

So even in the first few hours the foal is learning and probably absorbing information. This is called silent learning by psychologists and happens very fast and even when very young the foal is not acting as a result of reflex responses alone. What happens when he matures, how does he learn when we start to teach him particular responses that we want?

Equines are prey animals, specialising in movement – running away is their survival strategy. Thus their solution to almost any strange environmental change, is caution: to

It is advisable to get the foal used to contact with humans from very young, to encourage him to be interested and to have a head collar and learn to follow a human. Again, body language is crucial. Here, Chris relaxes with the 3-week-old foal who had not been touched by a human before, and encourages the foal to be interested and make contact, allaying fear and encouraging curiosity.

escape, and run away. If they are prevented from doing this by physical restraint for example, they will often fight harder and become hysterical: unable to learn or attempt to solve the problem, they leap, thrash about, and even throw themselves down. This may continue until they either collapse or 'freeze' immobile, which is a response that occurs in most mammalian species when they have reached the zenith of their fear and terror. During their thrashing about, they will be oblivious to any other object, even injury to themselves. This is not just 'stupid', it is hysteria and humans behave similarly in similar conditions. For example, French law has always recognised this type of behaviour, even if it has resulted in murder, it has been called 'crime passionel', where it is judged that when sufficiently provoked emotionally, it is considered inevitable that the individual will no longer be responsible for his actions.

It is particularly curious that the technique for 'breaking' horses has often particularly in western United States, Australia, and South America been just this. 'Breaking' is usually used to refer to 'breaking his spirit', or 'teaching him obedience and who is dominant'. The animal, who is often adult, and has had little previous experience of humans (and thus is suspicious of and unfamiliar with them), is physically restrained and then provoked to a point of extreme terror, until he reaches the fear-freeze point, after which he is said to be 'broken' and will do what is required. There is no evidence that this type of approach enhances learning thereafter, in fact it is likely to have a negative effect on learning and teach the horse to be, quite rationally, suspicious of the humans; this may take a very long while to overcome. There is no evidence, either, that it is quicker which is often given as the argument why it is done by Western US cowboys. Lucy Rees, one of the small band of people interested in improving horse teaching techniques, made a television film comparing the time to ride quietly a previously untouched feral horse to one trained by a top Western trainer in the traditional style. She worked with her wild horse by familiarising him with humans, and by cooperative teaching. At the end of the six weeks, the western cowboy was still not able to ride his horse, while Lucy was sitting on her's riding relaxedly only in a head collar quietly up the river into the sunset!

The approach of 'breaking' and 'dominating' the horse has certainly been encouraged by human cultural attitudes. One of the most important beliefs is that to overcome and 'dominate' a large animal who fights all the way will ensure higher macho status in the human community. It has always been associated with men, to enhance their status among men and, perhaps, attraction to women. The traditional Rodeo sports so beloved by US Western traditionalists, are based on this 'overcoming' of the beast by man, although now with equal opportunity legislation women are joining the men. It must be borne in mind however, that many of the horses as well as the humans have been taught to behave as they are expected in the rodeo (see chapter 15).

In parts of Europe, particularly France and Britain, among certain sections of the population, this approach to horse 'breaking' has not been standard practice for some centuries, although they have retained the use of the word 'break' in

England ('dresser' = to train in French). Trainers have generally tried to condition the equine more gradually to restraints
and to carry people on his back, or pull. In the latter case, the
traditional practice for training particularly heavy draught
horses, was to have the experienced horse teach them by
harnessing the youngster adjacent to the working horse, but
not attached to the implement.

Ideas on the teaching of horses are at last beginning to catch
up with our knowledge and understanding of how learning
works, and the communicative skills of equines. There are a
number of people now outlining alternative strategies for
teaching horses in different parts of the world. I have already
mentioned Lucy Rees who has been using cooperative teaching
of horse and rider for some years. Monty Roberts, whose
origins were in the rodeo circuit, is one of those who has
understood the horse's quick ability to read visual cues, and
developed particular body postures to teach the horse to go
away, or come towards him. This works remarkably quickly,
and dramatically; but as with von Osten and Clever Hans,
people find it difficult to accept that there is not a trick
somewhere! Maurice Wright of Australia has written on the
Jeffrey method of training with success (Wright 1973 and
1983) again developing handling and teaching strategies based
on body language and positive reinforcement: pleasure rather
than pain. Linda Tellington Jones (1995) has developed an
approach she calls the 'TTeam' approach which, although
becoming rapidly obliterated in a dogma, seems to rely largely
on better handling and positive reinforcement for the horse.
Alternative therapies, including radionics, communication by
telepathy, laying on of hands, shiatsu (see Kaselle and Hannay
1995) and some others are all becoming of increasing interest
to equine owners and even some trainers. One thing they all
have in common and which may turn out to be the most
important for the successes they claim, is that they all approach
the animal with empathy and have developed sympathetic non-
invasive ways of handling, and ensuring that this goes on for
some time, with minimum physical or pharmacological
restraint and no pain, thus effectively teaching the horse that
humans can be pleasant rather than unpleasant, and
consequently, relaxing the subject in the presence of humans.
This, in itself, never mind the particular explanation of each
alternative therapy (e.g. energy movement, lymphatic

distribution, thought transfer, and so on) can have dramatic effects on both the physical and mental health of the equine, or any other animal.

As scientists (those interested in increasing knowledge) we need to study these methods more carefully, and assess their successes critically, rather than dismiss them. We also in my view need to extract the important aspects from them, and then develop a cooperative training strategy in theory and practice which can then be thoughtfully taught, without the practitioner having to become too deeply embroiled in the dogma attached to each. This is something we, at our centre, have been working on and practising for some years. We certainly do not yet have all the answers, but we can already ensure quicker, easier, less traumatic and pleasurable education for both horse and human.

We will outline some well-known, and some not so well-known ways in which this can be achieved and how from the point of view of the animal's welfare and health this can progress from the foal onwards. This is used as an example of how important learning and the environment is in the psychological development of the foal, and how 'instinct' and 'learning' interact in the life of an equine.

The development of the foal and his learning: equine developmental psychology

It is important that the foal has learnt to be familiar and confident with humans before the formal teaching begins if the learning is to be free of trauma and therefore successful. The easiest way of ensuring this is to take trouble to form a *good or positive emotional bond* with the youngster and *handle* him so that he is never frightened or learns not to trust the human. The role of emotions in affecting learning is important although not completely understood yet. This also involves the human handler in learning *how to handle well*, another area of animal teaching that needs much examination and questioning. Has it always been done in the best possible way? Are even the most advanced and best teachers as good as they could be? Research is just beginning to scratch the surface in our understanding of this and how to do it. Here it will suffice to point out some general rules, some of which some people may use, some may be new.

The first thing to consider when teaching an equine is *how the equine perceives the world*, and secondly what particular characteristics of learning he is likely to have. Then we must structure the handling, and learning around this.

One obvious example, which we have already mentioned is that, unlike humans, equines are very sophisticated visual communicators, but not very good at verbal communication. They do not verbalise, but that is not to say they may not be able to comprehend language, or at least some of it.

We know that how the human moves and what he does with all parts of his body, where his attention is directed and so on all give messages to the equine which may not be obvious to the human. Thus the human has to learn a completely new language without a translator. If you like, she has to try and learn Chinese without an interpreter. It is hard, and easy to dismiss the equine on the grounds that he is 'just stupid and cannot understand' when, in fact, it is the human who is not understanding and perhaps not even trying. One of the tendencies when one is not understood by other humans speaking a different language is to shout louder and get more excited because one is not understood. By so doing with the equine one is also communicating a bunch of messages they will pick up concerning one's emotional state, which is not at all conducive to them doing anything but trying to get out of it and run away. . . would you not if the Martians started tying you up and then getting very excited and shouting, gesticulating and even leaping around?

Improving and teaching good handling skills is an exciting and exacting field of enquiry, but suffice it to say here that there is much room for improvement by even the most able equine handler. The message to be transferred to the equine when being handled, is that *he is to do nothing*, however frightening or interesting the situation that arises, he should just stand still; he must learn that is the safest thing to do. How to behave in order to achieve this is the problem for the human. It should be seriously taught to the human handler over a period of months, not dismissed in an afternoon's work which is usual, even in veterinary schools where the students are being prepared to be veterinarians who, even if they do nothing else, have to handle animals. Nor is it necessarily best learnt 'by experience' any more than learning to program a computer would be.

The next stage of the equine's education is to teach him to do something as a result of some stimulus. This is best done by *conditioning using positive reinforcement (reward)*. Traditionally in some equitation schools in the American west, for example, negative reinforcement is often used (if you do this, you will be hurt, or frightened). In certain situations, there may be a place for using negative reinforcement in the advanced teaching of equines, but certainly not at the beginning of their learning life with humans if the aim is to teach the animal quickly and to have a reliable student, highly motivated to learn.

Punishment is not negative reinforcement; it comes after the act not before, and its effects are not well understood. At present it is frequently used in horse training, and often with quite inappropriate results: the animal is taught not to do the desired behaviour as a result of the use of punishment!

There are some general rules which can be used to great advantage when teaching equines; these are summarised as follows.

General rules to help with handling equines

(1) Understand that one may be sending messages without knowing it to the animals, because of their ability to respond to visual cues. Study and learn whole body language but also the messages that can be transferred by positions and movements of parts of the body (the head, gaze, hands, feet, and so on).

(2) Understand how both Pavlovian and Instrumental conditioning works.

(3) Construct the situation so that the equine is *motivated* (wants to do whatever it is), and also is *attending* (see pp. 169–88 Kiley Worthington 1987). The use of positive reinforcement at appropriate times, whether this is food reward or verbal or tactile praise is very important here.

(4) Be consistent with the conditioned stimuli (aids), and never ignore the equine's response.

(5) Develop appropriate schedules of learning to perform

more complex tasks. Thus to start with, when the animal *begins* to give part of the desired behaviour, he is rewarded, then he needs to do a little more, and then one action followed by the start of another, before reward – and so on.

(6) Because the equine is a fast learner, it is very important to understand that if he is not doing it correctly, this is because the teacher/trainer is not presenting the problem correctly and therefore she must think again and try a different strategy.

(7) Because the equine learns fast, it is important not to repeat the action very frequently, or the equine may invent new actions or 'play up' in order to increase the interest.

(8) It is particularly important not to allow the action to be repeated incorrectly as the equine will quickly form a habit and if this is not what is required, it will need hard work retraining. It is always easier to *teach the right action* than to correct the wrong.

(9) Escape from the belief that the equine will 'try to outdo or overcome you' and build up cooperative relationships with the trainees, as one tries to do with other humans, not by domination, but by cooperation and reciprocity: 'you do this for me and I will do that for you'.

(10) Most individuals (equines or humans) do not particularly want to have to make decisions and 'lead' all the time, they wish to have a consistent and acceptable code of practice to follow, and even obey and follow a particular individual without too much questioning. Most of this behaviour is learnt from each other, some may be individually assessed, but the important thing for the teacher/trainer of equine or human, is to establish the appropriate mutual respect so that the students will listen, learn and then with respect perform well and follow leads.

It is important to realise that the equine is not only very quick to learn, but, because of this he will equally quickly *learn the wrong response* if he has been *inadvertently* taught. This is one, if not *the* most common cause of behavioural problems in equines (when driving, riding and working). For example, they have learnt to buck, rear, bolt, not go into the trailer, or stable; to bite or kick, and so on because they have been *taught to* by humans who have not understood how conditioning works.

The equine also has an ability to *learn from one trial* as many prey species have. If they get it wrong they are dead, so getting it righter means staying alive, and consequently the behaviour is learned quickly. Predators can make mistakes chasing and catching their prey; they can nearly always have another go. If the prey makes a mistake and is caught, he is eaten; consequently prey must learn in one trial, and this will be selected for because those that do this live long enough to breed.

Perhaps for the same reason, they also *form habits very easily*. If it more or less works once, then it will be performed again, because, at least the performer is still alive. But, from the human's point of view, the wrong as well as the right habits are very rapidly formed, and once these are established, they are difficult to change, although it can be done with time and skill.

Equines also *remember for long periods*; it is not only elephants that can do this! This ability would presumably be useful and mean the difference between life and death, and therefore be selected for by a prey species. One experience, particularly a frightening one (but it can work the other way where the animal has a *pleasant, free of worry experience* doing something rather difficult during his early life) will be remembered and result in the animal either getting very scared at any similar situation, or not batting an eyelid. We have recently been collecting information on the latter (pleasant experiences) in our young horses, and assessing what happens years later. For example the foals are taken out with their mothers on the roads and on the moor with bogs, trees, wire, and water to negotiate. When they are ridden for the first time, provided they have had no unpleasant experience at these times, they will without hesitation go under the trees, through the water, even walk over low suspended wires, and this may be two years after their first unconcerned experience with these things.

As we have seen (chapter 7) learning is not just the result of conditioning. Equines are of course also picking up all sorts of information from their surroundings all the time: *silent learning*. The social, physical, emotional and cognitive environments are all very important if learning is to progress easily and quickly, and the animal is to learn to do complex tasks.

Finally, one thing is also clear for equines, *they learn to learn*. That is, the more the equine learns, the more he will show abilities to learn more. In fact he appears, like humans, to have a growing need for intellectual/cognitive stimulation as a result of having exciting changing, stimulating experiences. This can be useful; for example a circus horse will need to learn new and different routines and movements, not just repeat the known ones. Provided a dressage horse is allowed to progress (and not spend his life trotting circles before he is taught to work on 3 tracks or airs above the ground), this can be true for him too. For horses working on the land it can also be important so that they learn how to cope with different implements. A recent example here was given by our Arab stallion, Carif, who has had a reasonably cognitively interesting environment. Throughout his life he has been a pilot subject for some of our research and has been learning many different movements and types of work. Recently, he had to learn to walk in the furrows pulling the potato plough to make them deep to plant the potatoes. Once the potatoes were planted in these furrows, he then had to walk balanced on the top of the furrows in order to split them so that they covered the potatoes. It was hard work pulling the ridger, but having to learn this skill perhaps kept him going better. He quickly learn to do this, within ten rows, although some of our other Arabs who have had less experience at being taught and learning complex task experience did not learn this skill in the time available. One of the controlling variables may have been the individual horse's different abilities, but just as important may well be our increasing skills in teaching what is required. As a result of the research we have been conducting over the last four years, we are very much more careful, particularly how we use language.

On the other hand, we must not interpret equine behaviour in a totally human way. For example, a popular concept used (and taught in equine training manuals) is that he is 'trying to get away with it' or 'trying to outdo' the human. This assumes:

(1) That the equine will not desire to do what ever it is that he is doing, and therefore must be made to . . . not encouraged to want to.

(2) That he will have these relatively complex concepts, because they are expected and common in western human culture. This concept depends largely on the individual having a very competitive and often manipulative view of the world, (which is the way humans, and possibly primates view their world and judge others by). Equines are unlikely to have the motivation – since their world is not one dominated by

concepts such as how to improve it by manipulation – either to want, or, perhaps, be able to do this.

Thus if they are not doing what is required, it is much more likely because
(1) They are scared or suspicious, or
(2) They have learnt to do, or not to do, something as a result of inappropriate teaching by the human. Remember they learn in one trial, so if once it has been presented wrongly and the animal has done the wrong thing, he is more likely to do the same next time. Soon this will become a habit (which equines form very readily) and it will be difficult to reteach him.

The equine is not trying to 'win points', why would he want to anyway? This is certainly a human concept and view of the world, which, at the end of a long day, one is inclined to agree with many trainers, is sometimes very difficult not to use as an explanation for equine behaviour. It can look very much as if the horse is trying to be a nuisance in order to annoy, but there are other explanations. If we think about it, we can often realise what these are and, perhaps, also remember the previous incident in which the equine learnt to behave in this way; but it can be hard work for the teacher to do this.

Understanding and acting on these ideas, as far as training and handling equines goes, is one of the most important advances that can be made, from the welfare of the equine's point of view. There would clearly be benefits reaped by the humans too as accidents can and would be avoided. The important thing is to understand the equine and how he learns. If the human teacher had just sat down and thought about why she is doing this or that, in this or that way, and analysed the equine's past experience, as far as she knows it, it is more than likely that s/he will come up with recognising her mistakes, and a way forward to teach the equine.

At our research and teaching centre, we are at present researching animal teaching and how to think about and improve it; the first steps perhaps in the 'science (understanding and knowledge) of animal educational psychology'. We will be able, with further study and the help of philosophers, scientists and interested trainers, to go much further. This is a beginning, pointing out how an assessment of equine teaching is necessary and can begin to be of benefit to both the equines', and the humans' welfare.

Part 2

Are current ways of keeping
equines cruel?

9

Equine husbandry: current establishment practices

The prime consideration, so it is repeatedly declared by horse owners in different establishments throughout the world, is 'the welfare of the horse'. This may be a thoroughly morally correct position but the problem arises in determining what *is* best for the horse's health and happiness? Is what is written in the innumerable text books, and endless string of articles by well-known and respected members of the horse-owning establishment correct, and how do we judge this? Are we so sure that the horse would be in agreement, or are we just making judgements concerning his welfare on the grounds that:

(1) We know what is good for him as he is, perhaps beautiful and lovable, but an unthinking, 'instinct reacting' (almost idiot-like) sentient creature who is not capable of making any judgements or decisions concerning his own welfare. This is what I have called the 'big brother knows best' approach. It is probably the most commonly held belief today. Despite (or perhaps because of) his believed thoughtlessness, silliness, or infantilism, we do sincerely love our equine very much. He is treated like a pre-verbal infant, something to be cherished, adored but also very carefully protected as he is incapable of looking after himself or making decisions for his own good. Often the more the equine is loved and 'cared for' the greater the restrictions that are put on him and the fewer decisions he can make for himself . . . the less freedom he has if you will. It results in *overprotection*, which ironically can itself increase the amount of suffering.

(2) We have convinced ourselves that the way we keep him and look after him is the best way for him because it is more convenient and easier for us. This can be called the 'belief of convenience' approach. There is nothing inherently wrong with this approach; after all if we have horses in the western world it is usually because we like them, or at least want to have them for various reasons. If this is to continue it must clearly remain a pleasurable experience for us humans. The question is – is this in fact the case; is it pleasurable from either the equine's or the human's point of view? Is, for example, the horse much 'better off' in the way he is generally kept, in a single stable, mucked out each day and groomed and cleaned regularly, than a cow, in a field or yard with others, never groomed and mucked out once a year? Is it *really* easier for the human handlers to look after him this way and achieve what they wish with him, or is this apparent 'convenience' just wrong and potentially damaging to both human and equine, and their partnership?

If we are honest and *sincerely* interested in advancing the cause of equine welfare, even though we are sometimes confused and muddled, the first thing we must do is examine where and how we make the decisions we do concerning what is 'good' and 'bad' for the equine, what is in his interest and what, when and how may it be in ours.

Clearly both his and our interests must be represented if we are going to keep the equine in a domestic situation where we control his well-being. Can we take for granted that a 'good' top-of-the market riding stable, approved by the British Horse Society (which charges large amounts of money for lessons as well as livery, whose horses are always clean, tidy and fat) have got it right . . . as far as the horse is concerned? Or are we making a judgement as a result of our expectations? After all, we believe that they must know what they are doing, since they are doing it the 'approved' way and horse owners have been looking after horses for 5,000 years. Provided it is done in the well-known established way, surely it must be right?

Indeed the horse owner may not knowingly cause her horses to suffer, but has she paused to think? Is she not just doing what she has learnt, what everyone tells you, what the current mythology and belief system says? Is it not that what is considered a 'good' stable for horses is defined by cultural beliefs rather than the horses' preferences? After all slavery, racism and discrimination against women were considered reasonable, normal, and morally acceptable by the majority in the seventeenth and eighteenth centuries. If we are seriously interested in equine welfare we must examine these questions, even if we do conclude in the end that all is well for the equines.

We may be making a judgement on the 'goodness' of the stable because it fulfils all the criteria we have learnt to have in mind concerning a 'good' stable; it is neat and tidy, the horses are shiny, the clothes and tack are expensive, the yard is spotless: 'you could eat your sandwiches off it' . . . this has actually been said to me as an accolade of a stable! Never mind that all the horses have 'anti-weaving' bars fixed in front of their individual boxes and are fed only rationed food. Never mind the fact that almost all have neuroses and psychoses. Such occurrences are ignored or considered 'just one of those things', but it is not often considered anything to do with the way the horses are looked after. It is explained on the basis of 'just the genes' of the horses. Would the horses make the same decision as the human concerning the management of the yard as opposed, for example, to the gypsy encampment or the working donkeys along the roadside in Kenya, or tethered perhaps, grazing and having some free contact with each other? They may be ungroomed and unclipped, the encampment may be causing a problem to the land owner or the traffic police, the harness dirty, old and chaotic, no rugs or blankets on the horses, their feet unshod, no high protein cereal food given to them. But if not clearly diseased or wounded, are they worse off, are they suffering more than the others? They do not have to have anti-weaving bars, there are no individuals who have neuroses or pathologies or perform stereotypies, none on phenylbutazone, and some may be well over seventeen years old, around about the age when stabled horses become 'old' and 'retired' – or 'euthanased'.

How are we going to measure which suffer most or least, in other words, define the equines' welfare? In making a judgement in this instance what we are actually doing is indicating that we, middle-class, anglo-saxon caucasians brought up with established ideas and beliefs, *prefer* nice, neat, clean and tidy stables and horse. We will even claim, when asked, that we think the horses are happy this way and that this is why we like the yard. Are you convinced they are 'better off' than the gypsies' horses or the working donkeys pulling carts around the streets in Morocco? And if so why and how?

Modern, aptly-named 'cages' in a British yard where students are being instructed in 'equine science'. These are the types of solitary confinement loose boxes which cause the highest levels of behavioural distress. In a quick survey one evening (1 minute with each horse), the author noted of 12 horses present, 3 were showing evidence of behavioural distress.

One of the Sheik's high status new stable blocks for breeding Arab horses in Morocco. The horses spend 90 per cent of their lives behind these ornate doors in isolated cells or loose boxes, and when they come out, are pathologically excited and difficult to handle. The irony is that this stable yard was modelled on a European style, and advice taken from 'experts' in Europe!

These are the questions that must be addressed in a serious assessment of equine welfare. There are many issues to debate, many ideas to air, many thoughts to consider. The point is to sow the seeds of thought and concern about these issues, not to dictate.

There are always exceptions that can be made to every rule, it may be that Mrs T or Colonel J can justify why and how they look after their horses with rational well-thought out arguments, but what they cannot do, if they are seriously interested in the equines' welfare, is take for granted that they are *right*; and similarly *we*, the students, must not take it for granted they are because they happen to run a successful money-making horse establishment, or competitive yard, veterinary practice, farrier business, successful racing stable, teaching yard or even a horse sanctuary in the 'developed world' . . . particularly the latter.

A group of small farmers' donkeys grazing on common ground near Limuru, Kenya. The group has different sexes, different ages, and little behavioural restriction. The donkeys are in good condition, without rubs or bruises from their work, despite the fact that they work probably around 3 hours per day, and have no other food but the sparse grazing seen here. Are they not better off than those kept in the Moroccan stables above?

If I am trying to achieve anything by writing this book, it is to make people think more about their equines and what they actually *are* and then to try to make *better* guesstimates concerning their welfare than is currently the case. I realise I take a risk, it will be controversial and confront issues people would rather forget. It is not intended to undermine, to be dismissive, to be opinionated but it will challenge many of the current mythologies concerning equines and their management in order to try and encourage all to think about the equines' lot and to better it in the future. It is not my intention to stand on a moral pedestal, it is just that it might be better for you, me and our equine pals if we thought seriously about these issues.

Research on behaviour and the problems of animal 'well-being' have, to date, largely ignored equines. They have been primarily interested in laboratory, or farm animal welfare;

circuses and zoos have also recently received attention. As a result of two and a half decades of research on these issues, we now know more about the questions and debates. Indeed I argue (and many of my academic colleagues in general agree with me), that we do have some answers and can build on these at least to point out how we could most likely get it right for cattle, or even equines. Goodness knows, we may not fulfil all the criteria all the time (any more than we do for our children, our spouses or others we love). To recognise that you and I can get it wrong just as often as the Moroccan peasant or the gypsy can get it wrong is the first step.

Equine husbandry

Equines through the centuries have been kept in many types of association with humans. This is not the subject of this book, for it has been adequately covered elsewhere (see Dent and Goodall 1988, Barclay 1980). However the most commonly accepted husbandry for the equines who matter most (i.e. those most expensive, most talented or loved most) in Europe, much of America and now spreading into much of Australia, New Zealand, Japan, Asia and Africa is to keep the individual horse in an individual box, or stable. In relation to the equine's welfare, let us consider what the strengths and weaknesses of this system are.

Why stables?

Why are horses, and even donkeys, kept in individual boxes whereas cattle, sheep, goats, llamas, elephants are not? In fact no other hoofed animal kept by humans is traditionally kept in this way. Are equines so different, are they perhaps non-social, unable to get along in groups, or incapable of surviving unless they have such attention? Horace Hayes (1968) in his textbook on stable management estimates that the 'stable lad' should take 8¾ hours just looking after one horse! (p.332). Perhaps these horses can only survive with the aid of humans. But then what about feral and wild horses, how do they manage?

It is generally admitted by the more thoughtful writer on stable management that stables do cause problems of one sort or another but nevertheless Hayes states '. . . working horses have to be stabled, because the *necessary protection by clothing and the requirements of cleanliness would be unattainable if the animals were allowed to live out*' (my italics). Yet in the previous chapter he has stated that the horses are well able to adapt to very considerable temperature changes outside; he does continue '. . . it is evident that we should regard a stable in this country as a useful, but by no means an indispensable means of protection which should *interfere as little as possible with the natural conditions that are conducive to the health and comfort of the horse*'.

Sainsbury (1984) confirms this with no reasons or discussion, it is just so: 'A horse must be kept clean, in good lean condition, and regularly groomed with a short, clipped coat.' Why? Are we so sure that cleanliness is next to Godliness? What have horses evolved their thick winter coats for if they have to be clipped off? Certainly these traditions do not appear to be of any benefit to *them*; their welfare is not necessarily improved by so doing.

Sainsbury admits 'Considered only from the point of view of the horse's health, it would be better to leave the animal outside all the year around . . . However there are practical

Our horses out on a camping expedition on Dartmoor. The mares are in a single strand electric ribbon enclosure which is light to carry with us, and the young stallion is tethered outside, as one of the mares was in season and we did not want a foal.

reasons why a horse should be housed.' But these however are not itemised. What are they? The first essential of housing he continues is '*to give the horses as healthy an environment inside as they would have had outside . . .*' The second to provide '*a good environment and facilities for the handlers*'.

So it is admitted that despite the fact that horses will be healthier outside, they are stabled mainly for the handler's benefit and primarily so they can remain clean! The handler then does not have to walk around in the rain checking and feeding them . . . Instead of the one hour per day or so check-ing and feeding the outside horse, he has to spend 8¾ hours per day looking after a stabled horse! If he has several he must have little time to do much else. Perhaps this is the idea. Stabling of horses all began with the military. Horses had to be near and ready so that they could be jumped on quickly and galloped into battle. It was also important to ensure that the soldiers were hovering around, not down the town whoring or drinking. In this way they could be kept disciplined and in order and thus be better troopers. Jobs and work must be invented for them until the recommendation became absurd and thus came the 8¾ hour day looking after one horse. Gradually more and more things became 'essential' to do if horses were in stables or near at hand – from daily mucking out to three hours a day grooming and cleaning the tack.

The cavalry vanished, but their military attitudes were absorbed into the training of 'stable lads' or even 'stable lasses', the 'working pupil' of the British training system. To do it 'properly' it is necessary to do all these things and more. This is the 'proper' way which has now become associated with the 'good' welfare of the horse.

A historical background to a belief system which has nothing to do with the horse! Given then that we stable them to make life easier for us the humans (even though we may increase the amount of work we have to do very dramatically and it costs more – which in itself is a contradiction) does the equine benefit or not from this type of husbandry? To examine this we first need to consider what the horse's needs are. These, as in the case of humans can be divided into:

(1) *Physical needs* There is universal agreement that the horse has physical needs. He needs good health, freedom from pain, adequate food and water, a temperature he can adapt to, some

Yards for young horses.

exercise and an ability to perform normal maintainance activities (e.g. scratch himself). Stable management to date concentrates exclusively on how these needs are to be fulfilled with an emphasis on (a) an unnatural cleanliness of the coat (not a physical need that horses have evolved to have to survive) and (b) restraining techniques and equipment (euphemistically called 'tack').

(2) *Emotional needs* To date the emotional needs of the horse in stabled environments in particular have not been carefully considered. The equine, it is generally agreed, is a sentient being who can suffer and feel pain and discomfort, he has emotions and consequently emotional needs, but unlike in humans these are not generally accepted by the handlers nor are they often catered for. Horse management does admit that stallions have sexual needs and desires but these must be restricted and restrained, in fact if possible cut out, or only partially allowed where useful for humans (e.g. controlled in-hand breeding, see chapter 11).

Horse owners intuitively realise that horses have emotional needs and desires; they may also believe that because the horse acts by 'instinct' (whatever this is) he is unable to learn to control them, and thus he must be physically, pharmaco-logically or even surgically controlled wherever possible. Therefore it is considered quite appropriate to keep horses in individual stables and never let them have any free access to other horses or form relationships with them. In fact if they do manage to (just as humans often do when kept in restricted, confined conditions like prison) it is considered a nuisance and efforts are made to prevent contact. More usually the animals become pathological and aggressive as a result of the behav-ioural restrictions (see chapter 3).

It is often maintained that equines will inevitably bite and kick: damage or be damaged if allowed to associate freely. How is it then that horses manage to live in social groups in the feral and wild state? Few people ask themselves this question, and follow it up by the observation that humans will often respond in the same way if kept isolated, frustrated and unable to have free access to others; they too become very aggressive or unable to fit in socially. Their undesirable behaviour is the result of past individual experience; it is not something that is genetically programmed, otherwise neither the human nor the equine would after all be a social animal (see Kiley-Worthington 1987 for further discussion).

One reason why many of us keep equines is because they respond to us emotionally and often positively: they can like as well as dislike. They have complicated emotional relationships between each other and indeed even with other species including humans. They do indeed have emotional needs although they can also, like humans, learn to control them in many ways.

(3) *Intellectual needs* We have discussed the horse's mind and suggested that he has not only physical and emotional needs, but cognitive, intellectual needs too (chapter 7).

An equine has a brain; indeed we know he has because we use this all the time in dealing with him, riding, working, and so on. He learns, he remembers, he makes decisions. He has beliefs: he sees you going to the feed store and believes he will soon be fed and acts accordingly.

Wanless (1987) in her otherwise interesting book about people (riding), constantly repeats the belief 'remember you (the rider) are the brains, he is the brawn'. This does seem to be a radical misconception and irrational belief. If there is *one* thing the horse has to intellectualise about when being ridden and asked to perform quite complex responses, it is how to make sense out of the jumble of messages often given by one person, never mind how different people give them. To achieve a good performance with any equine/human interaction there has to be a cooperative 'understanding' (as Xenophon said in 350 BC); an intellectual understanding; a mutual respect: the human of the horse and vice versa; a recognition of the other's brain and being. It is no good shouting louder in English (or Chinese) at a Frenchman or a horse when he does not understand. The way to understanding is to try to explain and receive information adaptively, necessarily requiring intellectual exercise.

Humans and horses develop physical, emotional and intellectual habits. Those who are not taught much and encouraged, or do not have the opportunity of developing their physical, emotional and/or intellectual skills, will not develop them to a high level. They can become very idle with one or other of these possible skills.

We may not know exactly what a horse's intellectual needs

are yet (indeed we are a bit clueless about those for humans and they seem to vary greatly between individuals), but since our association with horses rests on their intellectual abilities (their abilities to learn to perform various different tasks) it is foolish to assume they do not have intellectual needs. Keeping them in social, physical and largely intellectual isolation – that is as in single stables – may not be the best way of fulfilling their needs and improving either the equines' welfare or ours.

We may not yet know the best way of teaching either horses or humans to use their intellectual abilities, but we do know that both groups have them, although they may be different.

We will now look at how these various needs of the horse are fulfilled in the stabled environment.

Physical requirements and problems of stabling

Temperature

The animal must be kept in an environment where the temperatures are going to be acceptable. Designing stables so that they maintain temperatures that the equine can withstand without disease, since he is unable to make any behavioural adjustments (for example move over the hill or under the hedge out of the wind), is itself a challenge and can be very expensive. Enormous amounts of time and money have recently been spent on developing vaccines against equine influenza whose prevalence is one of the consequences of stabling horses in numbers. Indeed, vaccination in Britain is now compulsory if one wishes to take horses to any race course, many show grounds or even visiting other stables. All of this has been very good for research jobs and the pharmaceutical industry, but I wonder if it has really improved horse welfare? There are many cases of horses who have been badly affected by the vaccine; I once had a little mare at livery who had been exercised too much too soon after vaccination and developed a cough for life.

Keeping stabled equines cool in hot climates can be an equally difficult problem. Natural draughts and chimneys must be constructed, and care taken when siting the stable so that the midday sun does not penetrate. It is however easier to allow equines – often donkeys in this case – to make their own behavioural adjustments by being outside and able to choose trees for shade, stand in water, change places to maximise the wind and so on.

Ventilation

This is another problem on which many books have been written: *how to make the ventilation in the stable as good as it would be outside*. There are a number of ingenious suggestions and particularly many businesses dependent on marketing various bits of equipment to help. However one of the major physical disease problems of stabled horses is coughing; usually the result of inadequate ventilation in a closed dusty environment. It is normal that at least one horse in the stable yard will have a cough and indeed it may be that the stable has a coughing epidemic almost annually. There are also long-term diseases of the lungs which shorten the animal's life as a result of this problem, and these are very much higher in stabled horses than those outside. One solution is to cut down on dust – another would be to keep the equines outside.

Exercise

Another problem for the stabled horse is how to exercise himself when confined. He is unable to move around freely, let alone change his gait or move fairly constantly as he has evolved to do when in his open plains niche. The horse is *par excellence* a movement specialist, he can move long distances at considerable speeds. Only recently as a result of Long Distance riding and the accompanying physiological research (see chapter 14) have we become aware of what horses can do with appropriate training and development: 100 miles a day at an average speed of over 10 miles an hour, sound at the end and with a heart rate only little above resting rate 30 minutes after completion. Equines constantly move about normally, even in a field of a few acres where even the cob or Dartmoor pony will move between eighteen and twenty miles every twenty-four hours.

But the stabled horse is lucky to be taken out for an hour's work a day, and then he may move less than a couple of miles although be expected suddenly to put enormous pressure on his previously inactive legs by jumping large fences, up to five feet. It seemed to me extraordinary that particularly in the race-horse industry (but wherever equine athletes are being trained), so few bother to think about this. One would not expect a human athlete to win a race, a high jumping or hurdling competition if we kept him locked up in his bedroom for twenty-three hours out of twenty-four; why do we expect it of horses and then invent ways of keeping them so this is the norm? Curiouser and curiouser. Hayes mentions what we all know – that horses' legs can frequently become full when they are stabled as a result of lack of movement. This in turn gradually gives rise to stiffening and finally unsoundness and early death. The situation that gives rise to this has been created in the interest of horse welfare; or even the human horse owner's welfare.

Horses' legs, even more than humans', have evolved to cope with constant movement. Enforced inactivity is unlikely to benefit them.

Feeding

The stabled horse, because he is unable to find and eat any food for himself (as he is confined), has to be presented with the food he must eat. Again this has been and is the subject of much research expenditure. How to make and market an even better balanced food for the race horse, event horse, endurance horse or what you will, each of course requiring (for the benefit of marketing) a particularly different formula, and each expensively produced often from imported products. Sometimes these are grown where it causes considerable environmental problems. One example of this is the importation and use of soya beans from Brazil grown where there used to be the Amazonian rain forest; another example is of fish meal, carefully treated to become palatable but often exhausting the fish stocks, even if it does create jobs in the process. There has not yet been an equivalent of BSE identified in horses, but where recycled protein foods are fed, there is certainly a chance of such outbreaks in horses.

Another assumption when feeding the stabled equine is that he must have high levels of protein in the feed if he is to perform well. The equine is a herbivore and has the possibility of digesting cellulose and extracting protein from this via bacteria in the gut. His digestive tract cannot use a higher level of protein than around 8 to 10 per cent; the rest is converted to uric acid and literally peed away – an expensive waste in terms of money and environmental constraints. It is also a welfare cost to the horse. He has adapted to eat for around sixteen hours a day, and this does not change very much if there is very little or a great deal of grass to eat (see p.48, fig. 4.4). In a stabled environment where he is ration fed high protein feeds and little fibre, he can eat everything he needs in two to four hours. What will he do with the extra fourteen or so hours, especially since he is confined? (See Kiley-Worthington 1987 for full discussion of these problems.) The horse often invents ways of self-stimulating, such as weaving, crib-biting and so on.

Another problem when feeding the stabled horse is that he will tend to eat everything that he is given if he is ration fed because his gut is relatively empty and therefore he is hungry much of the time. This can result in him eating poor quality, mouldy or bad food which makes him ill and which he would not eat if he had lived out and learnt about what to choose during his lifetime. Colic is quite frequent in stabled horses, and even death from colic, as a result of all these various difficulties.

There is a curious belief that horses 'must not eat their beds'. I have never been clear why this is such bad news, but I think it must be like saying the child should not eat the food he has dropped on the floor, as it might be contaminated. It is very curious, though, for people to believe this when horses in any case have evolved to eat off the ground – that is, to eat grass. If your horse eats his bedding which is straw, then you are conventionally advised to change it to sawdust or waste paper, or peat or anything . . . but *don't let him eat his bed*. If he has a need to eat his bed it would seem rather that he is not getting enough high fibre food, and the best thing is let him eat it, or give him more hay or straw in a net if you are convinced he must not eat what is on the floor.

Bedding

It is often recommended these days to have concrete floor in the stable although why this is so is hard to understand. Concrete is a hard, cold and unpleasant sleeping surface for horse or humans. Earth is much softer and pleasanter and does not have to become mud, or smell when in a stable under a roof. Earth floors also save money. The equine is then hopefully given a bed to lie on for the night. This may or may not be taken out in the day or swept against the walls. There are various products and methods used to bed the horse.

Straw beds daily mucked out

The conventional way of bedding a horse in much of Europe has been on straw which is mucked out each day. The idea is that all the faeces and urine will be removed and the floor swept before the straw is respread over the floor. The straw is usually banked up around the sides of the box; this is a curious practice which has its origins in a belief that this would make it more difficult for the horse to get 'cast' with his legs against the wall (stuck) and unable to get up, although how is obscure. Nevertheless this has become the 'proper' way to bed the horse. In the stable where I originally trained, many moons ago, we were also taught to plait the straw in the front of the box; not a bad touch as the aesthetics go and if there is time and inclination, why not?

The problem with the daily mucked out bed is that in order to have a really generously deep bed to encourage the horse to lie down (remember the floor is usually concrete underneath) it requires a good extra ¾ to 1 bale of straw a day added, particularly if much of this is to be unavailable for the horse's comfort by being spread around the edges. The result of this is that frequently insufficient straw is used, it can be expensive (approximately 2½ tons/year per horse, £100–£200, just for the bedding material never mind the labour) and, more importantly, it can in a large stable require an enormous covered space to house the straw.

Depending how the straw is made and how dry it was when baled, it can be dusty when shaken out in a confined box with the horse in it (for some reason it is not encouraged to take the horse out of his box even when bedding up and the dust is everywhere). The result is that straw beds constantly being forked about can encourage lung diseases and coughing.

Straw is often eaten by the horses. In fact when taking a horse to a competition or visit to another stable, the owner is asked if the horse has straw or sawdust in his stable. The current stable per night prices for a horse (bedding supplied but no food, not even a hay breakfast) is slightly more expensive than Bed and Breakfast for a human in a modest house.

Using a straw bed is perhaps the most ecologically sound approach since straw is a by product of cereals and used to be burnt when produced in excess; however, these disadvantages have either caused it to fall out of favour, or to be used very sparingly, which results in uncomfortable beds and reduced time lying down by the horse.

Sawdust

Recently in Britain, sawdust has become a fashionable alternative to straw. This will either be swept up each day and the faeces and wet sawdust removed or it will be generously spread, the wet and soiled bits removed daily and a little more added. This is a type of deep litter system which for some reason, is acceptable to put in a stable if there is sawdust, but not if there is straw. Sawdust which used to be free at the sawmill is now packaged and priced accordingly for horse bedding. It is often vacuum packed in plastic and thus can be stored out of doors although piles of plastic bags of sawdust does not necessarily add to the aesthetics of the stable yard.

Sawdust can also be extremely dusty, but it is less likely to have bacteria that may infect the lung in it since it is processed from inside trees rather than directly from the soil. It is also not usually eaten by the horse, although some horses can develop a pathology eating it when the fibre in their diet is highly rationed.

There are many other products that can be used for horse bedding in stables, ranging from peat, waste, shredded paper, to rubber mats. Few if any actually use soil or turf, the types of flooring the horse has when he lives in his chosen environment.

One ecologically sound alternative is deep litter straw which is usually frowned on by the people in the 'know'. The grounds for this is that the horses' feet will suffer since they will inevitably be in faeces and urine all the time. Another argument often used is that deep litter straw beds will be smelly and it will be even more difficult to keep them well ventilated. Thirdly, they cannot be kept dry and well drained, fourthly they do not look as nice as the conventional straw bedding with the high banks at the side.

Let us examine whether or not these claims are true or false. In the first instance do the horses have more feet problems with a good deep litter bed? We have kept our horses (a total of 164 horse years) for the last twenty winters on deep litter straw beds and have data now on this. Our horses are now getting older but all of them are still sound, and we have had remarkably few feet problems that might be related to the deep litter bed, or indeed the work they do. During this period we have had only one mild case of thrush which is said to be endemic in deep litter beds and very frequent in normally run daily mucked out stables. Thus, the claim that deep litter straw beds are unhealthy for the feet at least appears to be unfounded.

Is deep litter smelly? The litter needs to be initially very generously spread on the floor. The drainage has to be correct, although this is not as important as in a daily mucked out bed as an incline in the floor will quickly be obliterated by the bed build up and thus not cause a wet hole. The stable, must be well ventilated. There is little if any rational reason why horses are completely shut up with non-ventilated doors in their stables. Even a risk of theft (often given for locking the top stable door) can be coped with by having doors made from bars or rails.

Are deep litter straw beds necessarily wet? Provided the bed is built up gradually, new clean straw (around ¼ bale/day/horse) is added, they are as unlikely to have wet and unpleasant patches as the daily mucked out or deep litter sawdust bed.

Aesthetically, are they necessarily unattractive? Provided again these beds are kept topped up there is no reason for this to be the case. One advantage is that they gradually rise until mucked out and then lower. This allows rather different views of the horse and for the horse of the environment; perhaps something that could be considered to enhance the aesthetic value of the system.

Stable aesthetics are another neglected area of concern and the type of bedding used is only one aspect of this. The deep litter bed in a well ventilated yard (rather than single stables) has the advantage that it can use big baled straw which can be stored outside, it gives off heat and is warm, it is comfortable and the horses lie down more, it uses far less straw and much less labour (5 mins/horse/day compared to 1½–2 hours/day for conventional mucking out, sweeping up the mess, building the muck heap etc). It can be mechanically removed once or twice a year, and if the horses are properly educated, they can help move it onto the fields where it will encourage further growth of grass and cereals for the horses and other stock. It is much cheaper in materials, time and energy; this means the stable lad or lass can spend at least twelve more hours playing with or educating her horse, or even just reading a book or drinking coffee, not an unattractive alternative. It may be worth seriously considering after all.

Clothing and clipping

Clothing horses is not only becoming more and more popular, but almost compulsory for 'good welfare' in the winter. One of the main concerns the public has, reflected in reported incidences to the welfare organisations is that 'the horse was outside in the field without a rug and in the rain'. Here inappropriate anthropomorphic judgements are often (although not always) being made. We feel when we see the horse outside in the wet sheltering under a hedge, 'shame, poor thing, he must be so wet and cold' because in similar conditions because of our lack of natural coat and lifetime experience of heated buildings, this would be insupportable for us. Thus we generalise and assume, in this case, often incorrectly, that it is insupportable to the horse and he is suffering. What are the alternatives, and will the horse necessarily suffer less if clothed?

Hayes and Sainsbury both admit that horses are quite capable of coping with the normal temperature changes in Britain and almost anywhere in Europe without clothing if they are able to make their own decisions and use their own behavioural adaptions to do this. If so, they are healthy (are less often ill) than those clothed horses in stables.

The stabled horse is less able to do this, but since the stable should at least reduce the wet and the draughts, it would be likely that even being in a stable is not going to cause the horse to suffer from cold with his own coat on (Hayes 1968, p.252). The problem comes of course when the horse has been clipped. So why are horses clipped? The reasons given for clipping are not always clear. For example, Sainsbury (1984) assumes that horses must be clipped. Why not cows then, one wonders? The 'common' reasons for clipping are:

(1) The horse cannot be worked hard with a long winter coat because he will sweat too much and will not be able to run the speeds we would like, or retain his weight as he will sweat it all away.

(2) The long winter-coated horse is very difficult to keep clean and we must cut his coat off for this reason.

(3) The horse will be likely to suffer from chill if he is sweaty and his long coat is wet. It takes time for the coat to dry.

The evidence for (1) is slim. There do not seem to be any proper physiological studies that have been done on the effect of clipping on the horse's performance. When I was in Colorado, US, a few years ago, I was invited to witness a fifty-mile long-distance race in February over the prairies where the snow was from 6 inches to 2 feet deep on the track. None of the horses was clipped and the winning speed was an average of 10 mph with the heart recovery rate down to 48 beats per minute (see chapter 14) after thirty minutes. These are similar speeds and recovery rates to those we achieve with clipped horses although here in the UK the temperature is never minus 30°C as it was some of that day!

Also at the US ride (and with our own horses), it is not the case that having the horse in training for hard fast events without clipping has caused an excessive loss of weight, or a need for extra feeding compared to the clipped horses. Like people, some horses are fatter and fit, others leaner and fit, most thin or fat and unfit.

These horses not only had to perform in the race but just like the hunters and steeplechasers which 'have to be clipped to get fit' they had to have long hard training schedules, come in wet and dry out enough not to catch cold with temperatures down to minus 50°C some nights. If we are going to believe the statement that it is not possible to get horses fit with their coats on, we need some evidence. This is not something we can take on trust.

Since this visit, although we and our Arab horses were living in the Hebrides (with a rainfall of 84 inches a year and wind speeds often reaching 100 mph in the winter) and getting horses fit early in the season for Arab flat racing and long-distance racing, we have not rugged any horses in or out unless they were ill for some reason. We have done well in the events generally too, with four international level endurance horses! Thus there does not appear to be evidence of (1) above.

There certainly is evidence for (2). It is much easier to keep horses clean if they do not have their own coats; but this is not in the horses' interest if it increases the chances of ill health, and feeling cold, rubs from the rugs, or accidents as a result of getting tied up in the rug. One particular disadvantage of keeping horses out in New Zealand rugs (another reason for giving up rugging with or without clipping) is that however well designed and customer fitted the rug, it restricts the movement of the shoulders. It may be the rug could somehow be redesigned, perhaps with darts in front of the pelvic pin bones to stop it moving back, but so far we have not found a satisfactory rug which horses can keep on during the winter and move freely in. One of our young horses with particularly good movement, was kept clipped and rugged from the age of three for two years every winter by his new owner. His free flowing movement was reduced to a short-strided 'pit-a-patter' even without the rug thereafter.

If horses suffer more from colds and ill health if they are unclipped but exercised and sweated up, then this must be catered for. If when returning sweaty with a winter coat, the horse is shut up in a draughty stable with no clothing and no rubbing, he may well get cold before he is dry. When the horse comes in wet, it is sensible to rub or rug him in a way which will encourage his coat to dry, and keep him out of a cold draught until he is dry. We have not had any sickness we have been able to trace to not clipping the horses, although there are many cases of cold, cough, and influenza in clipped horses who are clearly much more at risk, 24 hours a day when they are either sweaty after work or just standing around in draughty stables or fields.

10

Feeding, exercise, care of the feet

Feeding horses

Practically every week or month some horse magazine on sale has an article on horse nutrition and feeding. Research on horse nutrition is one of the areas that has been well covered in the last couple of decades at least, but this is not the place to cover the nutritional needs of the horse in detail. We will rather concentrate on the *behavioural* needs the horse has in connection with his food and feeding.

The first step is to consider the structure of his digestive tract and the way he has evolved to use it. Unlike humans, there is no debate about the natural food horses evolved to eat: they are herbivores, they eat plants only. They can eat a large variety of these but although their four-toed ancestors evolved in the wet forests of the Silurian period, the modern horse, *Equus caballus*, moved out on to the grassland and became predominantly a grass-eating herbivore. Unlike cattle, horses have incisor teeth on the top and bottom jaw and are able to clip off grazing plants very short. This allows them to live in areas and climates where grazing competitors such as many of the ruminants (e.g. cattle) would find it difficult. They are not ruminants and they therefore have different digestive/feeding controls (see Kiley-Worthington 1987, chapter 7, for fuller discussion of this subject).

Horses evolved an ingenious way of digesting the relatively indigestible cellulose (the fibrous material that surrounds the cells of plants). They have bacteria living within the gut which eat it, and then they digest the bacteria. However to do this and obtain sufficient carbohydrate, protein and vitamins from the often nutritionally poor food materials they eat, they have to eat a great deal (around 25–30 lb: 12–14 kg/per 15.2 hh per day; 20 lbs: 8 kg for donkeys), and they have to have long and bulky digestive tracts to store it, and ensure its proper digestion.

They, like all species, including humans, have evolved behavioural tendencies to ensure that they obtain sufficient appropriate food. One of these is 'nutritional wisdom'. It means that given options (choices) and food which is not masked by strong textures or tastes, they will pick for themselves a balanced diet and seek out any particular mineral or vitamin needs.

Another behavioural tendency crucial to nutrition, is that they have 'typical time budgets'. This means that, given the option, horses will spend around sixteen hours a day eating. Even if the grass is very plentiful or very scarce, the time spent grazing only varies by a couple of hours one way or another. Thus, part of the equines' inherited behavioural make-up appears to be a pre-programmed tendency to eat for around sixteen hours in each twenty-four. Of course, in the old days when horses were working all day long on the farm or pulling carriages and so on, as donkeys do in many countries now, they had much less time in the stable to eat and sleep (sometimes insufficient time: they usually sleep for around eight hours in twenty-four). Indeed they had little or no spare time standing idle in the stable. The important thing for the stable manager was to make sure that they could consume enough food of sufficient quality to have the energy to work the next day and maintain body weight.

The result of this was the introduction of grains into the horses' diet. These often have a much higher percentage of energy-giving foods (carbohydrates), food for growth and muscle development (proteins), and lower fibre than the natural foods such as grasses, browse, and hay. Thus the horse can consume all his physiological nutritional needs in around two to three hours per day and eat much less bulk (10–15 lbs: 4–5 kg/24 hrs; 5–10 lbs: 2–4 kg for the donkey).

As a result of the research on equine nutrition we now know a great deal more about the horse's physiological needs and have developed diets particularly for stabled horses. These have reached a great degree of complexity. Nowadays, however, the normal horse owner has to know less about this than ever before because she can buy what is advertised as a 'complete balanced diet', or a 'cooling feed', or a 'race horse mix' or one of another hundred products. She can also buy innumerable additives; complete mineral mixes, special mixes, and if inclined to believe in alternative or natural remedies, even garlic powder and herb extracts, to ensure that her horse has the best possible diet. There are even products on the market advertised to cope with her horse's behavioural difficulties!

Hay or grass is now rarely considered anything but either a bulk feed that must be rationed or the horse will get too fat and eat too much, or in the case of grass, an area where he can run around and exercise and get the odd mouthful. As a result, it is too often believed that the real nutritional needs that the horse has can only be served by supplementary feeding of all these various products. This may be good for the industries making and selling these products, but it is debatable whether this is good for the equine. Does this approach fundamentally improve the welfare of the horse; the question which in the first place gave rise to it?

It is difficult for owners who may have very strong emotional bonds, and love their son, horse (dog, cat or whatever) deeply, to deny them their favourite food which gives them pleasure. But as with human nutrition, we are realising this may not be in the long-term interests of the object of love. This is clearly indicated in horses by the relatively high level of illnesses associated with eating and nutrition such as colic, azoturia, even laminitis (Robinson 1987) and behavioural problems such as stereotypies (Kiley-Worthington 1987, McGreevy et al. 1995) among others. Clearly it is not in the horse's long-term interest to be fed high levels of high nutritional quality food, low levels of fibre and have little choice.

A problem that can occur not infrequently is that although the horse is naturally cautious about what he eats, once he has been fed food and learns to expect it in his manger or food container, he may eat foods that are either poisonous or certainly will make him sick (such as mouldy grains) which if offered to him elsewhere he would reject. This destroys his normal 'nutritional wisdom'. He has learnt that things in the manger are good and his natural selectivity is thrown to the wind.

Another behavioural problem endemic to the modern way of feeding stabled horses, is that because they are often

rationed in the amount of fibre they have they are constantly
hungry. The result of this is that they will be less discriminating
about what they eat. If you are hungry, anything can be better
than nothing even though it is unfamiliar and may not be very
good for you.

Well made hay or grass at any time of the year can be a
sufficient diet for the maintenance of the horse particularly if
he is not growing, reproducing or lactating; provided it is in
sufficient quantity: he has as much as he wants. This is the diet
the horse has evolved to live on and the one his digestive tract
can cope with best.

What about his behavioural nutritional needs? Horses are
fussy feeders, again for evolutionary reasons. Since they are
unable to be sick, what goes down never comes up, thus those
who are not fussy enough about what they eat may not survive.
In this way there has been selection in the wild horse for 'fussy
feeders' over the last ten million years. In particular they are
very careful about unfamiliar food. Try for example giving a
horse who has never tried it, a lump of sugar or a polo; he will
reject it, although your own horse who is familiar with such a
flavour and likes it may work hard in one way or another to
obtain one.

Equines learn a considerable amount about what to eat by
watching their mother, and from each other in any environment. One horse will try an unknown food only after seeing
others eat it often. Whether their mother 'teaches' them or
whether they just watch and imitate her we don't yet know (at
least there is no evidence that she does 'teach', i.e. consciously
impart knowledge). Generally equines will not eat poisonous
plants if they are familiar with them – ragwort for example
unless they are very hungry indeed. The reason why ragwort is
a registered 'weed' is because it is consumed by all livestock
when in hay and this is when animals are usually poisoned by
it. However there was a case reported from South Africa where
a group of horses did eat fresh ragwort in the field and many
died. Again this appeared to be the result of imitation over a
period of years. But why food aversion conditioning did not
come into effect remains a mystery.

When the equine is confined to stables and unable to make
choices even in what he eats, clearly he is much more at risk
and there must be more responsibility taken by his
owner/trainer. There may be more knowledge than there was

concerning this, but the fact that diseases involved with feeding are relatively common in stabled horses, much more common than in feral, wild equines or horses at pasture, indicates that there are still many unknowns.

Until such time as more information is available, if we are really interested in the wellbeing of our equines, would it not be wise to allow them to make more nutritional choices and allow their evolutionary tendencies free range? Can we really improve on ten million years of evolution as a result of a couple of decades of high technological research? So far we have not shown this to be the case.

If the equine is expected to carry weight and cover 100 miles in a day; to gallop at his fastest for a couple of miles, to jump jumps; indeed he will need more carbohydrates to provide energy than if he were just standing in a stable or walking around a field all day. It is in this case sensible to feed *some* higher quality foods to provide the nutritional needs. But all horses are not doing this. The vast majority of stabled horses are not out of their stable for more than an hour a day and then, even if carrying weight, they may not cover as much distance as they would have if they were out in a field for 24 hours. Horses wandering around outside in sufficiently large fields, or feral, will cover around fifteen to twenty-five miles a day just eating, socialising, sleeping and wandering around their home areas. Take him out for a five-mile trot, and he has not even done that much; feed him 10 lbs of concentrate food for doing his five miles, and control the amount of hay and straw he can get, and you have a recipe for behavioural and physiological problems: over excitement, aggression, stereo-typies, box walking, over-reactivity, and nervousness. Eating inappropriate foods, lack of selectivity and over-eating if given the option, will result physically in under-muscularisation, and leg and foot problems as a result of lack of use, and then sudden short use. Such strains can result in colic, azoturia, possibly laminitis, insufficient physiological fitness to cope with unexpected competitive work, obesity, or lack of appetite.

There is no special drug or additive that will solve these problems; what will solve them is a consideration of what the horse's behavioural and physiological needs *are* and changing the feeding to cater for them.

An amazing story from our own experience illustrates this. We were at the 100-mile in one day race run by the Endurance

Horse and Pony Society some ten years ago with an arab mare, Omeya, who is a slight horse and who does not ever have a very great appetite. When she is in training and physiologically fit (as tested by heart recovery rate, respiration and so on) she is thin and her ribs show. We never feed our horses more than 15 lbs (6 kg) of concentrate 'hard' food a day but they have *ad libitum* access to grass, hay, straw, or silage. She was in training of course to do the ride, and she was very fit. However in a strange place in the corral with the others (where we always keep them when we go away for competitions), she was too interested in all around her, and paid no attention to her diet, despite our every effort. The sensible thing we had found was to give her access to a bag of her favourite food and let her and her companion (Crysthannah Royal, another pure-bred arab who had much the same problem and was competing in a sixty-mile race) help themselves to food; to grass, to hay and so on. She would then eat almost 10 lbs a day, particularly if we gave her some in our hand from time to time.

Another competitor saw this, and was horrified, rushed to the organiser to complain on grounds of welfare: 'the horses will be killed'. Had the horses been kept like she kept hers, in stables and ration fed with the amount and type of food very carefully controlled by the humans, consequently never having the chance to make their own decisions as to how much and what they would eat, she might have had a point: they might have gorged themselves and had colic. It had not occurred to this lady, and probably never will, either to ask us about what we were doing or whether the horse, like a human in a similar position, may be able to take decisions about *what* and *how much* he will eat. In addition he is likely to get it fairly correct, certainly more likely to get it right than if he has never learnt to make these decisions, or is relying on a member of another species (often with little nutritional knowledge) to make those decisions for him.

The proof of the pudding was in the eating: Omeya came sixth in that race having got lost and done an extra 10 miles (110 miles in 18 hours) at an average speed of 6.8 mph. The other woman's horse was eliminated.

As a postscript Omeya is now twenty, Crysthannah Royal nineteen and both still sound and competing in Long-Distance Rides.

Exercise

One of the major concerns in the minds of many horse owners, is 'should I do so much with my horse; am I not over doing the exercise he takes?' This question has become one of particular interest to the media lately reflecting the public's concern following the deaths of horses in the cross-country section of Combined Training Trials (e.g. Badminton UK 1992). Similarly Long-Distance competitive riding has come into the limelight: should horses be asked to race as much as 100 miles (160 km) in a day, even though physiological measures are taken throughout the races to monitor the horses' state of exhaustion (not yet the riders' I am glad to say!).

There are very good reasons why these two types of Olympic competitive riding may well be of concern to the general public in relation to the welfare of the horses. The usual grounds for sweeping their concerns away can be stated as: 'we (horsemen and women) know what we are doing, and we are good, upright (usually rich) people who care very much for our horses who are very expensive, so we would not want to harm them'. It is maintained by such people that the general public knows nothing about the subject and makes opinionated judgements. Let us examine what the arguments are, and incidentally why are we so sure that it is only the 'uninformed public' who make opinionated judgements on these issues? Horse owners and potential olympic riders are also human beings after all who will make 'opinionated judgements', and perhaps 'uninformed judgements' too.

First of all consider stabled horses, who are behaviourally restricted and therefore do not have the option of choice as to the amount of exercise they get. Do they get enough exercise? It is a matter of considerable concern for the horses' welfare certainly, but judgements on how much exercise they should have are often made with a mis-application of anthropomorphic reasoning; the owner considers that if she had that much work at that speed (or even half the work at half the speed) she would have had more than enough. Thus riding the horse twenty-five miles, or even as little as between ten and fifteen miles a day at around five miles an hour is more than enough for him it is often believed.

This concern not to overwork is an especially British

attitude and probably results from the horror stories of the overworked carriage horses, the most famous of which is Black Beauty, whose story most of us were raised on. This book drew the attention of the public to the plight of horses and was an important foundation stone in the development of animal welfare awareness and legislation in Britain. Certainly it is important to think about what and how much work our horses should do, but is the present advice and practice that is given on this appropriate and correct, as far as *the horse* is concerned? Or are judgements and assessments again made on grounds of convenience for the owner or stable hand?

A good place to start is to look at how much exercise the horse has evolved to take: how much time he spends exercising himself in a feral or wild state or when given the options; how far he travels. Even domestic horses allowed to move freely over large areas might help answer this question.

There are many groups of feral horses that have been studied now and also the time budgets and exercise taken by domestic horses at grass in paddocks or large grazing areas has been measured. The time spent exercising, the distance travelled and the speed can be compared with that of the stabled horses kept for their competitive athletic ability.

Time exercising

As a general rule the horse will spend about 8–10 per cent of the day walking and moving around; he will also be travelling slowly as he grazes (another 55–60 per cent) of the 24-hour day. He is thus exercising for around 2½ hours in each 24 hours with reasonably consistent travel. But for another five to six hours he will be taking steps approximately every 30 seconds (depending on the availability and palatability of the grazing); during grazing he will be moving gently for another 13 to 14.5 hours per 24. In other words he will be moving almost constantly when he is not resting or sleeping: that is around 15.5 to 17 hours in 24.

By contrast even the race horse, or international combined training horse will usually not be out of his stable for more than around two hours a day, sometimes less than that. When he is in his stable he can, unless stalled, move all four feet in sequence, but he has little incentive and as a result moves very much less than when grazing. Instead he stands idle and immobile for around 60 per cent of the time. Is this likely to be appropriate for an athlete whose limbs have evolved to be almost constantly moving and whose specialism is movement and speed?

Distance moved

Perhaps even if the time spent exercising the equines kept in stables (who have been apparently selected for athleticism and are considered very 'fit') is lower than for the feral animals, this is made up by the speed and distance travelled.

This is not the case either. The feral horse travels around 20 to 25 miles a day just wandering. If food, water or shelter is scarce the distance may well be as high as 35 to 38 (56 to 64 km) miles a day. It must be remembered when making these comparisons that these feral horses are not the pick of horses selected, fed and trained to be able to out gallop, out jump or out perform others. These feral horses are breeding groups either with foals, or pregnant, of mixed ages and sexes, from the very young to the very old. Males in bachelor groups competing for mares, or when with a group of mares, are occupied almost full time during the breeding season with preventing other stallions approaching, and cover even greater distances, although these have not been measured to date.

The race horse, competitive jumping, dressage or combined training horse will rarely travel (with his own energy) 20 to 25 miles each day even for a few months before the competition. Rather he is likely to cover fewer than 10 miles (16 km).

Thus, even though they have the very young and the very old with them, nevertheless feral horses often move greater distances every day than a great many of the equines kept in training for their athletic abilities and achievement.

The only exception to this is sometimes the Long-Distance horse who, if he is to compete in 50 to 100-mile races may well be trained every day over distances as great and sometimes greater than his feral horse cousins. Because his physiological performance in competition has been monitored in the last two decades we have learnt much about horse exercise physiology, from the pony to the thoroughbred.

Feral zebras have also been studied to some extent in this

respect and are similar to feral horses in the amount of exercise they naturally take. To date there has not been any serious study on the exercise physiology of either the wild ass or the donkey. It is however unlikely to be dramatically different to that of the horse.

Speed of travel

How fast then do the feral equines travel, and how does this compare with competitive stabled horses? This is the only variable where the stabled horse often does outdo the feral horse. The feral horse can of course gallop for a couple of miles at a speed of 20 to 25 miles (16–45 km) per hour if he has to. But the stabled race horse will be expected to travel at speeds up to 30 mph (45 kmph) for short spurts. It is interesting to note however that even with the higher *speeds* at which the stabled competitive horses are often exercised, they do not often approach the *distances* covered by the motley group of pregnant and lactating feral horses.

Again the top-level endurance horses will often be exercised for several hours at relatively low speeds (averaging 7–10 mph, 11–16 kph), resembling more the way the feral horse exercises. Exercise schedules have been developed for long-distance horses as a result of our knowledge of exercise physiology from research on competing endurance horses. As a result the endurance horse may be capable of going further faster than the feral horse. It is doubtful if this is true of flat racers, steeple chasers, jumping, and combined trained horses, despite the extra care, feed and so on that they receive . . . or perhaps because of this.

So the only area in which the selected stabled horse seems to be able to outclass the feral horse is in the ability to run faster for very short spurts, or jump higher again over short courses.

One wonders if the equestrian athletes kept to compete in major races with huge sums of money involved, or to compete in the Olympic horse trials and games should not be able to perform *at least* as well as their feral cousins in both the time spent exercising and the distance travelled as well as the speed. If appropriate management and exercise schedules were worked out to achieve this, it may be that the equine would not only perform better in his own discipline, but also live longer, and have fewer physical and psychological problems as well.

The horses' legs and general physiology have evolved to cope with this, they have not evolved to cope with sudden spurts of very fast and straining work followed by enforced immobility. If you wanted your son to succeed in the high jump, the cricket team or 200 metres for his school, the county, or the country, would you shut him up in his bedroom for even 20 hours out of 24, then send him out for very violent very fast runs for an hour, before being shut up again? You would be considered barmy, and your son is unlikely to be very successful. But humans have not evolved to move around all the time, but only for around 5 hours per 24. The rest of the time they are relatively immobile; lying down, sitting, standing about and sleeping a great deal more than horses. So if this would be considered unlikely to achieve the physiological fitness required for humans, it is even less likely to be successful for horses.

Thus it is unlikely that a horse will be given *too much* work (unless he is unhealthy, lame, or, as is often the case, much too fat). It is much more likely that the horse is getting insufficient consistent exercise over distances and for 2 to 3 hours a day to ensure he is sufficiently fit and his muscles, tendons and ligaments able to cope with the sudden high speed work required.

Why have trainers come up with the type of schedules they have then, if they do not look to be particularly rationally thought out when considering the horse's evolutionary abilities and skills? There are two reasons for this it seems. The first one, a very common one when it comes to investigating horse welfare, is that it has been developed primarily not for the benefit of the horses but for the benefit of the human caretakers. When horses are kept in single stables, individually mucked out and groomed and exercised daily, there is not enough time to take every horse out for 3 to 4 hours each day unless one employs one groom per horse. Thus the horses are exercised in a way which reduces the amount of rider/groom time needed. They need to be reasonably fit to perform (even though they might be able to be much fitter with a different schedule) so they are worked at speed (race horses often only go out for gallops) for short periods. Any other system is inconvenient or very expensive. In addition, the horses may not be taken through rough or dirty ground because they will either get dirty (and require more cleaning time) or strain their legs. As a result their tendons and ligaments never get the chance gradually to adapt and strengthen. As a result the horse is *more likely* to become unsound because of this protectionist policy.

The second reason why the majority of trainers use these strategies for training (which do not appear to be in line with the evolutionary strengths of horses and how to get them fit), is for tradition. This again is a very strong motivator for all horse management as we have already seen. The reasons for this I have already mentioned. It is the way it has always been done, and it more or less works. There is a high wastage of horses of course and their performing life is short (a few years only) but there is much inertia and opposition to change. After all, the changes might end up worse than the present system and there are considerable sums of money and status involved which no one is anxious to sacrifice voluntarily. If alternative systems were shown to work and improve the length of life of the horse, reduce the horse's other problems and consequent wastage, save money and so on, then things might gradually change.

Thus too much work for the stabled non-competitive horse is not usually the problem for him, rather it is too little work of the right type.

Weight carried

The ridden horse carries not only himself, but the rider. He may carry anything from an extra 30 to 35 per cent of his own weight. Thus he will have to exert more energy and be fitter than if he carried only himself. Consequently he will need more energy foods, and more careful fitness training to prepare him. However he is not only carrying extra weight, but this weight is concentrated on his back. Consequently, the muscles around his back must be carefully developed, he must learn to balance with this redistribution of weight, and care must be taken not to damage the structure of his back. The increasing fitness necessary and even the appropriate development of muscles can be coped with by training programmes, but what is very little known about is the control of the damage to the back. This is presently being exploited by saddle designers all of whom will tell you that their saddle is the one which is correctly designed for the horse, but when we know very little about the percentage of the body weight that the horse should be expected to carry (this varies greatly world-wide), it is difficult to be able to make informed judgements.

In fact there has been remarkably little emphasis or discussion on the amount of weight that different horses carry, and how they perform. This has been recognised in racing, of course, where the weights are seriously controlled, and in Long-Distance riding in the States, it is also recognised as being an important factor where there are different awards for those who are heavy, medium or light weights. No one knows the degree to which weight seriously affects performance of individual horses. What would be interesting is to look at the differences in the performance of different horses in relation to the percentage of their own body weight carried, and see if the usually held belief that certain individuals 'ride light' or 'ride heavy' is true or false.

The assessment of the amount of weight that an animal can and should carry in order to reduce risk of skeletal problems is therefore an area badly needing research. Again there are very many preconceived notions here. While adult human males do and have ridden Welsh mountain ponies of 12 hands right up and around the mountains for centuries, in the European horse world it is generally considered that if you are more than around 5 ft 6 inches (1.5 m) high, you really must have a 16 hh horse or you will be 'under horsed'. Are several children piled on top of a donkey too many? Is one 5-foot woman on an over-16 hh thoroughbred 'over horsed'? More assessment of carried weights, their effect on exercise and feeding, on balance and individual performance, badly need to be made. In particular there certainly do need to be weight controls introduced into long-distance riding otherwise soon no one will be riding in championships unless they weigh under 9 stone. It is almost there already in Britain with very few larger or heavier people riding longer distances. A proper assessment of the individual equines to carry or pull weights needs to be assessed in relation to their own body weight and size.

Further research is also necessary on improvements of saddle design particularly where the saddles will be on for prolonged periods and the animals are expected to go relatively fast. At present the best policy appears to be that of the

Western American: the saddle fits the human, it fits onto the horse by having layers of blankets underneath which allows the horse to move under it and padding to take up the individual's shape. Although it is good for the saddlers' business to sell the idea that the saddle must fit the horse, whether this is ever achieved is not convincing. For example, surely the front of the saddle flaps of the saddle should be able to move away from the horse as the shoulder muscle mass comes back, otherwise inevitably it will cause pressure there.

The saddle improves the comfort of the rider, and his security, but it must also improve the comfort of the horse. Provided there is proper assessment of the back of the horse after riding, and all is well then presumably this is acceptable.

Perhaps the best way at present of assessing whether or not too much weight is being carried by the horse is again to assess longevity, in this case, the working length of life. Is the horse still able to carry the same weights without signs of physiological stress, lameness and/or back problems when he is twenty or over?

What of the debates concerning the Olympic events and long-distance riding? Are these horses being asked to do too much? Should they have to run 25 miles (40 km) jumping high fixed tricky obstacles in the hunter trial phase of the combined training? Should they have to race over 100 miles (160 km)?

As far as the horses are concerned, is it and has it been possible to ensure that the horses that take part in these sorts of events are not going to suffer dramatically or die because of them? With our present growing knowledge of exercise physiology can we predict if an individual is likely to be able to complete the course and not suffer from exhaustion or other detrimental effects?

These questions are addressed in part III.

Shoeing and care of the feet

A thoughtful person, or someone who came from a different culture, may not consider it essential, if the equine is to be worked or ridden, that he be shod; after all the foot has evolved to cope with movement and shoeing may well have the effect of changing the balance and development of the foot. However, the establishment approach now holds that if the horse is worked or ridden *at all* he must be shod. Indeed another of the public's major concerns with equine welfare involves the foot. Unshod horses, it is often believed, are necessarily suffering. The fact that there is a great chance of suffering as a result of either incorrect shoeing, or leaving the shoes on too long is not often considered.

In Britain it is now illegal to shoe your own horses or anyone else's unless you are a registered farrier. This development has been encouraged by the horse welfare organisations and the qualification is controlled by the British Farriers' Council. They have one training school in Herefordshire, otherwise it is necessary to get a place as an apprentice at a training farrier's forge. Since this incurs costs for both the apprentice and the farrier, these places are scarce. The result of this is that there is a shortage of farriers in Britain. There are plenty of young people who would like to train as farriers but they are refused, not because they are not of sufficient standard, but rather that there is nowhere they can train.

It is extremely difficult to get a farrier when you need one and a set of shoes is expensive. There is the work for many more farriers to make a good living so why are the numbers so controlled? One is forced to consider that this is because the Farriers' Council wishes to maintain not only its standards (which may be commendable) but also their members' income. More farriers (as more veterinarians) would necessarily make for greater competition and hence competitive prices. In other words it appears that at present in Britain farriery (as veterinary science) is a closed shop. Yet one of the main reasons for these restrictions given by the Farriers' Council is that it is 'to improve the welfare of the horse'. In the official magazine of the farriers, *Forge* (8 May 1995), Colin Vogel (a veterinarian writes) 'I have lost count of the number of letters received via *Horse and Hound* asking what an owner can do about a horse with a certain problem because they dare not take it up with their farrier as the farrier might then refuse to shoe the horse and it is so difficult to get a farrier.'

Given that there is this concern and control over horse-shoeing in Britain, can we say that there are fewer foot problems and problems related to shoeing in Britain than elsewhere where these stipulations do not exist (e.g. the United States and Australia)? We do not have evidence for this, but we do have much evidence that there is considerable confusion about how farriers should shoe (Price and Fisher 1989) and also that fashions change. Now for example as a result mainly of work with long-distance horses, the fashion for long toes and low heels is changing, and emphasis is now being placed on a more upright foot. One farrier (Gatcombe Clinic, Devon) maintains with what seems reasonably rational arguments that the foot must be even and straight on both sides and that the best way to achieve this is to shoe the horse wide and long-heeled where necessary, whereas another will consider this is 'bad shoeing' and that the shoe must always be made to fit the foot (Hickman 1977).

In the 1970s my partner and I began to consider shoeing our own horses because one of our endurance horses, who had been shod by a registered farrier the previous day, had failed the farriers' inspection at a competitive ride. We felt that we could do as well or even better. My partner trained and obtained his licence; during this time it became increasingly obvious that farriery was not an empirical mechanical science as it should be (there are measurements that can and should be made); it was rather open to flux and fashion just like other aspects of horse husbandry. It appears that no engineer or other suitably qualified person has actually *measured* in detail the mechanics of the foot in order to have some empirical results on which to base good farriery – at least we have not found any references to such work, but plenty of theories.

There will of course always be good farriers and bad ones, as there are good vets and bad ones; but farriers, like vets, ought to have some reasoned empirical knowledge on which to base their teaching and practice especially if no one but they are legally allowed to shoe horses. At present this does not appear to be the case.

There is some evidence that the shoeing of equines can cause many problems. If in doubt therefore it would seem sensible – if we are interested in equine welfare – to shoe *only* where it is really necessary. This will be when the equine is doing much hard work on hard and rough surfaces particularly roads, and where there is no option; for example in some driving and draught work, or long-distance riding and trekking on roads. Even here it may well be possible to shoe only the front feet.

The shoeing of many teaching horses, dressage or even jumping horses cannot be assumed to be always necessary, least of all the shoeing of horses running out on grass!

Studs are often used to reduce slip in driving, dressage and jumping horses. This in itself has dangers since the angle of the foot is changed. Dressage horses habitually have studs fitted before competitions. It does seem absurd that this is allowed. Surely if dressage is about horse education/schooling, balance and so on – it is the *one* type of work where aids to prevent slip and help balance should no more be used than gadgets to hold the head in place, control speed or stop the head moving.

There is of course a welfare argument for shoeing equines where they will suffer without shoes as a result of their feet becoming short and sore. There is also an argument for remedial shoeing where the growth and conformation of the horse's leg or foot is such that it will cause lameness, and shorten his life if he were not shod.

We could argue that the animal should never be worked so long and hard that he needs shoeing in the first place. There is some substance to this argument if we are sincerely interested in the equine's welfare. On the other hand, in our relationship and working with the horse we do also have to consider human welfare. If the horse cannot be worked hard enough to pay for his keep for example without shoes, what do you do, kill him (because no one else will buy him) or shoe him? In this case it is likely that the horse would choose the latter provided the rest of his life was acceptable and he was not suffering. Provided also that the shoeing itself is done well and enough is known about it for it not to cause suffering, then there may be little rational objection. However to shoe for fashion, for showing, for changing the movement, or various other reasons where the *need* for shoes is not for the horse's benefit is not defensible.

The protection of the foot is no longer confined to shoeing. There are a whole range of products on the market which can be bought, and some of which are compulsorily used in horse establishments which are marked as 'protection' of the leg or foot. Various forms of boots: overreach boots, brushing boots, knee guards, hock guards, pads on the sole of the foot, and so on, fall into this category. If the horse has such bad action that he is bound to cut one leg by the other, then there may be an argument for the use of such guards. However if it is considered so likely that he will hurt himself doing what he is asked and necessary *always* to wear such boots or bandages, then there is an argument that states the horse should not be doing such work. It is causing suffering. Other examples include overreaching boots for jumping and galloping, bandages and leg protections in jumping horses and sole pads for endurance horses. If always protected how will the equine learn to move so he does not cut himself? Is he so likely to come to grief trotting around a circle? If this is really the case – then *why* is he made to do it?

Surely if we are serious about horse welfare we at least should not be allowed to use such protection for competition, although it may, in order to prolong life, be acceptable for particular handicapped horses to use them for ordinary work. This was originally the case with endurance riding in the seventies and eighties where the rules had originally been drawn up *with particular reference to the welfare of the competing horse*. However with increased emphasis in recent years on competition and winning, with the growing status of 'endurance riding' within the equestrian world these rules have recently been relaxed and in some cases disbanded. A retrogressive step if ever there was one. (See part III for further discussion of these issues in different equine 'sports'.)

Restraining gear: harness and tack

It is not often pointed out that the function of harness and tack is usually to *restrain the equine* in some way. This of course is not true of collars and traces which enable them to pull or britching and cruppers which keep a vehicle from running into the horse on the down hill, and of course saddles and all their bits and pieces (a whole study in itself) which are to ensure the comfort of the back of the horse and the behind of the rider.

It is however fundamentally true of all bridles, bits, head collars and a large number of extra bits of leather that are often attached between the bridles or bits of it and the saddle. The first questions to ask from the horse welfare point of view are:

(1) Are all, or any of these restraining mechanisms acceptable to the horse, if not why not, and what can be done about them? Where do we draw the line as to how far enforced restraint and control is acceptable?

(2) Are not many of these restrictions and restraints to compensate for the humans' inability to handle or teach the horse?

If so what can be done?

(3) Do all these restrictions and restraints not point in particular towards the idea of dominating the horse? If this is the main reason for humans having horses particularly when used for recreational pursuits, then there is a strong argument to back the position that equine riding is unnecessary and cruel. This position of 'dominating the horse' is openly accepted, even among these who are considered the most thoughtful riders – dressage riders. The marking of dressage tests includes a category for 'obedience' (out of 10) and 'submission' (out of 10).

(4) Do relationships between horse and human have to be governed by conflict, thus making it inevitable that the horse be forcibly restrained?

These questions are not usually, if ever, addressed by the horse establishment organisations or horse examination boards. In fact you can obtain a Fellowship of the British Horse Society, a BSc, and even an MSc, in Equine Studies never having considered any of these questions. However it is often made imperative to know the *names* of all the various gadgets and implements available to the horse owner. 'Nosebands' (a band of leather suspended around the nose which either has no function but decoration, or else restrains the opening of the mouth) vary from cavesson, to drop, to flash, kineton and puckle. 'Bits' are strips of, usually metal, that go in the horse's mouth and are to restrain them by pulling the mouth open, or by pulling the lower jaw down; rotating a curved piece of metal against the top of the palate; or pulling the corners of the mouth up; restricting the chin with a chain and so on. Elwyn Hartley Edwards (1963) in a useful analytical assessment of bits and their function mentions seven different areas of control or restraint used by different bits in different ways. These have even more impressive names: 'fillis', 'gag' (with or without Duncan!) or eggbutt snaffles, kimblewicks, Weymouth curbs, pelhams, bridoons, or 'normal cheek-piece snaffles'. You will not pass your examinations for instructing others how to ride and relate to horses unless you know the names of all these bits and pieces but you will *not* be asked if you have thought about the questions (1) to (4) above.

One cannot help thinking that it may be time to change the

emphasis somewhat and at least insist that teachers and students begin to think about these questions rather than just accept the *status quo*. This is doubly important if degrees are being awarded unless of course we are happy to have low academic standards and expect our equine studies graduates to ask no more questions than an army private is expected to.

A cooperative relationship between horse and rider will be marked by less and less restraining tack, ideally, surely we should work towards none . . . so that the horse and rider are working together at any pace with no bridle, rein, rope or head collar. We don't all achieve this of course, but we should perhaps at least aim towards it, and having less 'control', and more 'cooperation' that is if we are interested in improving relationships between horses and humans, and increasing their cooperation and mutual pleasure. This approach can be (and is in a few places) taught, rather than placing heavy emphasis on physical restraining methods, and teaching names of all the particular pieces of leather, metal, rope or webbing.

11

The stallion, castration and breeding

One of the areas of horse management which is wide open to ethical questioning is that of how, when and where horses are allowed to breed.

As humans, we consider that we all should have a basic right to be able to court, have sex and breed. This is part of being a human being, and should not be denied. The idea of castration of human males is considered with extreme horror, and societies who perform this as unbelievably barbaric. This particular cultural belief may be in part the result of our particularly male-developed, orientated and dominated culture in 'the West', but this is not the only reason. Rape of women, (sex against their will) is also regarded as particularly unacceptable; indeed a major crime.

The right to breed is also enshrined as part of human rights. When in India bribes were offered to human males to be vasectomised despite the fact that this did not interfere with the enjoyment of sex in any way, and that India desperately needed, and still needs, to control its human population, the West was outraged. Breeding must not be controlled it seems, even though it is clear that the major problem confronting the world now and into the next century will be the human population explosion.

Despite this inherent emphasis on the importance, particularly to the male, of being able to be 'whole', these same human males have apparently no compunction at all in castrating male animals. Why do they suppose that sex, and having the secondary sexual characteristics of a male mammal is only of real importance for *human* mammals? These same people will be outraged if a horse is shown to them having his ribs showing; this, they will argue is the result of 'cruelty' (suffering arranged with intent) while castration is not. Indeed many animal welfare organisations encourage it and devote a great deal of money towards castrating male animals and hysterectorising females to prevent them breeding. What basis is there for these dual standards and what are the arguments for and against equine castration?

There are many parts of the world, in particular the Mohammedan world, where male animals are rarely castrated. Castration is assumed in that male dominated society and culture to be an extremely unacceptable practice because it must cause suffering to the individual; he is no longer a male with male behaviour and status, and this is one of the most important attributes to have. There is no doubt that courtship, sex and breeding are crucially important evolutionarily speaking for the horse (and every other mammal). Indeed individuals are very highly motivated to breed. In the horse the social organisation of the males in particular revolves around this. The animals live in groups with only one post-pubertal male. During the breeding season the stallions spend a large amount of time competing to breed, courting and having sex. The mares are in season for much longer than many large mammals (e.g. cows 12–24 hrs, horses 6–10 days). It is therefore reasonable to assume that sex, courtship and breeding is emotionally very important to equines, indeed competition

A stallion (left), who lives with his mares, relaxing in the morning light.

between them shows that sometimes they will kill for it. It would seem reasonable to assume that sex is at least as important to stallions as it is to human males. It is indeed possible that it is of even more importance to the less intellectual horse than it is to the potentially intellectual human male. Should we therefore, without a qualm castrate male horses?

What are the arguments for castration? In the first place castration was probably introduced to prevent random breeding so that humans could have control in their horse breeding and select for particular desirable characteristics. It is however clear that it is not necessary to castrate horses if you do not want them to breed; it is quite possible nowadays, where they cannot often move wherever they want over unfenced land, to control who breeds with whom, without castrating males.

The other and most important reason for castration nowadays is to stop the horse behaving like a stallion – in other words becoming excited in the presence of mares. It is usually believed that stallions behave differently from mares in *other respects*. They are said to be more aggressive, unpredictable, and so on. The question is, is this inescapably part of being a stallion, or is it the result of the management system under which they are kept?

In order to assess this we need to look at how stallions behave in natural groups. The 'natural behaviour' of stallions running with mares has been described elsewhere in this book (and see Kiley-Worthington 1987, chapters 4 and 5 also Duncan 1980). It is clear that sex is as strong a motivation as hunger, thirst, fear, pleasure, and so on. Most of the time stallions behave like any other equine – and they are not excessively aggressive.

However, with the exception of the moorland ponies (and other feral groups that have been studied in the United States, Canada, France and Australia), stallions are rarely allowed to have free access to other horses, move and do what they like. They are restricted and isolated often from soon after weaning. Much of the behaviour that is in the publics' (and particularly the horse owners') mind, associated with stallions is in fact the result of the management systems under which they are kept. For example typically in the acceptable 'well-run' stud the young stallion (colt) will be weaned – separated from his mother at around 4–8 months from whom he has previously

A stallion trotting along beside two colts with an upright posture.

never been separated. He will then be placed in a stable alone and possible let out into a field for the day. When he reaches sexual maturity and starts showing interest in the mares he will probably not go out at all – some studs have small yards where he will be allowed to run sometimes by himself.

He will generally never again after weaning (or sometimes after sexual maturity) be allowed free access to other horses.

Stallions with herds do not behave very differently from mares except when it comes to courtship, sex and breeding. Stallions, like human males, can be trained to behave appropriately at the appropriate times. It is quite possible for stallions to learn to behave quietly and non-sexually and even ridden out with oestrus mares, geldings, and other stallions without problems. It is also quite possible for them to compete successfully in any competitive event. It would seem sensible if we really wanted to select particularly talented horses for breeding and improve competitive abilities, to retain competing males as stallions. It would then be possible to breed from two top competing parents, not just their close relatives. The owners of Red Rum and Arkle, two of the top racing horses in Britain in the last decades, must be kicking themselves that they were both castrated!

On the other hand, if stallions are going to be handled and ridden by novices and are bred with no chance of them going on to compete or be involved with professionals, then there is perhaps an argument for castrating some colts since the alternative might well be that they would have to be slaughtered. If stallions are not well educated, or are handled by children or novices, particularly during the breeding season, then there is an increased chance of accidents; a chance that human parents might not want to take.

It is true that the education of stallions to behave appropriately at any time can often take more time than the education of a mare or gelding because sexual motivations are strong. This can however be adequately compensated for by the extra possibilities in performance and in breeding. A valuable breeding stallion does not have to take months off to breed, as a mare does. Provided the stallions are properly educated and managed this need not be a great problem. If breeding with the competing stallion *is* a problem, then we need to re-examine the professionalism of the professionals in this area.

Unfortunately in Britain today there are pre-conceived traditional notions and a considerable prejudice against stallions taking part in general events. They are believed to be anti-social, aggressive, unpredictable, excitable and very difficult to discipline and train. This reduces the market for young stallions, and leads to self-fulfilling prophecies.

Over the last eight years we have been breeding top performing Anglo part-bred and pure-bred arabs and trying to sell the educated three-year-old colts as young talented potential performing horses with both parents top performing horses. People came to ride them and liked them, but when they returned to their stable to enthuse about the horse they would buy, their stable owner, husband, or general adviser told them not to touch a stallion, however much they liked him and felt he was just right! They then did not buy our horses. Thus we had to recommence castrating our very young horses in order to find good homes for them where they would not be behaviourally restricted and have a life of reasonable quality.

Castration is likely to be less traumatic if the horses are young, in fact as young as possible before their personality has become established and developed. The later the horse is castrated, the more ethically unacceptable it is because it is likely to cause major behavioural and personality changes. The physiological effects will be greater too the later he is castrated; the larger the operation and the greater the risk from it as a result.

In sum, castration is usually performed on account of traditional cultural beliefs, usually erroneous, rather than on account of rational requirements. Once a practice has become the norm it is difficult to alter. It becomes part of the system, the *status quo*.

Breeding

Domestic horse breeders generally decide whom should breed with whom; the idea being to 'improve' the particular type of horse that is being bred. Exactly what 'improving' means varies, and is not always clear even in the mind of the owner/breeder himself. It usually means conforming to particular standards that have been set by the breed society (these are sometimes curious and leave room for debate on welfare grounds). This has been the case with domestic animal breeding, particularly dog breeding, with the result that dogs have been bred that are physically inept; one example is the German Shepherd dog which has been selected for lowered hips unfortunately encouraging the selection of animals that will have hip dysplasia. Selection for particular characteristics of a breed which can and do cause physiological problems or an increase in disease risk occurs in horses too. For example, Arab horses are supposed to have very straight backs with a high set on tail so that the vulva is at a peculiar angle and this is said to cause problems at mating and is liable to become infected. There are many other examples in animal breeding.

There are some basic requirements for conformation (e.g. the horse must not be limping, must have a head and two eyes functioning, a neck, shoulders, hips and so on); where the line is drawn between what is really going to increase the ability to perform, and what is simply fashion is really not at all clear. There is no particular moral problem here except that it might be wise to recognise that the animal is being preferred on grounds of fashion and flare rather than possible abilities to perform, and that 'good conformation' is not something that can be agreed on at all, except at a very basic level. The moral problem comes in with people who either have preconceived notions about breeding and what is 'desirable' in terms of conformation and/or performance, or with people with little knowledge who pass judgement on horses 'rubbish and not worth breeding from'. I have yet to be convinced that a very well-loved sound, healthy and delightful mare with wobbly legs and rather cow hocks who has a mutually satisfying emotional relationship with her owner should not have a foal if she and the owner both would like one, and can provide an appropriate background and home for it. It would seem that such an individual has as much, if not more, chance of having a satisfactory and rewarding life than for example a 'top' show pony who may have her home changed a large number of times, be traded and carted around for large amounts of money, and suffer many of 'the slings and arrows of outrageous fortune' described as part of the 'horse industry' in this book. Or does it not matter that our horses have rewarding and satisfactory lives?

It would seem sensible and rational to assume that the animal being bred should have a good chance of leading a 'good life', that is, firstly that physically he or she has a very high chance of being healthy with no physical handicaps and secondly that emotionally he or she will have a good chance of being able to develop a healthy equine emotional and behavioural existence, and thirdly that he or she will have a good chance of sufficient mental stimulation to be able to develop his or her various abilities and 'intellectual' skills. In the first category problems can arise as a result of breed fanciers selecting for inappropriate physical criteria. In the second with much of the current horse-keeping establishments being as they are (see parts II and III) a healthy emotional life for many equines is unfortunately rare. The third category can be catered for in some cases for example by 'performance' selection for animals that jump well, run fast, have stamina and so on – nevertheless, there is often more that could be achieved 'intellectually' even by top performers. An awareness of the animal to be's 'needs' and how these are to be catered for is, in my opinion, the first essential when considering breeding with the horse's welfare in mind – as it is (or perhaps should be more frequently) for humans. Current practice in the planning of breeding does not seriously take into account other criteria than the physical characteristics of the parent. Although behaviour is the result of the environment that the animals are born and raised in, nevertheless there is also a genetic influence. If one parent has behaved inappropriately in one way or another, there is a chance that the offspring may have a tendency to develop similar behaviour if the social, physical and educational environment is not very carefully considered. The scientific debate concerning the relative contribution of genes and environment on the physique and behaviour of any animal, including human, is still going on – but whereas in humans the predominant opinion is that the environment has an enormous influence particularly on behaviour – to date we have not thought to apply this to animals the majority of whose behaviour and abilities are still believed to be controlled by their genes. Breed societies encourage this . . . not only will the 'X' breed be beautiful, sound, strong, healthy, easy to keep – but they will also be delightful companions, learn quickly, be good mothers, easy in the stable, quick learners, intelligent etc. This is claimed by almost every breed society and the fact is that this is largely true of *all* breeds – provided equines are kept and brought up appropriately.

There are a whole series of human held beliefs concerning this or that breed e.g. donkeys are stubborn, thoroughbreds are very nervous, arabs are scatty, Dartmoors are quiet, cart-horses gentle and so on. All of these characteristics are believed to be genetic, so there is nothing that can be done about them. That is the way those animals 'are' and the way people behave towards them reflects these beliefs, which in turn affects the equines' behaviour. This is not to deny that genes do play a part in determining equine behaviour, but it is a small part compared to that of the lifetime's experiences of the equine in affecting how he behaves with humans. Thus breeding from a particular equine is done because we want to select for certain physical traits, and not primarily for his behaviour.

Having decided which stallion will breed with which mare, the mare is sent to the stallion's stud. Here, the stallion is usually, particularly with 'quality' pedigree horses, kept in a single box often isolated from others, always with solid partitions between him and any other horse. He may live in this box for years; sometimes he may be allowed out to run by himself in a small yard or field. Sometimes he may be taken out by a handler to be 'walked' around on a lead rein. Sometimes but rarely if he is 'at stud' he may be ridden out.

At the stud the mare must suffer a number of examinations and tests, including human internal manual examinations of her reproductive organs. At some studs there is a full-time residential veterinary surgeon employed specifically to do these examinations which are performed daily in order to 'palpate the ovaries', that is to feel whether or not she will be producing an egg that day. If she is not, she will have no exposure to the stallion, even though she may be in oestrus and receptive to the stallion. The reason for this is that most stallion owners do not want the stallion to waste energy copulating a mare who is unlikely to conceive. However, whether or not this is an efficient strategy remains highly questionable (see below).

If she is ovulating, she will be 'prepared for covering'. This often means she will be hobbled (harness fixed from her withers) to each hind leg so that she cannot kick her hind legs out. She can also be twitched (a leather or rope thong placed around her nose and twisted). In addition her vulva will be further manipulated and washed by humans, and she may have padding placed on her neck where the stallion tends to chew during mounting. She is then introduced to the stallion initially behind a barracade. Sometimes to a 'teaser' stallion. This is a stallion who is not considered of sufficient quality to actually leave many offspring, and is kept in order for the managers to be able to diagnose oestrus in the mare. The stallion becomes sexually aroused but is kept behind the barricade and rarely if ever has the chance of courting a mare or mating. After this, she will be led around to the 'mating area' often with at least two people holding her. The chosen stallion will then be led in and, because of his past training, will only be allowed to smell her vulva to arouse himself sexually before leaping on her. She will be held motionless by often at least two people, the twitch and hobbles. A third person will probably manipulate the penis into the vulva as the stallion mounts the mare. He will quickly ejaculate (if he had sufficient libido, which in itself becomes a problem) and then leap off. He then has his penis washed with water and disinfectant before being quickly led away. She meanwhile has the twitch and hobbles removed and is led away. There is a belief that a quick trot about after ejaculation will help the sperm descend down the vagina and encounter the egg, so she may be trotted about for a while before being put back in her box. The next day the whole process may be repeated or not depending on the veterinarian's assessment of the state of her ovaries. It is not uncommon for a mare to be covered only once during her stay at the stud. She may then be sent home or kept for three weeks until she should return to oestrus if not pregnant. She may have a number of pregnancy tests done on her as soon as there is any chance of diagnosing pregnancy.

The stud fee for such a process varies from around £200 to £500,000 or even more for some race-horse stallions. Some stallions have a 'no foal no fee' guarantee and will allow a free return to the stallion if the mare is not pregnant, others do not, so it is economically often extremely important that the mare becomes pregnant; but how frequently does she? Is there a great improvement in terms of conception than from the way the equines themselves have evolved to breed? Is the type of breeding (a) economically and (b) ethically acceptable? When compared with equines breeding themselves the behaviour is very different. In the first place the mare is in season for up to ten days during which time she will be courted daily by the stallion who is familiar to her, and may have lived with her for years (Kiley-Worthington 1987 chapter 5). Only when she is sexually aroused enough (which for maiden mares may not be until her second or third season) will she stand for him to mount her. In the pasture or feral state she can get away when she wants – and does. She can also kick and discourage the stallion if she chooses.

It is clear that bonding between the stallion and the mare is an important relationship which leads to pregnancy in 90 to 95 per cent of cases – even in feral animals which are periodically poorly nourished. An interesting question which arises is why should horses have such a long oestrus period when they are receptive to sexual behaviour from the stallion? The only serious answer to this question that anyone has to my knowledge come up with yet, is that the period of oestrus must be important *behaviourally* for the mare. By being in oestrus for a long time, she will be courted for a relatively long time. A long courtship then must be of importance for her, otherwise it would not have been selected for by evolution. In the case of horses, the stallion not only has to fight off competitors to obtain the females, he then has to court her, often for several days during which both he and she may use energy and time in their cavorting around, risking injury to themselves or each other.

Courtship therefore is a costly business for horses (in terms of energy and time, not money as in the expensive 'stud' system) and must be there for very important reasons. These appear to be firstly, that during this courtship the mare may have to overcome her equine caution of slightly different and at least initially unfamiliar events, and fear of close contact with the stallion. Indeed in our experimental work where we have recorded the behaviour of both mares and stallions when running together, the maiden mares may not be covered at all during their first few oestrus periods with a stallion because they are apparently frightened and rush away. Secondly, during this prolonged courtship she has the opportunity of becoming sexually aroused herself so that she is more likely to ovulate and conceive as a result.

In addition to the restraint and manual manipulation mares are subjected to (and which are encouraged by the horse breeding establishment, see for example Morel 1993) – chemical restraint is sometimes used. More commonly chemical stimulants such as steroids to stimulate or synchronise ovulation are used in some studs as standard practice. However, the presence of the male has been shown in many species to increase ovulation and conception (see Kiley-Worthington 1977 for review). It would seem sensible therefore if high levels of conception are required to allow the natural physiological/behavioural mechanisms to play their role. Despite (or perhaps because of) all the restraints and manipulators the chance of conception in studs is often much lower than in feral horses (68 per cent compared to 90 per cent. Rossdale 1983 et al.). This alone would seem to mitigate against present stud practices as outlined above, let alone ethical questions of 'equine rape', manipulation and restraint. The unwarranted and unnecessary interference in the courtship and breeding of our equines is one of the most serious welfare concerns in horse keeping.

Equine breeding can be improved. The most obvious solution that will fulfil their physical, social and emotional needs is to allow them to breed running out in fields together. This has been called 'pastural breeding', and I am glad to say is becoming at least thought about as an alternative by some people now.

Here the stallion runs with the mares in fields, and covers them when they permit. This is the practice we and some other studs have been employing for the last twenty years. The disadvantages often quoted for this practice are:

(1) The stallion will not be able to cover as many mares, since he will waste energy and time with one, courting and covering several times. Recent research (Bristol 1982) however, indicates that even when twenty mares in oestrus were run with one stallion (a situation which is rarely encountered even in the busiest studs) he covered them all and their conception rate was over 90 per cent in the first season, a level that studs who cover in hand envy and never achieve even with the extra expenses and manipulations they try.

(2) It is believed that the mare and stallion will injure each other by kicking and rushing around. It is indeed important that the stallion is raised appropriately and educated in normal equine communication in order to be able to read the signals from the mare of, for example, how close to get and how to avoid being kicked. It is equally important that the mare has had some experience with other horses, at least if she is to be able to interpret his intentions. One of the problems is because stallions in many parts of the world, are now only used for stud, it is rare for mares to have ever in their lives encountered an entire male of their own species. Thus sex and courtship are very novel and terrifying experiences for them. An inexperienced pathological stallion with an inexperienced terrified mare is of course asking for trouble and one of the reasons why pastural breeding is considered to be so risky.

However, there is no reason why with appropriate upbringing and experiences the next generation of equines should not be able to breed at pasture with very little risk to either mare or stallion. On our stud, we have had no serious damage to either in the over one hundred coverings we have now had, and our stallions are as valuable as others at the top of any competitive tree.

(3) A disadvantage we have found which has to be coped with is when strange mares are introduced to the resident group who are with the stallion, they may not be accepted by the other mares who may place themselves between the newcomer and the stallion, effectively act as chaperones and prevent the

A stallion herding a mare with the typical 'snake face'. Note the mare's attention directed back to him (ears) and the swishing of the tail, indicating slight annoyance.

Affiliative greeting, nose to nose sniffing, stallion (left) and mare.

The stallion is investigated by the mare's filly foal, and a colt foal is keeping a close eye on what is going on.

Shereen, the grey mare on the right with her filly foal urinates to attract the stallion Carif's attention.

The mare urinates, attracting the stallion. Touching and nuzzling, licking and apparently whispering sweet nothings are as important to courtship and successful sex (rather than rape) in horses as in humans.

Foreplay includes mounting, and leaping about. Horse play is rough play, but if the animals have learnt to be normal horses, very rarely are there any serious injuries.

Mounting, intromission and ejaculation willingly entered into by mare and stallion alike, watched with interest by two foals.

stallion covering the new mare. One successful solution to this has been to ensure that the newcomers are not in season when they arrive, so that they run with the group for some time, sort out their relationships and become more accepted into the group before they come into oestrus, and the stallion starts seriously to court them. It is interesting that resident mares behave much like stallions to other stallions: they do not willingly tolerate other mares having access to their stallion whom they have lived with for some time until the newcomers have integrated into the group.

The practical advantages of this pastural breeding system are:

(1) The animals can exercise their normal repertoire of behaviour, and consequently be less stressed and distressed, and the mares can only be covered when they wish it. Thus it is 'better welfare'.

(2) There is a much higher conception rate (over 90 per cent, whereas covering in hand achieves around 68 per cent (Rossdale 1983), and artificial insemination even less).

(3) It is much cheaper both in terms of capital (no individual stables required, covering yards, etc.) and running costs (reduced labour, reduced veterinary care, etc.).

(4) It is easier to manage and run. However, the stockpeople/ horse grooms, must be good observers who have learnt the necessary skills and have a through understanding of normal equine behaviour. They must be able to predict problems and act on them, rather than just sweeping and cleaning. In addition, for this system to work smoothly and well both the stock people and the management must be seriously motivated.

(5) The final advantage of this system is that the breeding season becomes less hard work and stressful for both humans and equines.

Castration

There are two reasons why animals should not be castrated without serious consideration:

(1) For the individual's welfare, being a 'complete' equine and having the possibility, at least at some stage of his life, of experiencing sex which may be as important to equines as to humans, if not more so.

(2) To enable selection of appropriate traits more rapidly by having both parents performance tested rather than just near relatives.

In general, castration should be the exception rather than the rule. There are situations when the individual is likely to have a lower quality of life with fewer options and choices as a result of being castrated. If this is as a result of the stallion being brought up inappropriately, and not taught proper behaviour at suitable times, then the development of equine welfare necessitates that *both the raising and the teaching of the stallion, as well as his keeping conditions should improve*. There are enough examples of how this can be done worldwide now for it not to be ruled out as impractical, although certainly more time associating with the horse and teaching him is necessary. As a result of the past experiences of the present generation of stallions there are problems that may be too difficult to overcome.

The pre-conceived notions people have concerning stallions' behaviour also affect how they behave. There is no need to raise the next generation of equine stallions in a similar way and end up with similar problems. We can now, if we want, raise stallions so that they can be well adapted, useful and pleasant companions and take part in normal equine activities. If those involved professionally cannot do this, then perhaps they should not be professionally involved: if a dentist cannot fill cavities in teeth properly, then he should not be a dentist; if those who make their living from breeding, riding, teaching, competing with equines cannot raise, teach and keep stallions appropriately where they have considerably less behavioural restriction than at present and can take part in normal horse activities and events – then they should not be so involved with equines.

It is often argued that the bad, difficult or dangerous behaviour of the stallion is typical; that it is the result of 'instinctive'; behaviour he has no control over. I have pointed out this is not the case since there are plenty of stallions worldwide who behave well in a huge variety of situations. The other reason frequently given for not trying to educate stallions to behave appropriately and keep them in conditions which are less stressful for them, is that it is that particular genetic line which inevitably will be difficult and dangerous; certain thoroughbred stallions in particular are often believed to be in this category. The questions then are:

(a) Should such animals who are genetically programmed to behave inappropriately and psychopathically be bred at all? If the demands of the 'horse industry' are to select such horses, then surely there are strong grounds for banning the whole thing.

(b) Is this a belief of convenience? Is it believed because it has always been believed and there is a whole series of traditional practices of 'how to look after stallions' that has arisen, and there is money to be made in various ways by so doing?

(c) Mare owners (and others) like to see a stallion leaping about and behaving 'badly' – this is associated culturally with 'virility' and 'libido'. It is possible to teach the stallion to behave in this way at certain times of course – but there is no evidence that such behaviour is associated with higher libido or fertility.

There is an argument for castrating young equines who will otherwise have to be slaughtered. One of these is if they are to live and teach where there are novices or handicapped people around, or are going to be kept by amateurs who have little knowledge. But this is not the case for all male equines.

The stallion, how to raise and keep him

If then, many more male equines are not to be castrated, how are they to be raised, kept and used in such a way as to avoid problems? There are two areas of important change, which apply to other horses too but are particularly important for stallions, if their welfare is to be improved, and problems avoided.

It is emphasised again that, the current mature stallions may not be able to adapt to changed conditions rapidly, because of their inappropriate past experiences and their resulting abnormality of behaviour. There is no reason (other than vested interest, convenience and the maintenance of the *status quo*) why, if we are interested in improving equine welfare, stallion husbandry and management cannot change for the next generation of stallions being born and raised now. Whether this will happen is another question and depends upon you, the reader.

On our stud we have been experimenting with this, and now compete on stallions which have successfully been raised in this way. We will now run through the life of a young potential stallion and outline the important areas that need to be assessed and changed.

Birth

The mother should be living with a group of other mares, youngsters and a stallion (vasectomised if necessary to control breeding each year). When the foal is born, it lives with its mother and others. They should if possible be kept out at grass in large paddocks and if necessary extra feed taken to them. If they are to be stabled, then this must be only for short periods, during which both can be handled. They must not be kept routinely isolated from other horses for prolonged periods, although short periods away from others will increase the adaptability of the foal.

Education

He should be handled and spoken to gently soon after birth, so as to have some early pleasant experience with humans. Formalised 'early imprinting' handling (see Miller 1985) is not necessary or particularly desirable in our view.

Foalhood

He lives with his mother and other mares and foals, possibly with sub-adults and preferably, also a stallion. Mother can be taken away and used/worked for short periods, initially from even two weeks postpartum if the foal is strong and well. Gradually this period can be lengthened to 2–3 hours by 3–4 months old. There should be no panicking by the foal, or mother; if there is, the separation has been too long or too soon. It is vital that the foal remains with other adults with whom he is familiar and can form relationships.

Education

The foal should be taught to lead quietly, first behind mother, then away from mother and alone. He must be encouraged to form an emotional bond with the handlers and teachers so that he will follow them around and have confidence in them, as with his mother. Bad behaviour e.g. biting, leaping around, kicking, etc.) is unlikely to occur if the foal is properly handled, but if it does it must be quickly corrected as it is by other horses in the group (a quick hard smack on the head if bitten, together with a verbal 'no'). Words should be used consistently, and in situations where the meaning can be easily gathered so that the youngster begins the habit of listening and comprehending human verbal communication as well as visual messages. The youngster when leading well, can be taken on expeditions (e.g. roads, through water, rough ground, to visit other stables, shows, gatherings, etc.) so that he gradually becomes used to many different situations and is quietly introduced, so as to become familiar with change, and learn it is *not* frightening. This can be done with mother and other horses initially, and then alone as appropriate. A particularly useful educational exercise is to take the foal out when the mare is ridden, either being led from the mare (e.g. on roads, etc.) but where possible (e.g. on the moors, open space, woodland or down land) – running loose. This allows the youngster to learn about different terrains, water, hills, rocks, bogs, and from his mother and the other equines so when he is taken out later he is more experienced and anxiety and fear are reduced. If, in any situation, the youngster becomes excited and frightened or badly behaved (usually a sign of fear) then it is important to remain with him, calming him until he can cope, so that he learns that the situation is not frightening, at least when his handler is there. Taking him away from the situation immediately after 'bad' behaviour, reinforces him in his previous supposition that the situation was frightening and to be escaped from; in this way he has been taught to behave in an inappropriate   way.

Weaning

The foal should be naturally weaned by the mare. If she is in foal again, she will do this at around nine months. If not she may continue to suckle the foal for a long time. If this happens, then a period of separation at around nine months where the youngster is kept with his familiar group and his mother is removed will help the mare's milk to dry. When this is achieved, and she no longer permits suckling then they can be put together again. It is very important that the mare and foal are separated for periods so that they gradually get used to being separate and the foal can form relationships with other, mature equines. Sudden weaning at 5–8 months and separation of the foal from others, or even placing them in a group together should be avoided. It is one of the major causes of behavioural problems thereafter.

Education

The same education as above continues, the more the better at this time so that he has other things to think about than either his mother's rejection or her absence. This is a crucial time when the youngster is learning very fast. He must have *free access* to both other horses to learn appropriate equine social manners and behaviour, and to humans to learn their required manners and behaviour, and to fulfil his growing emotional, physical and cognitive needs which are particularly important at this time.

Post-weaning

Whether or not the mother has weaned the foal, or it has been helped because she is not in foal again at around 9 to 10 months, the foal must be kept with a *mixed group of other equines*. At this stage he will be becoming pubertal, and the resident stallion may begin to try and chase both the fillies and colts away from his group. The youngsters' general strategy then is to run around mother and mother will protect him by kicking out at the stallion and keeping him away. However the foal will move further away from mother, and then he is at risk and can get trapped by the stallion in corners. At this stage therefore it is important to take either the stallion or the youngster at risk and keep them with older equines. This group can then become equivalent to the 'bachelor' group of the feral animals. The young fillies will at this stage also usually be rejected by the parental group and wander around, often taking up residence with the bachelor group when members of the bachelor group will try to stay with her and keep the other males away: and form a new harem group. The fillies if thrown out of the parental group may try to join another family group, or may even manage to stay with their mother and her friends, particularly if the stallion is replaced. This is a time of much social activity for the young stallion (as for adolescent humans) and provided the group is carefully observed and its structure thought about carefully, there needs to be no danger of serious conflict between horses as the youngster will indicate clearly his juvenile submissive status when confronted by an older horse.

If there is not another stallion and the mares are not pregnant, then the colt will gradually start to cover them when he is approximately 12–18 months old. If this is not desired, then he must be in a group where the mares are pregnant, or a bachelor group. We find that to keep competing mares and stallions together, allowing them to have sex and form normal relationships in the group, the best way is to have a vasectomised stallion . . . one perhaps who has already had some foals and whom one does not particularly want to breed from again. This allows both mares and the stallion to live together, and be fit and working without the mares' becoming pregnant every year. In this way they all have courtship and sex.

Education

At this stage (12–18 months), the youngster can begin to be worked on a lunge or at liberty, obviously without over doing it, but a future athlete must begin to develop and work his muscles carefully when young, and develop the necessary physical skills with his body to be able to improve them when older. The advantage of this is also that the equine becomes used to the ropes, and harness of various types early on, he already has confidence in his handler/teacher, and he is needing considerable intellectual stimulation. If he does not have enough to do and learn, very like teenage humans who do not have enough to do or enough stimulation, they will make it and this may end up with anti-social behaviour.

If the youngster is well grown at this stage he can be backed for short periods, and learn to carry weight without trauma or jumping about. Subsequently he can begin to work in or out of the school, first with other horses whom he knows, with mother is the best, we find, then gradually by himself.

If he is not going to be ridden, or driven or work on the land, then he still must have stimulating and interesting experiences and learning sessions. Liberty work and lungeing is useful here, teaching him to stand in ways that may be required for the show ring, even to do various little things in and around the stable (such as pick up a bucket, or shake hands, put his head down when required etc.) can be taught, which not only entertains and stimulates the equine, but also ensures that both the equine and the human are having to concentrate on each other. The human is not just doing the 'house keeping' of stable routines and grooming. This encourages the human to think more carefully about that individual, his needs and desires, and also to learn to teach by thinking about what they are doing. This type of work is particularly important for the young equine intended to be a breeding stallion as he otherwise has an unstimulating, and an undemanding life style and will have insufficient physical, emotional and cognitive stimulation. As a result he will overreact, and develop abnormal and difficult behaviours. The more different experiences and education he has, the better for him and the easier the management for the humans.

Management of the mature stallion

The mature stallion runs with both mares and youngsters, and will have learnt basic equine manners in relation to mares so he does not rush up to them, and thrust himself on them. He will have learnt to read equine messages so that if the mare is going to kick, he can get out of the way first. He will have learnt how to approach, to associate with and finally how to court mares without trauma and without damage to either. There is always going to be a risk of kicking, but then there are even more risks where the covering is done in hand; for example lower conception rates, problems of behaviour ending up in the stallion having to be euthanased, loss of libido in the stallion, which must be offset against the risk.

It is important that the first mares he is to cover are introduced to him *not in season* so that he can become acquainted with them initially without the excitement of sex. Then they come into season and it is wise to ensure that his first experiences are with mature females who have foaled and had sex often before, preferably naturally.

The stallion, if he is well, will always take notice of mares who are introduced to him after being separated even for a few hours, but after the initial greeting which can be noisy and usually involves front leg lifting, and squealing from both, they will relax and continue with what they were doing before. It is important therefore always *to allow a stallion to greet mares*, as otherwise he will continue to want to, and if denied will become frustrated and excited. As the stallion becomes more experienced, he will even trot off if for example let out into a paddock with them, and investigate all the chemical messages left in the faeces and urine, before even greeting them. They will watch him carefully all the while awaiting a brief flirtation!

If the mares coming to the stallion have never run with a stallion before (and many of them haven't) it is wise to introduce the two of them on long leads, standing well out of the way, so that they can be introduced under supervision. It is also important to ensure that the stallion is running with more than one mare, when new mares are introduced. The resident mares will not absorb the newcomer in to their group immediately, but as long as there is sufficient room they will sort out their social problems over time. One problem we have had is the resident mares acting as chaperones and not allowing the stallion to get near to the visiting mare, by placing themselves between him and her and stopping his approach with evil face and backing into him. If this happens, we have had to separate the offending 'Mrs Whitehouse'!

Although it is advisable to run the stallion out with the mares all the time, nevertheless, it is still possible to bring him into a stable for part of the day or even at night if it is easier. He can also go away for a few days to compete or for a riding trip, or whatever. He can even pay his way as he travels by covering mares here and there as required!

Out of the breeding season he is available as a normal working horse to hunt, compete, work the land or whatever is required. He does not have to be a large expense nine months a year doing nothing; which is not good for him nor his owner.

A stallion (right) can be ridden out and be relaxed and easy with familiar or strange horses, whether mares, geldings or other stallions.

Here, the chestnut stallion is quite relaxed with a gelding he has just met on an endurance ride.

In this way it can be practical to keep stallions without the types of problems which are generally associated with them, and which result in male equines being castrated for behavioural reasons.

This type of system is less demanding in terms of human time, technology, veterinary help, capital equipment and thus less expensive, and possibly might seem a threat to many who make their living out of the present 'horse breeding industry'. Perhaps it is time that we began to consider changes as out-lined above as commercial possibilities. Not only will the stallion benefit, but the mares will like it too. We have found that they are very keen on sex, sometimes even trying to arouse the stallion when they are not apparently in season. What the single mare owner can do, which will have a considerable effect, is only send the mare to a stallion who does run with his mares, even if you do have to pay a little more. Failing being able to find one who does (they are at present scarce), make sure that the stud allows you to be there and witness her covering. If they do not want this, be suspicious, maybe they have something to hide, indeed, something that even they are ashamed of in relation to their practices.

Stallions can be raised and kept like other horses particularly if they are at stud and are in professional establishments with experienced personnel. It would not be advisable to have stallions and mares kept together where children or novices are likely to be with the horses unsupervised.

12

Horse welfare, insurance and euthanasia

One of the recent developments in the 'horse industry' is the insurance business. Ride or have a horse, and soon you will be inundated with invitations to take out various insurance policies for things as varied as: losing your tack, breaking down in a horse box, your illness, or veterinary fees for your horse, lameness, killing yourself or your horse. It is the last two alternatives which concern us here.

Horses (in Europe and the United States anyway), are expensive to buy, keep and particularly to have veterinary attention for. It is tempting, having saved up perhaps for years to buy your horse, to insure him against death at least so that you will get your money back, and be able to buy another if he dies or is killed. If you insure against accident not just death, the premiums will be quite severe, because of course it is recognised by the insurance companies that accidents for the horse are relatively common. It may well not take much more than five years before you have paid the price of the horse in the premium! The result of all this is that many people insure their horse but only against death or 'loss of use'.

There is a rather serious ethical spin off to this which is not often recognised, but must, if we are seriously interested in horse welfare and ethics, be acknowledged. Suppose your horse injures himself so that he will have to be out of work for months – and then may never be sound again; perhaps he breaks a leg or severely cuts a tendon. He could be treated for this, and certainly such injuries are not often life threatening but it will cost a great deal, firstly in medical care, and secondly to keep him while he gets better. At the end of all this he may not be sound. The result is that when the veterinarian is called out to look at the horse and assess treatment, the first thing he may ask is 'is he insured?' If he is insured, this will colour the vet's judgement on what course of action he will advise. If the horse has broken a leg or badly damaged himself, there may certainly be an economic case to be made for having the animal euthanased. But do not let us delude ourselves that this is anything but a case of economics. It is *not* in the horse's interest to be put down, unless he is going to suffer acutely for prolonged periods. Even then this could, perhaps, be controlled by pain killers. We are unlikely to assume a human who breaks his leg will always be in pain. Medical care will help heal the wound – certainly the man or woman will not be put down 'for his own good'! Here again we have dual standards and 'beliefs of convenience'.

If the horse is not insured, the vet will give a run down on the likely medical expenses, and it is up to the owner to calculate what she should do. The veterinary and keeping expenses would then have to outweigh his value before he is put down because this is the money that would certainly be lost if he were euthanased. You never know, there is also a chance that he *might* be all right at the end of it, or at least able to do something, if only to be a companion and friend, or if a stallion or a mare, breed.

Thus, the result of insurance against death or loss of use is that the animal has an increased chance of being put down, when he might not have been if he had not been insured. Let me give an example. My partner drove on his tractor past the end of a local bridleway where it joined the road. He was surprised to see a horse standing puffing and sweating at the end of the bridleway. The horse was standing on all four legs, and was hot and flustered, but did not show any obvious sign of acute life-threatening injury. An hour later he drove back past the spot to find that the horse had just been shot. What had happened may have been that the girl rider had probably been of insufficient skill or understanding to ride the horse unaccompanied, the horse had taken fright on the bridleway and galloped off; she had fallen off, the horse had come out onto the road and fallen over. He may have done himself some radical internal injury which my partner did not see, but even if he had, he could perhaps have been given the chance of surviving (a human would be). More likely, it was that he had hurt himself, was going to be off sick for a while, and perhaps had a chance of remaining lame. In addition, and often very important to the decision, is that the rider was terrified, did not want to have to do with the horse any more, knew she would be unable to sell him unless she spent a lot of money on having him reschooled, keeping him to get better and so on. Since he was insured against death or 'loss of use' it may have been better, from her economic point of view, to have him slaughtered.

If I were in this position, I admit I would be very sympathetic to her (although I would hope I would not have got myself into such a situation), and might indeed make the same decision. However, I would have very serious qualms about the morality of this decision. The vet similarly may have serious qualms, but on the other hand he can no more be blamed; there is no reason he is likely to behave with greater morality than the rest of us. If he argues that the horse might get better and perhaps from the horse's point of view, need not be slaughtered, he is not likely to retain the custom of this person, nor of most of her friends. Both the owner's and the veterinarian's pocket may be affected if the horse is kept alive.

This is just one incident, but such incidents do happen widely all over the place. It is not often done in a calculated cold-blooded way of course. Partly because there is the 'belief of convenience' of our culture – and particularly the welfare lobbies within it – that the animal would be 'better off dead' even when we certainly have little or no evidence for this and certainly we would not, and do not make this judgement for another sentient being: a human. The owner may genuinely believe this to be the case without thinking it through. This is not to deny that emotional responses enter into this decision; they often do: 'I really love this horse and do not want him to suffer' is a common statement, although the sincerity of this remark is sometimes difficult to judge, and more importantly, whether or not the horse is going to suffer more than he would profit from having more life is even more difficult to judge. I very much doubt that the horse would make the decision to die rather than live – even if he knew he would be in considerable pain for some time, and crippled afterwards – any more than humans usually do.

On the other hand, the human owner may balance up all the difficulties and problems and decide that for the greatest happiness to the greatest number, the horse must go, just as she may send 'Granny' to the old people's home, although she may know that 'Granny' does not want to go, but the strain of having her at home will reflect badly not only on her daughter, but on the rest of her family. Provided these arguments are made sensibly and honestly, it may not be the decision one would like to make in the best possible world, but it may be the correct, 'right' one for that set of conditions.

What I am saying here then, is not that all insurance of horses against death and injury is wrong, but rather that the individual cases must be seriously thought and discussed through before the decision to slaughter a horse is made. Despite statements that this is always done, we all know that it very often is *not*.

One cannot help adding however, that if the owner is inclined persistently to make these decisions, she should perhaps not have a horse at all – unless she is prepared to argue that it does not matter, since the horse is a non-sentient pre-programmed robot. But this is more and more difficult to do (see part I). Insurance for injury to horses can be good news for vets, because if the fees are covered by an insurance company, the veterinarian will be inclined to charge more than he might to a private, not so well off individual, and recommend a complex expensive treatment that may not nec-essarily be entirely in the interests of the animal. The owner will of course be a party to this, by insisting on some treatment, x-rays, specialist scans, and other high-tech processes now available. These may perhaps sometimes be the best thing to do – but should not always be entered into without question, if one is considering the best interests of the horse. Some remarkable successes of alternative 'low tech' treatment of equines support this view (e.g. acupuncture, homeopathy, radionics, chiropractic, osteopathy).

It is not only in the case of horse injury that insurance can become a pernicious effector. One of my life-long friends, whose children I taught to ride, admitted to me in conversation one day that if they had had a riding accident, she would have had absolutely no hesitation in suing me for negligence, whatever the circumstances! 'Why?' I asked, horror-struck, and worried. 'Because, of course, it is not *you* I am suing, but the insurance company', she replied. The effect of insurance is to negate the individual responsibility for action; as you crash you friend's old mini you shout 'it's OK I'm insured', your friend claims a bigger brighter car as a result. It can often be the same with horses; the only difference being that horses are sentient beings with desires and needs too! Should these be considered?

When should horses be put down? When their suffering is great and will be prolonged. But when is this? Perhaps this book has given some guidelines on ways of assessing and thinking about this. There are of course economic considerations and the benefit or lack of it to the humans and other species must also be taken into account and weighed up for that set of conditions.

'Pro-lifeists' would argue that never should a human be euthanased, even if they ask for it, and there are those who argue the same must apply to equines – but although life is precious to individuals, and this should be recognised – there is no shortage of it and ecologically speaking, hanging on when the quality is past is after all denying others a chance by using resources that would otherwise be available to them – this is not to say we seriously should say 'he is better off dead' quite so often – be he human or equine.

In general, welfare organisations spend a large amount of their bequests killing animals. One of the only organisations who does not, and will take in all donkeys it is asked to, is the Donkey Sanctuary at Sidmouth, Devon. This is a particularly interesting place from the point of view of developing advances in equine welfare. The limits of veterinary care of the donkeys closely reflect the problems presently confronting those involved with medical care of humans. Donkeys are not euthanased unless they are found to be profoundly suffering physically, even with the use of analgesics (which are used at this centre as they are in human hospices). This applies whether they are young or very old. As a result the sanctuary has several donkeys over fifty years old, still living active pensioners' lives.

Of course economic criteria have to be borne in mind in connection with the euthanasing of horses, young or old, but perhaps, if we are rational about our morality, as with human welfare, we could begin to use length of life as an index of the 'quality of life' and 'good welfare'. In which case, at present, horses score rather badly. The average age of death of our horses or working donkeys is very much lower than that which might be expected with modern care, although no survey has been conducted on this to date as far as I am aware.

Part 3

Are current ways of using
equines cruel?

13

Eventing, dressage, show jumping, cross country, showing

By far the majority of the horse-owning public as well as regular riders compete. In fact competition and success in competition has become almost the only yardstick used by the 'horse industry' to measure ability to ride, knowledge about horses, and even in some cases expertise at teaching! Almost everyone who buys or rides a horse regularly will be told that to progress with the horse it is necessary to compete; that without competition you cannot learn more and improve, and only the real beginners and incompetents (with one or two exceptions) don't compete. In other words being a successful rider is synonymous with competition. It is extremely difficult to disregard this peer group and teacher pressure. To encourage even the beginners in such an approach, there is a mass of competitions run for them, and 'grades' of examinations, all of which contribute to the emphasis on competition.

At the same time there is a growing number of people who own their own horses and really don't have any wish to compete. They have their horse for various reasons, usually related to having and knowing another sentient individual with whom they can escape from their normal everyday life, take care of, keep clean and tidy, enjoy the countryside with, and get to know other humans with similar interests. They may just want to learn more and more about another species, how to ride, look after, enjoy the company of, and delight in . . . they do not at all want to compete; there is already enough competition in their lives and one of the attractive things about being in the stables and out and about in the countryside is the *absence* of competition with either humans or horses.

Such people have great pressure put on them to make them feel that they really ought to compete, without competing they will never get anywhere or manage to improve their relationship with the horses or their riding. They are sold the idea that there has to be a challenge, it *has to be* a risking, nerve-racking business, when, in fact, it was because it was not that they had been attracted in the first place!

It really must be considered and respected that for many people satisfaction with their horses is and never will be involved primarily with competition. It must also be realised that some of the most knowledgeable people about horses, most considerate and concerned, best teachers and best riders, are not, and have never been, involved with competition. Putting the heavy competitive message across to anyone and assuming that whatever is done without competition is no good is clearly not only daft but disruptive to progression concerning horses and their welfare.

This excessive concern with 'competitive riding' is particularly curious in Britain with its long tradition of fox-hunting which was a non-competitive motivation for riding for the majority until very recently. This may have changed in the last decade or two when fox-hunting has become either unacceptable (because of the supposed suffering of the fox), unfriendly (because of the wealth and status consciousness of the hunting people) or unaffordable. In the hunting field, extraordinary feats of both horse and rider were often performed, where almost any type of riding (as long as you stayed on) went, and much of the point is to take risks. Both humans and horses have died as a result and hunting has not been the best model for horse welfare. Nevertheless, it does illustrate a non-competitive approach to horse riding.

In the last few years, the welfare of horses in competition has become a subject of important debate largely as a result of the public's increasing awareness and interest in animal welfare and televising of equine competitions. This has, and continues to cause some embarrassment to horse owners, and, as is common human practice in such circumstances, each side tends to entrench and justify itself in its particular belief system without seriously examining the arguments of the other. For example:

The animal welfare lobbies' position
They maintain that competing horses are cruelly treated, are expected to do far too much and it ought to stop. The animals

are owned often by people who are not primarily interested in the horses' welfare but in the money they can make (the 'horse industry' is a thriving money-making concern sponsoring courses at a host of agricultural colleges now) or the status and fame they may accrue if successful.

The competing horse lobbies' position

The horse owning public maintain they *know* about the welfare of our horses; they care about them, and often become very fond of them. Thus they would be the first to stop any 'cruelty', they believe and do what is right. If there was any cruelty, this would be spotted and weeded out by well-thought-out and comprehensive rules which they are constantly revising. Thus they will continue to do what they are doing and the general public are ignorant and often silly – so they believe.

The division of the interest groups into these two un-communicating camps is unfortunate from the view of the horses' welfare. There are difficult complex problems here and they need to be thought out with mutual respect, rational arguments and genuine concern to arrive at mutually accept-able conclusions.

Recently I attended a meeting addressing just this subject which had been organised by the Eastern Region of the British Horse Society. It demonstrated only too well the horse owning and competing approach.

The central motive of the meeting which was attended largely by people who were directly involved with training, riding, looking after or breeding competition horses, was *not* to question what was going on and what the public's concerns were, but rather to ensure that the sport continued. There was no spokesperson from the 'ban the horse in competition lobby' or even anyone who had knowledge of all the arguments against competition, let alone a rational debate.

The meeting began with a speech by the chairperson of the British Horse Societies' Welfare Committee in which she emphasised how all present (all members of the BHS: and many owners of competing horses) were *primarily* concerned with the welfare of the horse in all the competitive disciplines. It continued with a talk by a past Olympic eventer who pointed out that there were some changes to the rules that had been made recently, and how they were constantly updating the rules. There had been nine mortalities in eventing in the last few years. I was not clear if these mortalities were of horses or humans (it turned out to be humans). I asked how many horse mortalities there had been in the competitions or as a result of the competitions, no one either knew or would tell me and the subject reverted to how to control the number of *human* mortalities by making sure it was safer for the humans (a long talk on the design of the hard hats by a surgeon was then instructive but hardly pertinent to the subject of the meeting). The main improvements for horse welfare in eventing that were suggested were that the 'table fence' (one where several people had either died or been injured; no mention what has happened to their horses) should be carefully placed, and that the course building would have some minor changes introduced.

Since two or three horses had been killed as a result of eventing at each of the last four Olympic meetings, and the animal welfare lobbies were now trying to ban eventing as an Olympic competition, the meeting then turned to what was going to happen at the next Olympics in Atlanta where it would be very hot and humid, and heat and exercise exhaustion were likely. Because a wealthy wellwisher had seen the problems with the horses in Barcelona and given money for a research programme to be started at the Animal Health Trust in Newmarket, the problem of how to assess fitness and whether the Atlanta Eventing Olympics should go ahead was at last being assessed by the spending of a great deal of money on sophisticated equipment and salaries for some physiologists.

This is of course a laudable development. On the other hand it would be more economic and in fact better science to assess what was already known about fitness in horses and how to measure it, and then immediately to introduce physiological criteria that the horse has to reach before he is either allowed to start or continue in the eventing competitions. These criteria are already known and implemented at a sophisticated level in long-distance riding competitions. If eventers are *seriously interested in the welfare of their horses,* rather than the continuation of their unaltered sport, these criteria could be introduced and have to be fulfilled by every competing horse at every competition (just as they are for long-distance competitions). This would be a start to improving the welfare. Alterations can be made as more information is accrued. This has happened with long-distance competitions over the last decade and a half. It is really not necessary to wait two or three years before the physiologists have done yet some more exercise physiology research at very considerable expense (and with questionable welfare of their experimental horses). We already have the answers and know how to prevent the majority of horses dying or suffering as a result of doing too much too fast. What will never be able to be prevented by any amount of research is falls at fences (or anywhere else for that matter), accidents of one sort or another, but to ensure the animals are fit to perform what they are asked to do, physiologically, is possible and will inevitably cut down mortalities, injuries and accidents. So why is the knowledge that is already extant, and collected to a large extent from long-distance competitive events not used in eventing? Are the people just not too interested in being eliminated for the horses lack of 'fitness to continue': they have invested too much money, time and effort in getting the horse to the competition and therefore will argue vehemently for a continuation of the *status quo*. One tends to believe it is the latter concern which sways their judgements.

The meeting continued in the same vein with a champion steeplechase jockey giving his opinion on the use of the whip in racing (another area of recent public concern) but also maintaining that in racing it was the welfare of the *jockeys* rather than the horses that was lacking in attention. Then a vet mentioned how the welfare of the horse at home was important, but without giving any details on how this could be improved. The meeting broke up, the majority satisfied with the proceedings and confirmed in their belief that all was well in the horse competitive world. There was no reason to question whether what they were doing was open to debate, (at least on grounds of equine welfare).

I, and several others were not convinced: had the subject of the meeting really been about the horses' welfare in competition or about how to maintain the *status quo* and reduce the number of human mortalities when riding in competitions?

In this chapter, my aim is to try to seriously address the very real and important issues on horse welfare in various types of competition, not to take sides, but rather to try to debate the important issues and use the horse in competition as an example of how this can be done. I hope the result may be better informed and serious debate, not only for the competitive horses' benefit, but for other animals, either in competition, or public display of any type.

To do this we will take the various competitions one by one, starting with eventing (dressage, cross country and show jumping): the most controversial competitive event at present. Chapters on the welfare of equines in other competitive events follow. There will inevitably be overlaps so the reader will be referred back where necessary.

Eventing

Eventing or horse trials consists of three types of competition in which the horse takes part: (1) the dressage, (2) the cross-country phase where they gallop over fences around a course up to 90 kms long, (3) the show-jumping phase. In the less advanced competitions these events are all on one day: a 'one-day event'. As they become more advanced, they are spread onto two and finally three days; a day for each type of competition. Each phase will be discussed; what happens in the competition and in particular what often happens in the training.

Dressage

For a growing number of riders in Europe and throughout the world, dressage is becoming the aim of their competitive or even non-competitive riding life. Dressage comes from the French word 'dresser' which means to train, and what it traditionally meant during the ages of the cavalry (over 1,000 years or so) was the training of the horse and rider to be able to stay together and perform various movements of various difficulty, depending on their talents and needs, in order to be able to protect themselves better in combat and kill more of the enemy. However during the fifteenth century onwards, dressage became an end in itself for the talented horse person and many thoughtful, thought provoking and interesting books were written, mostly by those who taught the cavalry.

Soon the various schools of dressage developed their own dogma. The best known of these is the Spanish Riding School in Vienna now renowned as one of, if not *the* major 'classical school' of equitation. However the French also have their own approach, still taught to volunteers and conscripts in their cavalry centre in Saumur. The French elite cavalry riders are called the 'Cadre Noir' and they also tour and give displays. The riding school of the genuinely Spanish cavalry which stayed in Spain has its own particular approach; the Russians, the Prussians and the Germans all developed their own particular dogmas too for the riding and training of the dressage horse for combat.

The English came late to dressage and do not have a tradition of their own since their particular emphasis had been (and remains to a large extent) on fox-hunting; riding to hounds over fences (closest to the cross-country phase of eventing, see below) with its very considerable element of risk, surprise, luck, and sheer tenacity . . . some might say lunacy! Presumably their cavalry when it came face to face with the enemy galloped in wildly slashing, leaping and by chance twisting and swirling, and galloping away as soon as possible; tactics of surprise and plenty of good luck to stay on. The Charge of the Light Brigade, one of the only accounts of the performance of the British Cavalry in Europe seems to support this supposition. By contrast as a result of their controlled dressage training in arenas and lack of wild leaping and galloping about, the Europeans were expert at controlled leaping about in hand-to-hand combat.

Elevated 'passage' performed by a pure-bred Arab stallion approaching a mare. This natural movement would not obtain more than 5 out of 10 in a dressage test.

Thus it is the European cavalry traditions which provide the dogma for the competitive dressage arena of today. There is a certain way in which the horse must move and hold his head, lift his legs up, place his back: hold his whole body; a certain way in which the rider must move and hold herself, a certain way to dress, certain permitted restrictions of tack, and only certain movements are considered 'proper'. These must be done in a very specific way. Every aspect of what is done is highly controlled and often ritualised. The horses and riders often spend years and years learning, and often become so thoroughly inbred with the dogma that they don't consider any other type of riding is anything but messing around. They are usually the respected teachers and become the establishment members of the horse clubs/societies. As a result the particular 'dressage dogma' has rapidly become absorbed by the riding public in most countries: dressage is the 'art of riding'. There have been and there are some great sophisticated and thoughtful dressage riders through history. Many of the ideas concerning thoughtful riding and training the horse have their origin with them (see Fillis 1902, Decarpentry 1971, Burger 1986). On the other hand the way this approach is taught can lead to a very disciplinarian, unyielding inflexible approach for both horse and rider where any other skilled and perhaps aesthetically pleasing displays, such as western riding, circus riding, and so on are dismissed and considered to be second class. Such a dogmatic approach can seriously jeopardise the quality of life for both the horse and the rider.

This happens in particular, of course, where people are becoming increasingly competitive. Competition may make individuals work harder and think through the discipline harder, but where it can become a matter of high monetary and status gain, too frequently serious welfare problems arise for the horses.

Dressage horses are, in particular, kept stabled usually for their entire competitive career and for not unusually 20 to 23 hours per day. The reasons given for this are that the horses are 'too valuable' to allow them even out in a field or to move freely with others. The question we have already addressed is whether this approach itself does not create a much greater likelihood of problems and risks, rather than reducing them. Dressage horses are usually trained for many years before they are considered up to the necessary standard for the big international events. In their training various restrictive gadgets are sometimes used such as 'dropped nosebands' (almost *de rigueur*) 'german reins', bearing reins, particular curb bits and so on. These, as with other gadgets, are to compensate for inappropriate riding or training.

One of the major problems for dressage horses is that they have to perform the movements in a particular way, and carry themselves in a particular way. For many horses this particular carriage and the gaits expected are by no means natural to them. There is no particular reason of course why they should not learn to hold themselves differently for the dressage competition or during their training, just like a dancer having to learn to do an arabesque in a particular way, but if it is necessary to use gadgets, further restrictions and keep them in unacceptable environments where they show evidence of distress to do this, this is not acceptable. Is it the inability of the trainer to train the horse appropriately (in which case he should, surely not be doing it) or the horse having to be trussed up because of his inabilities? Clearly sometimes it is either of these. However it would seem, *if we are seriously interested in the*

A young horse chases llamas in an aggressive mood, while performing a reasonable collected canter such as required by dressage tests. In this case the movement is performed, albeit rarely, while the horse is free.

Carif, one of our Arab stallions, doing a passage in a dance display, not competitive dressage.

welfare of the horse that if the trainer can do it without the gadgets and positions for him, then that is acceptable since it causes no serious distress or suffering to the horse (if he can't do it well he will just be bottom in the class). On the other hand if it is necessary for the trainer or rider to use gadgets to obtain this end, then they should go back to the drawing board or give up dressage riding.

In fact the dressage rules back up this particular position. In the competition only a few gadgets are permitted. Martingales (to stop the horse throwing his head up) are forbidden and only relatively straight forward bits are permitted. Whips and spurs can be carried and worn, but spurs without points or rollers only are allowed. Drop nosebands are *de rigueur*.

It is very curious why some gadgets are permitted and others are not. On what grounds is this done? Surely if one is really interested in testing the ability of the horse/rider partnership to perform aesthetically and technically acceptably, no gadgets or complex bridles, bits, spurs, nosebands, etc. should be allowed. Does this mean there would be no one doing it, or is it not the challenge for the future?

If the horse is so bored with doing these tests (and some dressage horses are never given any exercise outside the arena, never hacked out into the country, never allowed a gallop, to leap and career about in the spring air) that he has to be ridden in spurs and kept indoors and fed a lot to make him sufficiently energetic to perform . . . should he be doing it at all? Perhaps we should have a dressage test to be ridden without saddle or bridle; that would be a real test of the horse/personhood and the educating of horse and rider.

The welfare problems for the dressage horse are usually not in the ring, but at home in his training and his husbandry. But the policing so that we could be satisfied that there are no serious welfare problems for the horse is difficult. Much of this policing comes from the general cultural beliefs of the moment of the people who have dressage horses and are 'horsey'. At present it is considered that dressage horses in the ring have few welfare problems compared to others such as eventers and show jumpers. This is not entirely true, evidence for behavioural distress can be very high in dressage horse yards where they are confined for almost their entire active lives (see McGreevy 1994). If these problems were seriously understood and taken on board, it would be possible to change the way the dressage horses are kept ridden and trained yet not dramatically change the competition itself. Whether this will happen is another question, but I am hopeful. For the last decade and a half we have been trying to put these ideas across by the way we keep our horses and what we do with them, including dressage, and although we don't win all the competitions, we do no worse than many others who are using 'crueller' methods.

Show jumping

Show jumping is perhaps the most popular equine competition, with more horses and humans competing here than in any other field at present. There are two pertinent results of this that reflect on the welfare of the horse. In the first place, the popularity of show jumping both for competitors and spectators, and now as a TV spectator sport, has resulted in considerable sums of money being either put up to sponsor individuals for advertising reasons, or as prize money. The result of this is there is a considerable amount of money available and competitors who compete for the money in many countries. Although there are some professionals who are particularly careful of their horses, and indeed some horses whose longevity in competition has been commendable (e.g. the grey British horse: Milton), there is also very considerable pressure on many individuals, not just for status and fame, but also for their income, to compete very frequently and to show results in the ring whatever goes on in the training. Although much of the abuse of the horse in show jumping is the result of ignorance and inability from those with less talent and lower down the winning tree, this is not always the case. But even if this were to be the case, there remain various questions concerning the suffering caused to the horses because of show jumping which are often taken for granted.

We have already pointed out that the way the horses are kept must be seriously considered. The valuable horses tend to be kept indoors in single stables the majority of the time and are therefore severely behaviourally restricted, physically, emotionally and intellectually. However, unlike some of the other competing horses, the jumping of different fences in different combination in restricted areas does involve a considerable amount of intellectual challenge; judgements must be made on distance, speed, take off and landing, turning, balance and so forth. Some horses, often the most successful, are encouraged and helped to develop these skills themselves, unlike the dressage horse who must only do what he is told when he is told to do it.

Another concern that many have concerning competing horses of many types, including jumping horses is what, if any, restrictions or unacceptable practices are used during their training. Jumping is no exception here. There are a series of gadgets on the market such as particularly severe bits, including gags; nosebands, particularly those preventing the opening of the mouth; bearing reins, and martingales to restrict head movements, which cause pain and prevent the head being raised at any time including when the bit is being pulled. The first step in the improvement of welfare of the jumping horse might well be to forbid the use of any of these gadgets in the ring. This has been done for dressage horses. This will not stop their use during training, but might increase the awareness of their undesirability to the competing and spectator public, a first step in changing the attitude of the trainer.

Another unpleasant practice often used in training is to use pipes, metal rails or even electric wires, to dissuade the horse from knocking the fences.

Major accidents resulting in death of show jumpers are relatively rare in the show ring, but frequency of lameness, an occupational disease, because of the extra pressure it puts on the legs, is a serious concern for horse welfare. It often results in the shortening of the horse's life, although there are no figures at present kept on this by the British Show Jumping Association. The main causes of lameness here are over-straining of the limbs and concussion of the leg bones. There is now some concern about this, and usually those organising competitions or course designers, insist on reducing the risk at the take off and landing areas around the jumps by spreading softer materials such as sand or sawdust. However, recent research indicates that concussion will increase, even if the material is very absorbant. The best surface is one that allows some slip and some give, for example a mixture of sand and sawdust (Barry, Landjerit and Walter 1991).

It has become standard that show jumpers are often lame; whether or not they should compete in such frequent or difficult competitions which cause this to happen so often has not been asked. In fact it is still permissible to feed analgesics at certain levels (e.g. phenylbutazone) to prevent the animal showing any lameness! It is time that proper statistics were kept on the frequency of lameness, and length of life, in training stables and competing yards for us to be able to compare this with other equine sports and the non-competitive horse, to decide if it is acceptable. The question is should the long competitive life of Milton be the exception? If we are seriously interested in the welfare of horses in show jumping competition, then this should surely be the rule, and pain killers should be banned in the competition at least. If what the horses do will so commonly cause problems, then we must ask the question whether they should be doing it at all.

There is much public concern about the puissance, where the competition is to jump the highest. Again I have not been able to find any information on how common lameness is, what the normal length of life of a puissance horse is, and how it compares to other horses, so we do not know if this causes particular physical problems. It is safe to say it does not cause particular psychological problems, unless, like anything, it is overdone, and the horse never has the opportunity to do other things.

The whip is often used in jumping events, particularly, but not only, at the lower level. Here again, there is an argument for banning the whip, or using it in particular style. Particularly pointless is the beating of horses after they have refused; this will not encourage them to jump the next time, it may well teach them to refuse though! (See chapter 8.)

Even on the international events which are televised, where it is expected that the standard of jumping is high, the riding is often open to question. Style and smoothness of performance often become a rarity. Although this may not do the horse a great deal of harm, apart from affecting his balance somewhat, it certainly can encourage the public to think of show jumping as a struggle, often interpreted as between the 'unwilling horse' and the clever dominant rider. This is a pity, since at its best show jumping can show great style, precision, accuracy and horse–rider cooperation and coordination.

Improvements in the welfare of jumping competitions are needed, in particular serious veterinary inspections to ensure soundness both before and after an event, the outlawing of analgesics in competition, and the collecting of data on the frequency of lameness in jumping yards. A control on the number of events that horses may take part in might be necessary to ensure that lameness and length of life is at least as low as in horses in other disciplines.

Cross country

Cross-country events involve riding around a constructed course which has various jumps and sometimes other obstacles in it. Usually the fastest time back wins, but in the larger events there are now controls over the time and doing certain sections either too fast or too slow incurs penalty points. There are also of course penalty points for refusing, for falling, for taking the wrong course and so on. The difference between cross-country fences and fences in the show-jumping arena is that the former are fixed. They rarely have even the top rail or any part detachable. The result is that when the horse hits the jump he may well fall. In addition, the horses cover several miles – up to 25 for the Olympic trials – and the terrain may vary in hardness, softness, muddiness, twists and turns; obstacles may be put at peculiar points and in extremely difficult positions.

For example, I remember walking around a course being instructed in course design construction and how to ride the course, where there was a 6-foot fixed bar to be jumped into a barn (into the dark) and two strides later a large table-like object (also fixed) with a 5-foot drop on the other side to be jumped from the dark out into the light and down a hill.

Judging from the mortalities of both horses (at present no one will let me know the figures on this) and riders (nine over the last three years in Britain) the fences and courses have become too difficult. In addition, it is clear that the horses are not physiologically fit enough generally to compete at the speeds they do over the length of course they do. This was evident from the mortalities and accidents at Badminton (one of the Olympic trial courses) in 1992. It had rained during the previous week, the ground was wet, but if the horses had been fit enough they should not have become exhausted and thus *fallen or hit fences*. At the British Equine Veterinary Association meeting I went to listen to the advice given to veterinarians who wished to learn about the psychological criteria of fitness developed for long-distance riding. Some of the vets there had been at horse trials. When asked how the eventers would compare on the heart-recovery rates and lameness criteria used for long-distance horses (even for the shortest long-distance competitive events: 25 miles), they said that of the eventers subjected to these criteria of heart rate and soundness, many would not be allowed to start, let alone finish without elimination!

It would appear only too obvious that the cross-country phase, if no other (but better would be all of the phases) of the horse trials *must* be properly veterinarily overseen with proper controls on lameness and measurement of fitness (e.g. heart recovery rates) if horse deaths are to be reduced or avoided, never mind all the other horses whose life is shortened because of taking part in events when they are not sufficiently fit. Again this is something that could be instigated *immediately*. It does not have to wait three years until the latest research findings are published. We already have very considerable guide lines by which to ensure that horses do not drop dead or have accidents because they are not physically fit enough to do the work they have been asked to do. Serious criteria, not cursory veterinary inspections should be introduced immediately (see rules of Endurance Horse and Pony Society for example).

The criteria for the long-distance horse are that the horse is vetted sound and his heart rate taken before he starts. Then the heart rate must be below 64 beats per minute (in Australia 55) half an hour after completion, and the horse must be trotted up sound otherwise he is eliminated, even though he may have done the best race at the record time (and this may be as much as 100 miles). In addition, there are stops every 25 miles (40 km) where the heart rate is assessed and soundness looked at. If the heart rate is not down to a set level for that place and time, the competitor has to re-present after 10 minutes rest. After two presentations, the horse and rider are eliminated if the heart rate has not recovered sufficiently to meet the pre-set standards. Lameness at any point immediately ensures elimination. Elimination can, and does, happen for the novice or experienced rider and horse, and there is no disgrace attached, one just tries to get it right the next time. The consequences are that the speeds and fitness of the horses have improved dramatically over the last two decades, and very few horses have died.

Why cannot the same criteria be used for eventers? At least then the competitors would have to make sure their horses were fit enough to take part in that event at that time. These criteria could then be elaborated and developed for the particular needs of eventing. The important thing is that horses are not killed or permanently maimed as a result of taking part. One of the major causes of accidents and death appears to be lack of fitness of the horses at these events. We have the information and could reduce or prevent this happening tomorrow. If the competitive horse lobby wishes these events to continue, these criteria will have to be rapidly absorbed into the rules of the game, or quite rightly, the cross-country phase of the horse events will have to be banned.

Showing
Genetic changes

The central idea of showing was originally to help individuals select better animals to breed from and to 'improve the standard' of equines. It is difficult to know exactly how these 'improved standards' were to be measured, and who was to

Showing in hand. The horse is encouraged to run with a long extended trot when the whip is raised. Here the handler has got it wrong, over-used the whip, and the horse has changed direction and stride as a result. It would be more impressive if handlers were not allowed whips, and the horse learnt to perform the correct movement on a verbal command.

make the measurement of them. There is however, a general belief that 'standards of the horses and ponies in show rings have improved', in other words that certain characteristics have been selected for as appropriate and others as not, and that this has had an effect on the gene pool of the animals registered for each particular breed. This is something it is difficult to take on trust and needs to be looked at in more detail. There are many ways of measuring 'improvement'.

One of the major problems which is becoming increasingly evident is the breeding of animals to conform to certain artificial standards set by the breed society which may (and sometimes seriously does) endanger their health, their ability to perform their own behaviour, and breed successfully. Such breeding programmes of course select particular genetic combinations, and even sometimes freaks.

In the case of equines, the effect of breeding for artificial standards set by breed societies is by no means small. Shetland ponies for example have all the characteristics of dwarfs, large heads and short legs. In Europe Arab horses for years have been bred to be displayed in the show ring in hand, not to work or to be ridden or even to move around by themselves. One particular characteristic that as a judge one is expected to look for is a very straight back with a high set of the tail. This can result in a curious angle of the vulva which causes infection and sometimes lack of breeding ability. Dartmoor and Exmoor ponies have been selected according to various set standards which were developed in order to try and produce the aesthetic 'ideal' of those who are interested in them. The result is that they are less able to live on the moors where they evolved.

There is a growing amount of information on this subject. It is not the intention to go into detail here about what these characteristics are, but rather to question the ethicacy of any of them. As a result of the direction and competition in shows are appropriate animals being bred and selected which will enable the individual animals to have lives of quality? Or are the showing standards primarily about using equines to serve human ends (however spurious, trivial or serious) without concern for the equines themselves and the suffering that may result?

So far with equines, this is not as big a problem as with dogs, but it is growing and it is something that needs to be very seriously considered before anyone starts to breed an equine of a certain type because it catches their eye, or amuses them. Modern technology such as genetic engineering and embryo transfer can make such changes occur very rapidly, even before the ethics of such developments have been properly considered. The technicians who have vested interests in such developments are not the most appropriate people to make decisions on their efficacy.

The inherent genetic defects that are emerging may be worrying, but at present they certainly do not cause as much pain, suffering and distress in equines as the way the animals are bred, bought up, and kept in order to be shown. These are the questions that we address here.

The effect of showing on the equines' lifestyle and experiences

The welfare of equines that are kept and bred particularly for showing presents many of the same problems as all the other equine competitive disciplines in relation to how they are kept at home in the stables. In fact with in-hand showing (where the animals are presented on a lead in the show ring, and not ridden, and are judged as a result almost entirely on their conformation) this can reach an extreme.

One of the particular problems for many equines (and other animals shown in this way, for example dogs at Crufts show in Britain) is that they are kept in environments that are highly over protective in order to ensure that their bodies are not damaged in any way which will be penalised in the show ring. The result of this is that frequently the animals are severely behaviourally restricted. If contact with others might cause one to bite or kick another then no contact is allowed; one rubbing another's tail thus ruffling it, is prohibited. Even any self-rubbing, the mane or other part of the body is prevented by restrictive clothing or physical prevention.

Showing animals must look their best, which in itself is not harmful to the animal, in fact, it might enhance welfare (as is usually assumed). However, the way the animals are judged and the cut and thrust of competition is not always conducive to the best management of the animal in relation to its welfare.

For example, the use of drugs (as tranquillisers, sedatives, or even excitators) is not monitored, and consequently it is not unusual to find these being used. A story that is around is that some arab horses are made cocaine addicts to ensure they correctly follow the stick around with their heads and thus pose in the particularly curious position required by in-hand arabs; this happens particularly in the United States.

With some breeds there is an assumption that they cannot be improved by human interference. This is the case with the indigenous ponies of Britain, and with Arab horses, who are traditionally shown with their manes and tails long and loose as they grow, with little or no other trimming of other areas. On the other hand for many breeds of horses and for most performing horses, it is considered that their appearance *can* be improved by human interference. For example their manes are pulled so they are extremely short and straight, their tails are trimmed and pulled at the top, and or plaited, and the hair of their fetlocks is cut off. Heavy farm horses have an elaboration of fitments placed into their manes and tails (and they used to have their tails docked. This still happens in some countries although it is illegal in Britain.). They also have a veritable pandora's box of harness, brasses, bits and pieces placed all over them . . . almost to the point where it is hardly possible to see the horse underneath! These types of changes to the equine do not always cause suffering and, provided this is the case, there is no reason why such traditional practices, if they amuse and are approved of by the public should not continue. It is where they *do* cause distress to the horse that such practices are unacceptable.

One very common practice which is almost universal establishment practice is the cutting off of the vibrassae around the nose (Spooner 1979). As in cats, the vibrassae in equines are used to judge texture and distances to things, they are used as an additional information gathering technique and are well supplied with sensory nerves in the skin. Cutting them off clearly does not benefit the horse. This should be disallowed when showing at least – rather than encouraged. It is perhaps time that pressure is put on show judges for change as has recently been the case for dogs, where, until a few years ago, many breeds had to have their tails docked before showing. Now veterinarians are supposed to be the only people allowed to dock dogs tails in the UK, and then only if they consider it will benefit the animal physically to have its tail cut off. This change is taking time as those with a particular attachment to traditional practice find it difficult to accept, but it will happen (although at the time of writing we found it very difficult to find a pedigree Spaniel puppy for sale who had not had his tail cut off).

Apart from behavioural restriction and the show animal never being allowed to run outside, and mix freely with others, other techniques are used to try and 'improve' the appearance of the animal. He may never be allowed to roll because it takes too long to clean him afterwards, he may never go in mud, he may have to wear a rug throughout the year with the restrictions that this entails. Before showing the animals may be kept in the dark so that when they come out their pupils are enlarged – and so on.

There are some particularly unacceptable practices with some breeds. For example Morgan horses who are supposed to have a very high head and low tail carriage may have their tail de-enervated so that it hangs loose. Tennessee walking horses have particularly unpleasant restrictions exercised on their legs in order to ensure they show an elaborate movement of them, and pacers (who move two legs on one side instead of diagonally in the trot) have the legs on one side tied together so that they are unable to move normally and have to 'pace'. This is allowed even in the races of trotters. I am sure there are many more of these types of restrictions and expectation of which I am unaware, as a result of not being familiar with everything that goes on in the show world. The important point is that it is necessary to begin to question if the way the animals are presented in the show ring and the treatment they have received beforehand is acceptable as far as the individual horse is concerned. There may as usual be arguments that can be made for some of the current practices but there are certainly others which are not, and it is for the horse owner, breeder, competitor and the general public to examine what is done and why. If they are unable to present the horse in the show ring as a result of not doing one or other of these practices which cause some suffering to the animals directly or indirectly, then there would be a strong argument against showing of this kind.

Another seemingly universal characteristic of show horses is that they are usually fat, often too fat. The reason for this is fairly obvious; it is much more difficult to spot conformation faults if they are fat, and fatness is often associated with good health in horses, just as in humans. However as in humans overweight and fatness can be dangerous for health. One of the major causes of ill-health many veterinarians argue is over-weight. This has ironic implications. For example, we have performing arab horses but, because our horses have to be fit for their other work (long distance, working on the land, etc.), they have no chance of being placed in any in-hand or show class, even though the horses' that are shown in the in-hand classes conformation is judged largely (as any book on confor-mation will point out), 'for performance'. Yet the frequently overweight winners have often never been ridden or driven, or performed at anything at all except walking and trotting a little in the show ring! This is not something that we worry about, except that surely if animals are being judged for performance, if they show evidence of performance this should be considered. The British Arab Horse Society have recently recognised this, and introduced an in-hand class for performing horses.

There is nothing wrong with judging the equine by whatever criteria are required: the shininess of the coat, the dolefulness of the eye, the straightness of the legs, whatever, provided it causes no suffering to the animals and is an honest, not hypocritical judgement. This latter may not be the case for the emphasis in in-hand showing. Here the set criteria are those that are said to ensure 'good performance' – however the animals who consistently win in performance competitions do not often resemble these in-hand horses – they often display severe conformation faults which make them unshowable!

Having said this, there is much potential for fun, enjoyment, pride and joy for both animal and human when showing if that is what both want to do; it is just a question of working it out satisfactorily and at present there *are* many practices which are wide open to question in this regard. It is not just what happens on the day but also the quality of the life the animal lives most of the time as a result.

As a footnote a particularly important concern is the behavioural assessment by the judge of an in-hand horse. A horse that walks and trots quietly and gently and behaves as one would wish most ridden and performing horses to behave, will be unlikely to 'attract the judge's eye'. This is especially the case with stallions or young horses who are often therefore encouraged and taught to leap about and 'show off'. Of course this in itself is not questionable from the point of view of the horse's welfare – but how it is *done* can be. If the handler has to carry a stick and hit the horse with a stick, or uses other violent means to encourage him to behave in ways she would normally discourage him from performing – this surely is unacceptable practice and the horse should not be placed in the ring as a result.

Provided the horse has not had to suffer physically, emotionally or cognitively in order to show him either 'in hand' or 'ridden', there is no reason why there should be any welfare concern here. At present this is by no means the case.

14

Racing and long-distance riding

The race-horse 'industry', perhaps because of the amount of money involved and consequently the obvious economic temptations to have horses win (or lose) races at almost all costs, has previously been the area of horse competition which has come under some public scrutiny. One particular area has been drug use.

Drug use and detection

Traditionally there have been drug tests for race horses and stringent rules concerning which drugs are permitted and why. Horses are tested randomly for drugs at race courses. As a result there is, and has been, a very careful use of restricted drugs. Certainly it is not in the interests of trainers in particular to be pulled up for the use of illegal drugs. These rules for race horses have been in effect for a long time and as a result their policing and implementation is relatively effective, and understood by drug companies. The drug rules for race horses are generally more stringent than for horses competing for example under the Federation Equestre International rules, where some drugs are permitted up to certain concentrations (e.g. phenylbutazone, and analgesic), but none are permitted for horses at the race course.

Interestingly, what drug companies now do to sell their drugs is to mention the withdrawal period before racing – because of possible detection. They also try, of course, as any good capitalist does, to stay one jump ahead of legislation – develop, sell and use the drug before it is banned. This is not to say that drug companies are trying to undermine welfare; this is clearly not their intent. Their intent is quite reasonably to try to make as much money as possible within the law and try to improve performance and pain reduction.

The problem arises, as with human drug use, when the drug is seen seriously to reduce the short-term or long-term benefits to the horse. It is the long-term effects of drugs that causes most dispute in medicine. It is becoming increasingly obvious that improving performance/nutrition/reproduction, even pain relief, with the use of drugs may jeopardise the health of the equine in the long term. When drugs should be used and what for, then becomes a more complex debate. There are no easy answers, but in line with the position of 'evolutionary continuity' taken here as a general rule, the first priority for equine welfare which will encourage good health and consequently optimal performance is to ensure that the animals' physical, social, emotional and cognitive needs are fulfilled. If it is necessary to treat the animals persistently with drugs of any sort, or stimulant feeds, to achieve these ends, then we must surely examine whether we should be doing this.

Drugs are increasingly used, prescribed and permitted in ordinary everyday life for horses and humans. Almost any kind of drug will affect training and performance. However there are also drugs used in training which have either physiological functions (e.g. to increase muscle mass, or improve the physical effectiveness of other parts of the body) or change behaviour and affect 'the mind' in order to ensure the individual continues to train, or to perform better (e.g. tranquillisers, anti-depressants, sedatives and excitatory drugs).

Continual vigilance is required to keep up with the latest development in drug use both in medical and veterinary practice in order to try to assess the permitted as opposed to the illegal drugs. The result of this is that there is a continuous debate as to which, if any, drugs should be permitted in horse racing. But when does a chemical application or voluntary intake become a 'drug'? For example, what about mineral licks, or electrolytes; should they be permitted? When is an additive a 'drug', when is it 'a mineral supplement', or a mineral food additive? It is no longer the case that we can safely say that horses are not treated routinely with a number of drugs on a day-to-day basis. In fact during the research for this book I have been surprised to find how much routine drug therapy is

A relaxed endurance horse coming into the finish in a competitive trail ride. But why does he have so much gear over his face and neck?

used in stables of all kinds. Certainly there is a need for a thorough examination of this. The increasing interest in and use of homeopathy and alternative drug therapy for equines indicates not only that conventional drug therapy is widely used but also that there is some concern among equine owners and trainers as to its over-use.

The use of the whip

The use of the whip and its effect on the welfare of the race horse and the issue of whether or not horses should be raced at all, is as far as the horse is concerned, probably of less consequence than drug mis-use. Particularly in Britain, the use of the whip is carefully monitored and jockeys are not infrequently taken to tribunals for excessive use of the whip.

Horses, as we have already discussed, if allowed access to each other and to develop into normal well-integrated equines, are tough with each other. In feral animals, or those raised in groups, there is relatively infrequent evidence found of serious damage to each other as a result of this rough behaviour. This is usually because the horses are able to read each other's intentions and act on them. Even affectionate behaviour can be relatively rough, for example the stallion licking and nipping the oestral mare who comes back for more.

Thus it is unlikely that the whip that is carried by jockeys and used in the race does cause any particular suffering to the horse. Physically it is very unlikely (unless barbs and other attachments have been hidden in it) to cause any serious physical pain. On the other hand, because horses have learnt to avoid the whip during their training and also because it has often become a symbol of disapproval and/or anxiousness and excitement of the human, the use of the whip could cause some stress in some race horses. If the whip were to be used throughout the race this might well be described as 'distressing', or if the whip has to be used continuously to get the horse to enter the race at all then there would be an argument to suggest that racing for that horse is distressing and therefore he should not be raced. On the other hand if, as is usually the case, the whip is used at the finish to encourage the horse to run a little faster and indeed to generate 'stress' so that the General Adaptive Syndrome is affected, then there does not appear to be any argument for not allowing the use of the whip at the finish on the race track. But is it likely to reduce public interest, and would the quality of the race change if no whips were used or carried at all? It would be interesting to see.

Should horses be raced at all?

The question that arises from the debates concerning drug use and the use of the whip is whether horses should race at all. Do they like it, or is it that only by means of whips and coercion of one sort and another that they do it?

As in every animal/human (or human/human) interaction there are always cases to show how bad things can get: there are cases of abuse of animals, including race horses, and of humans – and even parents of their children – but does this make an argument for changing the rules, or even banning the pastime? Or, as in the case of bad parenting, banning others from having children? Clearly this reaction is an over-simplification and provided there are ways in which practices can be improved so that both parties can enjoy the activity, there can be no grounds for over reaction. But can horses *ever* enjoy racing? What about the large jumps, what about Becher's Brook in the Grand National, what about the number of horses who are killed, or put down as a result of racing, surely this, coupled with the clear and frequent use of the whip, indicates that horses do not enjoy racing and never can and therefore it should be banned. Is this true or false?

For evidence of either case the simplest and most accurate way of assessing whether or not horses are likely to enjoy racing is to look at equines out on their own; do they like galloping about in groups, and even jumping over obstacles, and going as fast as possible, or is this something they can really only be coerced into doing by humans? There is only one answer to this. Equines are after all prey animals whose great specialism is running at speed, galloping and turning, twisting, jumping, leaping and so on, to avoid predators. They play by galloping about and doing all these things as if escaping 'pretend predators'. They do this from a young age, and it continues throughout their lives, if they are given the opportunity. In particular, being a social species, they appear to take pleasure in doing this in groups. Let fit healthy horses out into a field after being shut up or even just into a new fresh field, and the first thing they will do is to gallop around, through, and up and down it as a group.

There is little doubt that running fast in groups is something horses usually do, if they are given the opportunity. Therefore provided the animals are fit enough to race for the required distance, and provided they have not had such bad experiences doing this that they have to be coerced into it, there does not seem to be an argument for banning racing at the competitive venue . . . the race track.

But a number of horses are killed in races, others die or are put down afterwards as a result of the race. Recently there have been efforts made to cut down the number of horses killed or falling at jumps on the race track, which is the most common cause of death, and efforts are made to keep track of this by the veterinarians responsible and the betting levy board. It is interesting that the same concern does not exist at present for the number of horses killed in, for example, combined training, and there are no legal requirements to prevent or reduce this.

Inevitably there will be some horses killed (and some humans too), as a result of racing and jumping. It can be said that the human makes the choice to do this, the horse does not. In fact the horse does make choices concerning what he does and what he does not do. If he really does not like racing and jumping, he will not do it, and he will not be good at it. As a result the time, effort and costs to get such a horse to the race track will be greater and his success much less likely than racing and jumping a horse that is willing to do it. It is therefore incorrect to assume that the animal never has a choice; animals do have some choices, and even if they are coerced into doing something they dislike this can be seen, and could be disallowed.

On scrutinising a video of the Grand National for the last two years, I have been struck by the number of humans who fall off. Why do so many horses fall at the jumps, and why do so many riders fall off? If one looks carefully at the riding of the horses, those that fall are usually those that are too close to the others and unable to see over the fence. Surely the job of the rider, if he has one at all, is to help the horse get over the fence safely by directing him away from the crowded areas, and particularly staying in balance with him and helping him rather than hindering him to balance (something that every BHS jumping student is taught the importance of in their first lesson). Careful assessment of the videos of horses racing over jumps does indicate that often neither of these things is done by the jockey. In the case of the 1994 Grand National I was particularly interested to see an older woman riding whose odds were heavily against her at the start. She and her horse finished together, despite the odds, because she appeared to be more in balance and rode away from the scrums. This raises many questions: Why is this not done more often? Are the jockeys just not good enough at riding? Surely from everyone's point of view it is better to finish than to fall off or cause the horse to fall?

The other interesting thing is the number of loose horses who continue to run and often *win the race*, but are not even acknowledged. Surely an indicator, if anything is, that they enjoy it. It would be great fun to instigate an award for the winner of a race, either ridden or not. The jockeys would then have to make decisions on when they were being an advantage and when a disadvantage to the horse, and bale out at the proper time . . . Now that would make for fun racing indeed, and select horses that like to do it!

Interestingly, the famous Palio race in Sienna where the horses have to gallop around and around a cobbled square, is won by the horse, whether or not he has a rider. Perhaps similar races on race tracks could be introduced in other places which would certainly increase the betting interest.

Although there has been much public debate concerning the use of the whip during the race, there has not been debate concerning any other equipment that is commonly used when racing. Many race horses are raced in hoods over their ears and heads, others with blinkers to prevent them seeing other horses behind. Should these types of restraints be acceptable, or should they be against the rules? If blinkers and hoods are allowed to prevent individuals seeing or hearing, then why not drugs to do the same thing?

Having said this, however, compared to most other competitive horses, the race-horse tack is relatively minimal and unrestrictive: small light saddles strapped on with extra straps to prevent sideways slip and breast plates to avoid backward slip of the saddle. No martingales or other hard restraining harnesses such as elaborate bits, nosebands and so on which are commonly used, if not compulsory, for other competitive horse events.

Here again there is an indication that race horses and the rules governing their racing are ahead of most other equine sports as far as equine welfare is concerned. However the area where very considerable inquiry is needed and rules introduced, as with most equine sports, is in *the method of keeping and training of the race horses at home, not at the race course.* This is where there are many welfare problems as far as the animals are concerned. It is clear that there are very high levels of behavioural restraint in the way these animals are kept in single stables; they are fed restricted low-fibre diets, disallowed free contact with others most of the time (if not all their lives after weaning), and so on. Race horses are not unique in this as we have already mentioned several times, but they are leading the way and it is crucial that changes are made *if there is a serious interest in equine welfare.* If the race-horse 'industry' does not do this themselves, then it is unlikely that public opinion will support racing in the next decade and this might well end up by being the end of racing. It may be wise, if the reader is in any way involved with or interested in equines, to consider these factors. It would be interesting, and fun to see if by raising even middle-of-the-road thoroughbreds in appropriate ways (see part IV) the horses would have as many racing successes, if not more, than conventionally raised and trained animals.

Other problems with race-horse management and training

One other area of important concern for equine welfare in racing stables is in the training, and in the racing of very young horses. Curiously, racing horses are aged from the first of January. There seems to be no reason for this except a historical one. Why could they not be aged from the first of May say? The result of this is that all try to have their mares foal very early in the year so that when they race as two-year-olds, they are at least near being two years old rather than 18 months, an obvious advantage. This means that the mares have to be covered by the stallion early in the year since the gestation is 11 months. At this time of year the mares are not normally coming regularly into season. This has encouraged a large investment in veterinary research to try and bring the mares into season earlier by using changing light regimes, drugs and manipulations (see chapter 'Breeding'). In fact this has become an important industry; as a result many jobs have been created, and much money is generated. For example most larger studs have a full-time veterinarian on hand during the breeding season. In addition the stud spends large sums buying drugs including steroids to encourage early onset of oestrus.

Breeding difficulties have also meant much experimentation with foetal transplants and all the other modern reproductive manipulations. This has stimulated investment in research. The concerns which have to date been relatively neglected is the ethics of these practices. Should we drug, manipulate daily, implant a foetus, operate, etc. on mares? Can this be justified, and if so when and where? These are serious questions which should not be ignored.

Potential race horses are often taken away from their mothers relatively young (around 4–6 months) and then kept isolated from others in boxes during the night, although they may go out as a group of youngsters during the day. As we have already discussed, this is not the appropriate way for young horses to associate since they retain very strong inter-generation bonds and rarely spend much time in peer groups (see Kiley-Worthington 1987).

The young animals are fed high protein foods often with controlled levels of fibre on the grounds that this will make them grow bigger faster. The problem here is that they may grow taller faster, but their bone growth can suffer, as has recently been found in the broiler chicken bred for very fast growth on high protein foods. The development and ossification of their bones does not keep up. The result is that the young animal can be irreversibly damaged when trained or raced.

Age of starting racing

The young thoroughbred race horse is expected to race at two years old (calendar years; the animal is rarely two years old). At two years old equines are still growing and are very immature both physically and mentally. In order to race with a rider at two years old, they have to be 'broken' beforehand (at around eighteen months they start carrying a light rider). The word 'broken' is a suitable one for the way this is usually done in thoroughbred stables. Because there are high prices for keeping and training horses, labour is usually short (or at least is employed so busily on the stable housekeeping jobs) that there is little time (and unfortunately often little skill) available for proper handling (and learning about handling) the young horses, in order to teach them appropriately. The result is that the young horse is frightened, and in order to try and get away leaps, cavorts, and uses any technique he can think of. Since the animal is already distressed as a result of his keeping conditions, such training sessions can be extremely traumatic for both human and horse, and indeed are expected to be.

Another reason often given for why thoroughbred backing and training is such a risky business (for the human) is because, it is argued, it has to be done so fast. Yet horses are very quick learners and there is no reason why thirty minutes should not be enough to get the horse mounted and started quietly and without restraint, excitement, or violence in any form. Monty Roberts from California does displays with thoroughbreds to show how this can be done using appropriate body language. So it is not shortness of time, but shortness of skills and thought about how to improve the training of all young equines, not just race horses but the problems are more evident in race horses.

The result of starting to work hard and racing the animal at less than 2 years, is that there is a great wastage in horses that are born to race and those that actually get to the race track . . . This of course costs a lot of money, so it must be reflected in the cost of having a horse trained. It would surely be more satisfactory from everyone's point of view, including the equines' to cut down wastages of this type.

This can this be done by:

(1) Improving the keeping conditions of the horses to cater more for their physical, emotional, social and cognitive needs (see chapter 19).

(2) Changing the training techniques that are often used (see chapter 8).

(3) The racing of immature horses of two years old could be changed to three or four years old, as in Arab Horse Racing.

(4) Changing the calendar year of registration from the 1st of January to the 1st of May would ensure that the animals were more likely to be, in reality, the age they are expected to be when they first race. This would cut down the use of drugs and manipulations which attempt to bring the mares into season earlier in the year than naturally.

(5) Reducing the drugs and manipulations in breeding, and allowing the stallion to run with the mares is not an impossible idea for race-horse breeders to develop, particularly for the next generation of stallions and mares who can then be brought up in ways where stress and distress is less common. Such techniques would very likely dramatically increase the conception rate which would cut costs.

These ideas are not 'airy fairy' impractical suggestions, they are quite possible realities which may initially cause outrage among the traditionalists, but then so did the abolition of slavery and women having the vote. This is an area where those interested and active in animal welfare could pressurise, publicise and eventually cause change; surely a better solution for human and horse to banning racing entirely.

Competitive long-distance racing

It is only in the last two decades that long-distance riding has become a competitive discipline. Before that, there were tales of long journeys ridden at remarkable speeds by various people: but the truth of lots of these feats was that the horses died as a result (Lawrence 1980), although the human became a hero! Non-competitive long-distance riding for transport, war, pleasure, tourism and for learning has been continuing ever since writing began (e.g. *Travels with a Donkey*, Stevenson, *Tschiffely's South American Journey*, see Lawrence 1980).

Until recently those who were involved in long-distance riding were primarily motivated to see different countries, different places and different people. A consequence of this was that much time was spent with the equine, without whom the traveller would be stuck.

Endurance riding competitors, all from our stud!

As a result of the introduction of competitive long-distance riding things are changing very rapidly and there are some extremely important equine welfare questions that must be faced now rather than avoided and involving the horse in suffering for the future. The reason of course why this is happening is that there are now Olympic events for long-distance riders, there is a World Championship, and an opportunity (many riders believe) to succeed in international competition where they have not in other equine sports. Fortunes are beginning to be made or lost, sponsorship offered, horses bought or sold for substantial sums, and status accrued. Careers are being built and maintained on the strength of success in long-distance competitions.

More than any other riding discipline competitive long-distance riding has taken on board concern for the physiological fitness of the horse, for obvious reasons: it is very easy to cause equine suffering through exhaustion. It is even life threatening. From the early stages long-distance competitors and organisers were seriously concerned with the welfare of the competing horse. The distances started relatively short: 25 miles (40 kms), but soon 50, 75 and 100 miles (160 km) in a day were being ridden. Clearly the assessment of physiological fitness became of paramount concern. Those interested in organising the first competitions were aware of this, and as a result it was the veterinarians who were appointed to be the judges. Initially the knowledge of exercise physiology in the horses was not great, and the veterinarians used a whole host of measures, including much subjective judgement to assess the horse's fitness. The crux of the judging was that the horse had to be 'fit to continue' when he was vetted at the end of the competition. Failure resulted in elimination even though the horse may have come in first.

This judgement was made initially by assessing temperature, dehydration, respiratory rate, heart rate, behaviour, lameness, rubs, cuts and bruises. However there was not much knowledge of what the criteria would have to be, to be 'fit to continue' for any of these measures. The veterinarians having been appointed as judges acknowledged the difficulties, so judgements were therefore made well within the margin of safety. These competitions – where the veterinarians were asked to judge – sparked off a host of studies on exercise

*Veterinary inspections in Long-Distance rides are
every 25 miles (40 km) at least. The horse must be
trotted up on a hard surface to ensure soundness.*

*The heart rate is monitored, the untacked horse
inspected, for rubs or sores. Failure means
elimination, even if the rider has just won the race.*

physiology in horses in many countries (USA, Canada, Britain, France, Germany, Australia, e.g. Equine Exercise Physiology Conferences; vol. 3, eds. Persson, Lindholm and Jeffcott 1991). Blood samples were taken, weight loss measured, respiratory, dehydration, temperature, gaits, and heart rates and murmurs, were measured and assessed over the next decade and a half.

This has been a marvellous example of the way cooperation between the scientists (in this case the vets) and the riders has sparked off a great accumulation of knowledge for the benefit of the horse. This resulted in good criteria for the measurement of mechanical and physiological fitness, and how to identify insufficient fitness for the work done. As a result, despite the extraordinary demands on the physiology of the horse over periods of exercise up to 24 hrs, the numbers of horses that either die or suffer severe distress in the long-distance events at any level are relatively low in Britain, although there are no detailed figures available at present (Long Distance Riding Group of BHS and Endurance Horse and Pony Society, UK). The number suffering long-term damage as a result of the competition is also unknown, but some of the first competitive animals are still competing fifteen years later, which is not the case in many other equine sports.

Some of the horses are being asked to travel 100 miles a day, carrying a rider, and the record speed (which of course is largely the result of the course) is an average of around 12 mph (17 kmph). Unlike the speeds in racing, the average speed has risen from 8 to 12 mph in the last fifteen years. Not only are these races safer for the horses, but they are also completed much faster than twenty years ago. Many of the ideas on how to measure fitness and construct training schedules have developed from the work on human athletics which has also advanced dramatically in terms of its records and successes over the same period.

If we are interested in horse welfare in competition (and with the disastrous record of mortalities and shortening of life in other horse discipline competitions we should be), it does indicate that the involvement of physiological criteria in assessing the horses *before* they are allowed to begin the competition as well as afterwards would be a great step forward, and we do have the knowledge now. If we are seriously concerned with the welfare of our competition horses veterinarians or other trained personnel should be assessing *all* horses in high level competition to *set criteria*.

There are still questions to be asked concerning horse welfare in Long-Distance events. Although the physiological criteria are reasonably well understood now, there are areas that need careful consideration. In the first place, if the horses can do 100 miles a day, what is to prevent someone sooner or later saying that they should then do longer distances still, say 120 or 140 miles a day? Would this be acceptable for the horses' welfare?

Another concern is the use of after care. It has now become impossible to be seriously considered for an international team, or major event without having a team of around 4–6 helpers whose job it is to meet the horse and rider at every possible stop, to offer the rider food and drink, wash the horse to cool him, give him electrolytes (these are the only chemical permitted). Initially no protective gear for the legs or soles were permitted, but now many are (FEI rules permit false soles, overreach boots, leg and knee boots). At the end of the ride the rider has usually half an hour after coming in before presenting the horse to see if it is fit to continue. During this half hour the half dozen or so helpers, or 'crew' will massage the horse, walk him, wash him, clean him, fix his legs or body up if they look a little worn or bruised and so on. The horse is then presented to the vet and his heart rate is taken. The recovery rate of the heart is the best indicator of fitness and in Europe it must be below 64 beats per minute; in Australia below 55, or the horse is eliminated, even if he has broken a record. He is then trotted up and if he is not sound he is eliminated. Many horses, or humans, will stiffen up after half an hour; however if the horse is given particular treatment of massage and general pampering for the half hour after he comes in, he may well manage to pass the vets. But once this is over, he can be thrown into his box and everyone adjourns to celebrate. There is an increasing problem with this, is the horse 'fit' two hours later or even the next day? In fact to accumulate points in Europe the horses must be vetted the next day as well.

With all the crew attention he may be able to pass as fit when in fact he may not be. Although the crew is supposed to be there in order to help the horse (and rider) the result is that their presence may well actually mask the problems the horse may be having.

Another problem is how many of the long competitive races should the horse be allowed to perform? It might be to the benefit of the horse not to allow either any protective gear, or crews at all. In the USA there are special awards for this, but in the UK it is *compulsory* to have a crew if taking part in a race longer than 30 miles. It is highly debatable that having crews is in fact necessarily in the interests of the horse or its welfare. If the horse needs a crew to continue and satisfy the various physiological criteria of the judges, I suggest that he should not be competing.

The crews also have a dramatic environmental impact. In order to ride 50 miles often in beautiful unspoilt countryside in National Parks or mountains and moorland, state forests, since the riders prefer this, the lorry or large car and trailer may be driven around 200 miles (or more even). In addition each competitor will have one, two or more cars brought along for each horse's crew. The boxes are parked somewhere at the venue, but the cars are then used to cruise up and down the minor roads to meet the riders, often streams of them blocking the minor roads obstructing the competing horses as well as others who have managed to get away from the city and the traffic jams to enjoy the weekend in particularly unspoilt countryside . . . only to find themselves in another!

Then the riders pound along the bridle paths that are often both bridle and foot paths, overtaking, and sometimes in their zest and hurry, frightening walkers and their dogs. At the end of the day the competitive rider when talking to the organiser or assistant will in typical competitive mode, say 'I did not come here to see pretty countryside' . . . (an actual statement made at a recent 2-day 50-mile competitive ride in the Welsh hills) . . . The public may well have well-founded concerns about the development of this competition using an unnecessary amount of the scarce countryside resources that should be available to all.

The Endurance Horse and Pony Society (the first and friendliest society with the toughest fitness requirements for the horse) has a competition which is a race only against yourself. This is called a Competitive Trail Ride (CTR). The idea is that the horse after completing the ride must on the physiological criteria assessed seem not to have done anything: his pulse must be down to resting rate half an hour after completion. Penalty points are accrued for any bumps or bruises, sorenesses or heart beats higher than the resting rate set for the day. The skill lies in doing the ride at the required speed (usually for the open events 7–12 mph) and obtaining no penalties. The horse must look as if he has just walked out of the stable for the first time that day when he is presented to the veterinary judge half an hour after completing the 25, or even 100-mile ride – now that is a challenge! It means that you have to think very hard indeed about your horse and your speed, throughout the ride, not just bat along, keep up with the others and hope that all is well at the end.

Having done the race rides up to 100 miles in a day and the Competitive Trail Rides, I am now convinced that the CTRs are much more difficult, and more of a challenge, and at the same time safer for the horse.

There is however another area that needs debating concerning long-distance competitive rides and this is the psychological well-being of the horse. Do the horses really like and want to do these very long mileages? We do now know when they are suffering from exhaustion or pain, we can measure this, but what about the horse just not wanting to do it, just wanting to stop? The horse does to a degree have a choice here, if he really does not want to do it, he can stop and refuse to move further. The kicking and even whipping that may ensue is not going to cause him any very severe suffering (although further developments by competitive riders in this direction e.g. use of drugs, restraining or encouraging aids must be watched – at present spurs are banned). But is this enough? Should the horses be ridden on and on when they clearly would prefer to stop?

There are some horses and ponies who, even when they are experienced and know that the rides can go on and on, do keep going on their own and, provided one rides with another horse, or thinks carefully of the strategy to continue to motivate them (for example ride the last ten miles previously so they recognise it and know they are going home), they will keep going willingly and happily. But when it comes to distances of more than around 75 miles in a day, such horses are in the minority. The majority of the horses, particularly the experienced ones, want to stop. They may not be physiologically particularly tired (their heart rates may be fine, they are not lame or dehydrated) but they may be bored and mentally tired. Should they continue to be pushed on, even if there is a Gold

Medal for England in the offing; and how much pushing is too much?

Over the last years I have been watching how the horses go after around 75 miles on a one-day ride. At this distance, 80 per cent of the horses are having to be seriously pushed on to keep them going, although when they come down to the crewing points or veterinary gates, the riders may be careful not to show too much of this. Is this good enough? Perhaps what we now need is a serious programme on how to motivate the horses to keep going: 'psychological fitness' and how to measure it. These results might be useful for the other equine competitions. Again long-distance riding may lead the field in the welfare of horses in competition, but it must be very careful to retain its primary concern with horse welfare, with the rapidly growing pressures on many of its participants in competition for Olympic accolades, status, and even money.

15

Rodeos, polo, circuses, zoos, wildlife parks

Rodeos

The welfare of equines used in rodeos has received much attention in the United States, where rodeos are a traditional entertainment characteristic of the West. In some areas they have even been banned, because of the 'unacceptable practices' that are common. During a rodeo the horses are made to buck by the addition of extra straps under the abdomen which it is argued can cause pain and suffering, and under which various severe irritants are sometimes placed (e.g. prickles, nails, chemical burning agents, etc.) Horses can be taught to buck in appropriate circumstances without such practices. If the people taking part, or providing the horses for the rodeo cannot teach them to perform at the appropriate time, then rodeos should be stopped.

Banning them outright does not seem to be either necessary or desirable provided there are enriching experiences to be had for both equine and human – which there is no reason o suppose could not be had any more or less than for competitive jumping, dressage or any other equine sport. As with these other competitions, there is a serious need for change in the way the competition is conducted; the way the animals are trained, the way they are kept and the policing of them to ensure the rules are properly followed. Failing this rodeos should indeed be banned as should all these equine sports.

One of the least desirable effects of rodeos is that of their nature they reinforce the competition and fight between man and animal in which the successful human 'overcomes' the animal who is set to try and 'outdo' him or her, and thus the human finally 'dominates' if he is successful. The same attitude is fostered in the bull ring. In Spain the bull ends up killed; rodeo horses often damaged. There is a strong argument for the banning of rodeos on the grounds that it fosters and encourages the development of an attitude of conflict with equines. One wonders if attitudes were considered more, and cooperation between horse and human developed and admired, there would be rodeos? There are skills independent of those to do with human/animal conflict that are developed in rodeos. It might well be that those could be developed and exhibited to demonstrate the cooperation of the horse and rider as in fact can happen in some western riding exhibitions and show classes.

Polo

This is a game which has been played by humans on horses or ponies for many centuries. It started with particular ghoulish practices of Syrian horsemen competing for the head of a dead sheep or goat, and has now evolved into a particularly 'upper class' sport for the well-to-do with much social éclat. The game requires the person on the horse to chase a light wooden ball around and hit it with a long-handled stick with a mallet on the end. It is extremely difficult to hit the ball, and the whole game takes place at a fast canter or gallop, if one is any good. It is, there is no doubt, an exciting and fast game with risk and fun attached. The 'chukkas' are usually seven minutes and then the player gets off one horse onto another. The player therefore needs a string of 'polo ponies'. What are the welfare implications of this game?

There is no doubt that there is considerable risk to the horse playing this game; the ball can hit his legs, and often does, he can be hit by the polo stick of another player or even the person on his back, and it is fast and can be an exhausting game. However, there are ways in which the horse could be protected from the many bruises and wounds he might get (which the human can also receive, being almost at the same risk). The horse can, and usually (at least in Europe), does have leg guards. There is no doubt that horses are sometimes lamed and surely some have been killed in polo but this is not a common occurrence.

However, what is common and perhaps should be changed in the future is the rough riding, often by not very competent or balanced riders, who become extremely excited during the game and therefore are not as considerate as they could be to their mount. Not only do they tug and pull the horses around, but they also use bits that can cause considerable pain and damage to the horse's mouth; they also use many gadgets to restrain and restrict the horse such as martingales, and so on.

Ironically the horse, as any polo player will tell you, learns the game: to follow the ball, to place the rider in the right position to hit the ball, to ride others off the ball and many of the normal techniques that are used. If he is able to learn the game in this way, then if the horse's welfare is of concern, the bits and restraints used should surely be carefully controlled. The horse should not have to suffer because of the inabilities of the rider or the trainer. In the game of polo (as in most other equestrian sports) we should surely aim towards a situation where the horses are ridden with no bridle at all! Both they and their partner know the game; what a challenge that would be for learning and understanding of both horse and rider.

Meanwhile, it would seem appropriate, if the horse's welfare is of concern, to severely control the tack and restraint used in the game and any other painful practices that may arise in the training of the polo pony. Equally, as with the other equine disciplines, the keeping of the horses/ponies leaves much room for improvement of the equine's welfare.

Again there is no rational reason for banning this game, even though the main reason for playing for many players is the human social status with which it has become associated. The main area requiring improvement is where the polo pony spends most of his life: in his stable in the summer.

Circuses and zoos

The importance and role of animals, including equines, in circuses and zoos has been discussed in depth elsewhere (see Kiley-Worthington 1990 and 1995). Here, there is a place only for the conclusions of these studies; those who wish to investigate the arguments in more detail are referred to these works.

It is clear that the conditions for keeping equines in both zoos and circuses are not ideal, in fact they may be very poor, just as they are in conventional horse management. The changes that have been suggested to ensure that the animals' physical, social, emotional and cognitive needs are catered for must be made. If this is done (and there is evidence from many circuses and zoos that they are now attempting to do this), then there is no need to assume that equines, wild or domestic, should not be kept in circuses and zoos, provided there is no sign of prolonged distress, little behavioural restriction, the animal husbandry and training conform to the criteria outlined, and their keeping or capture does not cause ecological problems (chapters 19 and 20). In addition, both the equines and the humans must benefit.

It has been repeatedly maintained in the last decade or so that although there may be a biological argument for zoos (the conservation of endangered species) and therefore a serious reason for their continuation, there is no similar justification

One of Mary Chipperfield's circus zebras, who have been handled and work a liberty act, having his feet cleaned out. There is no reason why zebras in zoos should not be handled safely for everyday veterinary and foot care, rather than taking the risk, expense and welfare implications of immobilising them.

for circuses which are primarily for the entertainment of humans, a function which is considered trivial and frivolous by many. My work in both these types of institutions indicates that provided the husbandry system is improved, which can often be done very simply in circuses particularly, there is no justification for banning circuses rather than all competitive horse events, and/or keeping rare animals in zoos. That there are important conservational ideas as well as ideas on what different animals 'are' (their *telos* in Aristotle's terms) that can be conveyed to the public through circuses. This can outline the animals' cognitive abilities and needs which are not generally conveyed to the public in other captive environments.

Both circuses and zoos allow humans to approach near to the animals, allow the animals and the humans to exchange awareness and interest in each other as living emotional, sentient beings. Animals and humans can even exchange emotional experiences which is not generally possible with animals in the wild. Such direct personal experiences can be very influential in ensuring future interest in the species and its survival, which is not necessarily the case from watching the animals at a distance, even if one has the money to be able to do this, nor from seeing wildlife television movies.

Thus although circuses with animals may perform 'to entertain' they may also have the function of being extremely important educationally, and enriching the lives of both the humans and the animals there. For example, there is no reason why such animals should go hungry, thirsty, have disease or wounds untreated, or suffer in many ways that wild animals do. In addition it is possible (as we have argued in chapter 7) that learning new and different things can be an enriching experience for both the animal and the human, provided it is done properly (see chapter 8). This can apply to species that are wild in origin just as much as those that are traditionally domestic.

The most important concern in this respect is a consideration of the animals' individual experiences as well as their species characteristics in order to design and provide a suitable environment. Thus adult animals that are wild or feral in origin if they are going to be caught, transferred and then live in very different conditions from those in which they have spent their life, are likely to suffer more than younger animals who have not yet become established in their environment.

The effect on the environment of having these animals in circuses or zoos must be considered as well. If the alternative is death, as it often can be for wild equines, then even if there are likely to be problems initially for the individual, there is often an argument that it would be to his advantage. However if the effect of the capture and sale of the animal is to create a market and thus to threaten the animal in his natural environment, this is not acceptable from his point of view, or the worlds' general environmental welfare. Each individual case, must therefore be considered carefully and the arguments made clearly and understood before animals are caught in the wild to be transferred to circuses and zoos. Having said this, there is no reason why zebras, wild asses, Przevalsky horses, mules, feral horses, quaggas (if only they were still around) or other wild members of the equine family should not be in circuses and zoos, and be taught to pull carts, be ridden, work at liberty or do any of the other things that other equines do, provided it is done without suffering and is mutually beneficial that is, they have a pleasant time. There is equally, no reason why this cannot be achieved, but it does need application and often a rethink of conventional traditional practices in circuses and zoos, just as in conventional horse-keeping establishments.

Some of the liberty work taught to equines in circus which is then performed without any tack or equipment and even on occasions without a 'presenter' (a human in the ring) can be one demonstration of a cooperative relationship between the human and the horses. Another interesting approach taken by some circuses is to allow the animals in the ring at times to do what they wish, and thus to be creative and innovative themselves rather than, as is the case in the majority of equine competitions, to insist on particular performances in a particular style with submission to the humans' will and unquestioning obedience. Further discussion of all these issues is given in Kiley-Worthington 1990.

Wildlife reserves

There are a number of problems with equines in wildlife reserves in different parts of the world. One of the major problems is what happens if, even though the reserve may have been created for them, the numbers rise so that either they threaten their own habitat or the survival of other species by changing the habitat? Does one 'cull' them: kill certain of them, or are there other possible approaches?

There are different views taken on what should happen in this case, well-illustrated, not by the equines, but by elephants at the present. Here in East and Central Africa, it is generally considered that even though the elephant population is out-growing its reserve, and changing the habitat (in the case of elephants this is by opening up forests, and breaking down trees), nevertheless, because these animals are relatively scarce on a world view, they are extremely large, exciting and cognitively advanced animals, they should not be killed unless no other solution is possible (e.g. Leakey 1993). In South Africa by contrast, the 'elephant problem' is considered of little importance; if there are too many, the wildlife experts will assess how many is too many (it is not necessarily agreed how this is done, nor is it necessarily done by any objective mea-sured criteria) and then send people in to shoot them. The only problem the South Africans see, as far as the elephants go, is that it is no longer at present possible to trade in ivory, no money can be earned from ivory sales, therefore there is less money returning to help with the conservation of the elephant in the future (see Wildlife Conservation 1993 for articles from many points of view).

This discussion of elephants might at first sight seem somewhat irrelevant to that pertaining to equines, wild or domestic but this is not so. At the moment for example, although these debates rage over the rhino (another odd-toed hoofed mammal, a close relative of the equines) and elephants, equines, particularly the zebra, have not as yet attracted the same attention, despite the fact that many of them are endangered (e.g. the Asian wild ass, the Grevies zebra, mountain zebra) or have become extinct due to man's previous irresponsible actions (e.g. the quagga). This is despite the fact that they are clearly a cognitive advanced group that have lived in association with humans for some fifty centuries. At the moment, it is considered that the greatest value of the zebras in Africa, together with the bovids and most of the antelope (except for a few very rare species that are on the endangered species lists), is in their meat. They do have some small tourist value, but once there are too many of them, then they can be culled without a qualm, and their meat sold in the local tourist hotels particularly (since many of the local populations do not like zebra meat much) as a tourist attraction . . . roasted zebra.

Yet, at the same time, in Britain and parts of the US, there is a general taboo about eating either dog or equines such as horses or donkeys. The origin of this appears to be in the long association humans have had working and living closely with these species, having them as companions, friends and work-mates rather than potential supper. It maybe that this taboo has little rational origin now since the majority of meat eaters do not have anything to do with either species group, but it does indicate that humans still do, in a way, care about which animals they slaughter for food. Those that become very familiar as a result of living and working with them, are generally not raised and kept only for meat.

There is no reason to believe that zebras are any less cognitively able than other domestic equines. They can and do learn similar liberty movements in circuses. There are cases of them having being taught to be ridden, to drive with a famous photograph of a duke who drove four zebras in hand to Buckingham Palace at the beginning of the century. If then, these other equines are cognitively similar to Flicker, or Dobbin, then perhaps we should not value them primarily as meat, particularly if equines are more mentally able and more similar to humans than we previously thought.

The problem of over-population remains with the increasing restriction of wildlife areas, but there are alternatives to killing. One of these is selling off at least some of the extra animals to circuses and zoos where they will help to educate others on their existence, importance, beauty and abilities. Another is to develop good educational strategies so that they can be used locally for many things that other equines are in other countries: what about zebra races, zebras used for transport, zebras for tourists to ride and see the other animals from, and so on.

Of course this type of approach may not cater for the whole of the excess population, but it might allow a few more animals life, and an enriching life if done appropriately, as well as enrichment of the humans' life who work with them.

The management of the feral horse populations of the United States and Australia are also having to face problems of overpopulation. There is much more concern from the public about killing them for meat. Various groups have been created

Zebras live in family groups, and the spare males in bachelor herds. Here, a group of bachelors graze on Imire Wildlife Ranch, Zimbabwe.

The mare suckles her foal while watching us. He is probably suckling because of our intrusion, and his consequent slight unease. She is wagging her tail, indicating annoyance.

Grazing, tied to a tree, after capture from the wild.

The stallion leaps and kicks out at the mare, and she responds in the same way. These are the kinds of interactions which are most dramatic and easily observed, though they are not as common as affiliative social bonding behaviour in any group of equines we have studied to date.

Zebras show the same complexity of social relationships and visual communication as horses do. A mare with her foal orientating towards the camera, although the foal is also interested in his zebra neighbour (note right ear positions).

Zamitaye, the young zebra stallion 24 hours after capture. Note the relaxed posture of the animal and of the people around him.

(Above) A mare, her foal, and probably her 2/3 year-old daughter stay close together, almost touching, cementing the bonds between them, while the foal defaecates.

(Opposite) The stallion (centre) barges into a mare while she grazes. She takes no notice, while he swishes and turns his back on another mare and her foal. The right-hand mare avoids him and leaps off, while the foal keeps on the safe side of her.

The young zebra stallion, two days after capture, being scratched between the ears.

Flehmen: the young stallion has smelt the mare's urine and now lifts his head to allow the fluid to run down onto the gland on the back of his palate, which allows more thorough investigation of the strange smell or taste.

A young zebra stallion who had been darted and brought in to be handled two days previously. With appropriate handling, even a completely wild animal can be quickly accustomed to being handled and learn to do what is required without aggression or unpredictability. This zebra was the subject of an experiment to see if the preconceived notions concerning the difficulties of training zebras were well founded. Within two days, this zebra was handled, scratched under the tail, front legs lifted, groomed, led and tied up. Within a week, he was learning to lunge and to long rein, and had a saddle and pad on.

to encourage adoption of at least some of the young horses by members of the public. But this has, needless to say, raised much controversy among ecologists, and animal welfare organisations because of how it is done. Again, there does not seem to be any particular reason why this cannot be done in a way which will not cause long-term distress, although it may indeed cause some short-term stress. It does need further thought on *how* it is to be done, particularly using what we know about about how the equine perceives and interprets the world, his cognitive abilities, and how to develop cooperative handling and teaching using reward (see chapter 8).

There was an interesting television film to illustrate this point made with Lucy Rees (an author and one of the small band of cooperative equine teachers), on the catching and training of a feral horse in the western United States a few years ago where she succeeded in six weeks, while the cowboy had given up with a wild mustang. Her approach was contrasted with that of the professional cowboy, whose argument was that he 'did not have time to spend letting the horse get used to him and doing things quietly, he needed a horse to ride to do a "job" '. What more needs to be said? Feral horses, provided they are properly taught and kept in appropriate conditions, are just as pleasant and able companions, work mates, and performers as those born domestic, provided they are handled and taught well . . . but then this is the case of course with any equine.

Farming equines for meat

If any higher mammals are to be farmed for meat then, provided they do not suffer during their lifetimes, there is no particular reason why equines should not be farmed for meat. There is no reason, except for cultural prejudice that they should be exempt.

However, the arguments about whether any animals should be killed for meat for what Singer (1976) rightly calls 'trivial' reasons, since we certainly do not need meat to survive or live well, are debatable. One of the problems of abandoning raising animals for meat, will be that there will be very few of them around. We will end up living in an even more anthropocentric world where we can have even less relationship with other sentient beings. Those animals who do survive will be kept isolated from humans in 'animalistans': nature reserves, which as a result of continuing human population growth and consumerism become smaller and smaller. This is likely to result in a type of Animal Apartheid, separation of animals from humans which is already the aim of some organisations, for example the 'anti-dog' lobby (see Kiley-Worthington 1990 and 1995 for further discussion).

There is, of course, another option, that higher mammals at least are no longer farmed for meat, but they live with humans and earn their living in other ways than giving their lives, for example by supplying energy, entertainment, relaxation, companionship, fibre, milk, and other products which do not cause suffering or require their death. This is already the case for many equines, but there remains the problem of what to do where there are too many, and not enough resources to support them. But then we are confronted with the same problem for humans; perhaps the answer in the long term will have to be population control but not by castration, rather by contraceptive methods which still allow these animals to perform all the behaviour in their repertoire.

One unnecessary development is the transport of live animals to be killed, whether they are equines or any other species. Why is it acceptable to transport calves, pigs, cattle, sheep either to live in inappropriate environments that cause suffering and are behaviourally restricted, or to be killed after a long journey when legislation has been passed to prevent this for equines, at least exported from Britain? Again the horse has special status, but is this anything but a cultural belief, is there any evidence that they suffer more being transported? Often this is to the contrary, many horses for export will have previously had experience of being handled, moved about and even transported which has not always been a bad experience (even to and from competitions) whereas cattle or sheep from the highlands of Scotland or the out back of Australia, and even closer to home from the home farm, usually have not.

This is not to say that the export of live horses for slaughter is acceptable: two wrongs do not make a right; it is rather to argue for the unnecessary practice of exporting animals of any type live for slaughter or for rearing in unacceptable conditions for slaughter later. Today with the ready availability of freezer trucks, and other high-tech ways of keeping meat fresh, this is unnecessary even if the animal is raised for meat – if we are interested in the welfare of another sentient being. The main reason for its practice is to generate more money for the producer at the animal's expense. It is also practised for human cultural/religious reasons (e.g. the method of slaughter by Jews or Muslims without pre-stunning) which again is open to very serious reconsideration with our growing knowledge and understanding of these animals' sentience and cognitive abilities – at present these religious groups are the only people permitted to kill the animals without pre-stunning. It is the *method of killing* that causes unnecessary suffering to the animal, not whoever kills the animal, for whatever reason.

16

Fox and deer hunting with horses

This is an area related to equine welfare that has received much attention from the public and media in Britain to date. The arguments both for and against hunting foxes and deer with horses and dogs are often more involved with human society and its expectation than directly with the welfare of animals. We will quickly outline the arguments as, although they do not at present revolve around the welfare of the horse, the debate has given rise to much thinking among the public and some horse owners concerning what we should or should not do with animals and is therefore very relevant to the debates on equine and other animal welfare.

Both the anti- and the pro-hunting lobbies are united in basing their arguments exclusively on whether or not foxes or deer should be hunted at all, and if they are how they are hunted . . . This has, ironically, to date included nothing about the welfare of the much more numerous horses and/or the dogs (hounds) who are key to this sport.

If the anti-hunting lobby wished to point to the *total* sum of animal suffering as a result of hunting then they need to assess the amount of suffering in the stables and kennels as well as that of the hunted fox or deer. They will, as we have already pointed out, find some evidence of behavioural distress and therefore suffering in the stables, and probably the kennels too. Use of this evidence would make the case against hunting on utilitarian grounds – the *total* amount of suffering – a great deal stronger than the normal assessment of the suffering of the one, two or three possible hunted foxes or stags per day's hunting. The anti-hunting groups have not entertained these arguments, presumably because of the usual consensus that:

(1) Only wild animals count when it comes to suffering. After all domestic animals, they argue, have evolved to live with humans, are so different from their wild counterparts that they can't suffer in the same way. Yet that domestic animals do suffer has been recognised (see Harrison 1964). Often the reason for the suffering of millions of poultry, pigs, cattle and horses raised for meat is that it is 'necessary': because humans require plentiful supplies of cheap meat, cheap animal protein. Current husbandry practices for meat animals are neither the most efficient method of raising animals, nor the most desirable; nevertheless they are usually justified on account of an acceptance that human interests trump animal interests. The case for the nutritional need of animal meat for the health of humans was abandoned long ago when it was shown that many societies of not only vegetarians, but vegans, were found to be perfectly healthy and have long lives.

(2) It is often stated that fox and deer hunting serve no valid purpose and are done 'just for fun'. The second part of this statement is generally true. Despite arguments from various pro-hunting lobbyists, fox and deer hunting is followed by the majority 'just for fun'. On the other hand why are we so convinced that animals raised for animal protein are not raised 'just for fun'; would their existence be threatened if this were the case? It is curious that the killing of less than one wild animal per day's hunting 'for entertainment' outweighs the issue of raising of thousands of animals to be eaten (sometimes by the protesters as well as the hunters!) in conditions where there is evidence and demonstration of suffering, behavioural distress and all are behaviourally restricted. Thus we hunt and allow animals to be kept in their millions where there is clear evidence of animal suffering 'just for fun', or as Singer (1976) points out, 'for trivial reasons'. One of the most common 'trivial reasons' is to make money.

These arguments have been developed and explored at length over the last two decades (see Midgley 1976, Singer 1976, Rollin 1989, Clarke 1978, Leahy 1991, Kennedy 1992) to name but a few; but many of both the anti- and pro-hunting lobbies continue to ignore them unabashed.

It would seem that there are other arguments at the base of this dispute which do not involve animal welfare. One of these seems to be related to human privilege and money. Anti-hunting activists have a quite valid argument when they state that they do not see why some people should have so much money that they can spend one to four days a week galloping around chasing foxes or stags for fun, especially when this ritual is accompanied by conspicuous expenditure in terms of transport, horses, harness, clothing and in particular land ownership. If there is to be such an unjust distribution of wealth, the anti-hunting lobbiest will argue, then at least *the haves* should behave towards *the have-nots* with a degree of respect, and manners, rather than with arrogance.

Interestingly, the defence of fox and stag hunting uses that of 'traditional practice' most strongly . . . It is right if it is traditionally part of 'British Country Life'. However, traditional practices and behaviours have been changed because society has changed. For example 300 years ago it was normal practice to have slaves, 100 years ago to deny women the vote and to rule their own lives.

Perhaps all that is needed is a greater consideration for others demonstrated by the hunting (and often horse-owning) fraternity.

But what of the arguments on animal welfare grounds which are central to the anti-hunting position? Is it such bad news for the fox, or the stag? There are many arguments here on both sides that can be mentioned. On the side of the anti-hunting lobbyists:

(i) Foxes and deer clearly suffer from physiological stress when they are chased and hunted by dogs or humans.

(ii) The killing of the captured prey is often not clean and particularly quick; it depends if the dogs get there first, or if the man with the gun to dispatch the animals is near. Thus there is some suffering during capture and death of the prey.

(iii) Fox and deer hunting with dogs and horses do not control the population by culling, which is often given as a 'conservation argument' by the pro-hunters.

(iv) It is morally wrong and a bad education particularly for young humans, to learn that fun and enjoyment come from seeing or taking part in the suffering of other sentient beings. Kant in the eighteenth century, argued that people should be nice to animals, not because the animals mattered in themselves very much, since they were not capable of rational thought, but because, if people were nasty to animals or witnessed this, then they might generalise and be nasty to other humans, which he considered morally wrong (see chapter 1).

(v) It can also be argued that hunting creates environmental problems (e.g. churning up paths and countryside, blocking roads, etc.).

In answer to these arguments the pro-hunting fraternity may use the following:

(i and ii) These wild animals will indeed suffer when chased and caught but this suffering is of short duration, and in any case they have evolved to cope with the hard facts of the living world, and they are still living natural lives so, why should they not be hunted? It is more 'natural' than being shot, or poisoned and may cause less suffering. Life after all is difficult, particularly for wild animals, but that is the 'law of the jungle'. The suffering, however, is not prolonged and measures are taken to dispatch animals fast when the opportunity arises.

(iii) Even if the populations are not controlled by hunting (which many pro-hunters argue they are) nevertheless the fact that fox and stag hunting occur ensures that these animals which are a threat to agricultural production are not exterminated which they otherwise could easily be, and in some countries have been by poisoning, shooting and snaring. This is a strong conservation argument.

(iv) It does no harm to young humans to witness such 'facts of life', in fact it can help them realise that human beings, particularly country dwellers, must contend with witnessing death and other natural occurrences and come to terms with these occurrences.

(v) Hunting encourages landowners to preserve the traditional countryside with its hedges, coverts, woods, arable and grassland – and traditional values. That it is environmentally helpful, not harmful, and stimulates interest in the countryside and its maintenance (MacDonald and Johnson, 1996).

All these points serve to demonstrate the separation of the urban from the rural dweller. One quite divorced from the 'natural world' and often proud of it, believing that nature can be improved on if it comes in contact with humans, and must be, although it must also be left alone in some areas entirely undisturbed; the other, by contrast, rurally employed, believing that life just exists like this and that is the way it is, and there is nothing that can be done to improve it for wild animals. But these humans will also accept the urban over-protection and manipulation of nature in the interests of humans, economic gain, or leisure and pleasure.

Although there are some reasonable arguments on both sides, the most rational position appears to be the following: that getting enjoyment by galloping across country at the cost of another sentient being's suffering, and sometimes life, is unnecessary unless there are greater benefits to be gained from this (than mere pleasure for example), to compensate for that suffering. For example, that the dying of one stag in this way will save many others. But this has not, to date, been demonstrated. There are other ways of ensuring the survival of red deer than by hunting.

If one wants to gallop across the countryside in groups wearing 'traditional costume' and using 'traditional language', provided this does not cause suffering or distress to any other sentient being then why not? There are other ways in which it can and is being done, for example drag hunts, hunter trials and team chasing. These activities could be encouraged – provided all sentient beings involved have a good time and their life is free of prolonged distress.

The suffering and distress caused to other animals in the system needs also to be assessed before one can be convinced that hunting in the traditional way with dogs and horses is really justified. How are the hounds and the horses kept and managed, are we sure that there is not distress and prolonged suffering induced because of (a) our belief that the horse and hound must be kept in a certain way if they are going to be able to gallop about and (b) are avoidable accidents and disasters adequately assessed and considered?

On the other hand it is clear that change is not likely to come by engaging in confrontation, violence and abuse. A better direction might be to try and make those involved on both sides consider carefully what they are doing and defend it rationally. This is happening here and there. If the anti-hunting lobby has done nothing else, it has made the odd hunting person a little more polite, and perhaps even a little more thoughtful.

As a postscript there are without doubt many recorded and un-recorded twists to these arguments. Recently a neighbour of mine wanted to downgrade a bridle path over his land to a footpath – not because it was over-used – he had already made it impassable for horses. There was considerable opposition from local riders since there is a great shortage of bridle paths in the area. The owner countered, so I understand, by going to the local hunt telling them that if they did not write in support of his application then he would stop them hunting over other open areas of his land. The local hunting fraternity (which still has considerable influence in the neighbourhood) did this and despite the opposition of the local riding group, the non-hunting riders, the land owner had his way. Another bridle path was lost, with consequent less rideable area for hunting and non-hunting riders alike!

Humans will be humans and such curious unexpected outcomes of confrontations, such lack of discussion and rational thought will continue. Who benefits in this case? Neither side, nor do the equines themselves. Such outcomes could be avoided by more careful and systematic thought – but as a respected mentor of mine says (Midgley 1992) 'thinking is hard work'.

17

Horses in riding schools

The training of humans concerning horses and their welfare is at present conducted in various institutions. These are:

(1) Veterinary schools where the training is primarily centred on physical diseases and their cure. After graduating with a veterinary degree, it is possible to specialise in veterinary practice with horses where the qualification is relevant to coping with physical diseases primarily, and remarkable advances in surgery have been developed. However some veterinary schools now have courses in Animal Welfare and Ethics, although they are not always taught by people with a good philosophical background, and are therefore often sketchy. The first and best of such courses that I have encountered is at Colorado State University, Fort Collins where the students have to complete a full semester's course taught by a well-known philosopher in the field – Bernie Rollins. Despite their frequent lack of training in animal behaviour or ethics, it is generally the veterinarians who are believed to 'know about animal welfare'.

(2) In what used to be called 'agricultural colleges' and which are now often part of universities. As a result of student demand, courses have recently been developed with such titles as 'Equine Studies', and are very popular. These courses are either taught at a diploma level, or there are now even degrees both in the UK, as well as the USA, where qualifications in Equine Studies are given. These vary greatly in the expected standard and content (many concentrating on the business aspect of the 'horse industry'), and in whether they have a practical component or not.

(3) For the majority of those who are interested in learning about and training with equines, the traditional way has been

through the riding schools. These schools vary in size and splendour from the historic centres of riding, such as the Cadre Noir at Saumur in France, or the Spanish Riding School in Vienna, down to one woman and her horse in a tiny yard.

In most of Europe now there is an inspectorate for recognising riding schools as approved training centres by the establishment horse organisation (in Britain the British Horse Society) and they prepare students for examination which incorporate both theory and practical riding. This is geared to the main establishment competitions, such as dressage, jumping and eventing. These courses even at the highest level, the Fellowship, do not include many other aspects of working with or using equines, such as driving, working, western riding, long distance, farriery. They are geared towards producing teachers to continue with the *status quo*. It is possible to obtain some training in light horse and carriage driving for showing by approaching the British Driving Horse Society, and a student who would like to learn to work horses, might be taken nowadays as an intern on one of the few farms who still have heavy horses, or the occasional one with light horses.

There has been much criticism of the BHS examinations and, as someone who was trained and took some of them, but also has been involved in university examinations, I know that the criticism has often been justified. Recently, however, because of the efforts to have some courses approved by other examination bodies, there does seem to have been an effort to upgrade these examinations and introduce a more stringent, less subjective way of judging candidates. It is vitally important, if equine welfare and the integration of equines into society is to continue and grow, that the upgrading and broadening of these courses continues, so that a proper scholarly grounding in all aspects of management, welfare, behaviour, teaching and use of equines is presented. It is possible to give an introductory assessment in a week, but I hope that if this book has done nothing else, it has shown the complexity and wealth of questions still remaining to be thought about and discussed.

In riding schools, how the equines are kept, trained, ridden, and what else they do, are on public view almost every day. As a result, the welfare of horses and ponies used in riding schools has come under public scrutiny rather more than many other equine-based pursuits. Indeed riding schools in Britain have to have a licence to operate, and this can only be obtained through the borough councils and planning authorities. The main reason for the inspection preceding the issuing of a licence has been to ensure that the welfare of the horses and ponies was adequate.

Because of their teaching role, the riding schools are in a unique position to be able to review, revise and change the current husbandry practices and attitudes to and relationships with equines. Equally, they are very powerful in maintaining the *status quo* and influencing the next generation of equine keepers.

The member of the public goes to a riding school for a 'riding lesson', she does not go for a 'lesson with horses'. The horse she is to ride is usually brought out of the stable for her; ready to ride, tacked up, clean and shiny, and she is told how to mount almost immediately. She then spends the next hour being taught how to stay on the horse, which is then taken away from her and put back in the stable while she may chat to the groom or pupil doing this. People may have lessons at riding schools for years without ever having anything else to do with the horse, even how to put a bridle or saddle on, never mind have some understanding of him as a sentient being, other than when they are on top of him! When being taught to ride, only

Riding free.

too frequently an analogy is made by the teacher to a motor car 'he has no brakes', 'you just have to push the right buttons', 'he is the brawn, you are the brain', 'you must have control' (all quotes from top trainers). One has to question whether this attitude fosters the wellbeing of the horse, and good inter-species relationships.

In the first place it encourages the human to assume that the only thing worth doing with a horse is to ride 'it', secondly that one must dominate 'it', and thirdly that riding 'it' is really more or less like a cross between driving a car and hang gliding, and with practice one will get good at it. Then one will take 'it' to competitions and perhaps one day win (with the help of the pit crew), and this will be rewarding.

When being tested to pass examinations to be a teacher in a riding school, the student is assessed primarily on his teaching of *riding*, not on whether he can teach how to communicate and relate to the horse, to handle him, or what a horse is, and what he can do emotionally and mentally, as well as physically. The student or client is not introduced to the horse and expected to converse, she is given a leg up and off she goes, like getting in to drive a rather old-fashioned bus.

If the welfare of the horse is of a high priority, the time has come for the basic entrenched teaching of riding and about horses to be broadened. The interested child or adult should be taught, not only how to ride, but how to relate to horses, to handle them and to communicate with them from the ground. One simple step surely here is to ensure that the student/client is taught how to prepare her own horse to ride, and untack him and put him away afterwards. At least then the student/client will have had some time individually getting to know the horse, and learning a little about what he is other than being an unreliable machine and method of transport. There are some riding schools who do this, but this type of teaching requires as much skill, patience and time as teaching people to ride, if not more. Handling is not something which is learnt in an afternoon. There is much need for development in the thinking and practice in order to improve the knowledge and abilities of all, from novice to professionals (Kiley-Worthington and Randle, 1996).

One of the pressures against this type of approach is that the emphasis in riding and having horses, is heavily on compe-tition, in particular jumping, dressage, cross country and racing. Thus the 'top' riding schools with the 'best' horses, equipment, and so on, aim primarily to teach people to compete. Although education for humans in many spheres has lately become 'training' (i.e. acquiring of skills, particularly technological to fulfil the industries' needs or ensure higher salaries), education through history, has not generally implied this. It has involved 'giving intellectual and moral training'. It has been about allowing and helping the student to develop his ideas, skills and thinking abilities so that s/he can benefit and have an enriched life. There is little doubt that equines are not interested in money, but they certainly respond to appropriate, or inappropriate emotional, physical and intellectual environments. Perhaps there is room for a romantic here and there, to consider that learning to associate with and understand equines better, could take us away from the overriding materialistic concerns of the present culture . . . expose us to different ways of thinking about the world and even living. But these benefits for the human student will not be apparent if they are not recognised and taught. Those who go to riding stables to learn, generally are attracted there because they would like to get to know horses better, so they are already predisposed to being taught about them, and having to do with them . . . not just hop on and gallop off.

The stables often talked about as the 'best', are those which charge much money, have large, often modern buildings and facilities and sometimes have good teachers (although this does not, by any means necessarily go together). In such establishments the horses must be kept in the conventional way and establishment practices must be strictly followed and taught to residential students. If this is not the case, the riding school will be refused a licence. Thus it is in such institutions that the establishment practices are very closely adhered to in the name of 'good management'. The more that is done, rather than *what* is done may be taken as an index of success and good horse welfare. The result is open to all the criticism of conventional horse management (see chapters 9 and 10). Many of the problems for the horse, as in the majority of horse keeping establishments, result from a lack of knowledge concerning the horse's needs, and over-protection.

One important factor here is that the riding schools who also have residential students often have much labour available, and they are consequently in the same type of situation as the cavalry: they need to invent jobs to keep all the people around the yards busy. This in itself is not harmful, but the difficulty is that the students emerge from such training with little experience of being able to make judgements as to which practices are seriously beneficial either to themselves or the equines, and which are disposable, and thus the *status quo* is not only maintained, but often enhanced. Here the solution may be to invent other jobs that the students can learn and which will be of greater mutual benefit in order to keep them busy, rather than the emphasis on sweeping, shine and polish as if daily there is to be a military march past.

Like all other institutions there are 'good' and 'bad' riding schools, judged from the horses' point of view, as far as we know at present. The cheaper establishments may have less equipment, fewer clean stables and horses, may be less well organised, and the ponies at least may live out in fields in groups for most of their lives when not working; these 'cheaper' schools may in fact be 'better' for the horses, who may show less evidence of stress and behavioural distress (see chapters 3, 4 and 5).

A particularly important problem for riding schools is what to do with animals who are not very well, or even very well but thin. They will attract attention and complaints, as on all occasions when animals are exposed to public scrutiny, however careful and concerned the owner/manager is. It is extremely difficult to have old, thin or even slightly lame horses on view or doing appropriate work, even though this may be the best thing for them by, for example, keeping them occupied, and interested. There may well be appropriate jobs in a riding school that old horses are a real asset doing. For example an old or lame horse can teach people, especially the less athletic, how to handle and relate to him, and to communicate with him perhaps with the help of a human teacher, and even to teach him to perform various little movements.

Associating with equines, working with them or just enjoying their company does not have to be connected with youth, athleticism and sport, a particular sex, or alternatively 'the handicapped'. This is not to deny the enormous contribution that riding for the disabled and their organisation do; but rather to ask them to extend their approach to the non-handicapped. Associating with, and learning about and with equines can enrich the lives of people of all backgrounds, ages, sexes and abilities, help them with their physical, emotional and intellectual problems, and even educate them about the world, whether they are normal, or handicapped, sporty or non-sporty, adult or child.

It is in the riding schools that there is a chance of some 'community integration' between species, and surely this should be fostered, not just in specialist organisations (e.g. 'the handicapped' or 'children's holidays') but in *all* riding schools, particularly those considered at the 'top' of the range, teaching the teachers and 'competitors' of the future. Until the leading edge institutions start to consider this, as well as change their equine husbandry systems, the filtering through of such ideas is slow, and both the humans' and the equines' welfare will continue to suffer.

The role of horses as work partners and energy helpmates has been so forgotten in the 'top yards', that not one of them that I am aware of actually uses the horses for a whole variety of work around the yards. For example why do they, almost without exception, all have a tractor and harrows to harrow the school before the competition or next lesson? Why do they not have a horse that does this, or even several, even the horses that they use in the lesson? Why do they not teach the students how to look after the yard, bring the straw, distribute the hay, harrow the fields, move the muck – using horses? The students might well enjoy learning to do this and the horses would be doing some useful work rather than having to be taken out on exercise. They would also be doing something different which in itself may be beneficial, the teachers would have to think clearly and carefully about their handling skills, which would improve their teaching. In addition the money would be saved from buying the tractor and employing the tractor driver!

One of the complaints concerning the welfare of riding school equines is the monotony of the work they do. They are ridden around slowly, often in enclosed areas, teaching humans to ride for several hours a day, and they may do this for several years. This is considered 'bad' for the equines, to such an extent that some horse owners will be heard to say when parting with their horse 'I will never let him go to a riding stable'. An interesting coda to this belief is that even if the horse did not suffer from going there (which is believed to be highly likely) nevertheless he will be 'wasted'. The owner considers that it would be much 'better for him' if he were to be sold to a competitive yard, and suffer the rigours of this life and its risks (see chapters 12, 13, 14) rather than amble around a riding school arena or around the country. Indeed it would be better for every equine to have some variety in their work and rest. The job of the riding school teacher/owner/manager is to ensure this happens, and perhaps to broaden the experiences both the humans and the equines can have at the establishment.

The other reason why people believe the life of a riding school horse to be inferior to that of a competitive horse is because he will be ridden by people learning to ride, and they will crash around on him and pull him about. However, what is often forgotten is that riders in riding schools are more usually supervised than private riders or at competitive yards. The onus again is on the teaching. If riding is taught to be a discipline which inevitably involves domination of the horse, kicking, controlling, pulling and trying to 'overcome' his desires, then indeed there is an argument that from the equines' point of view, all riding should cease . . . they are better off not ridden. There are a growing number of alternative type riding teachers and trainers, however, who are developing the practice and teaching of more enlightened approaches (e.g. Sally Swift 1985, Monty Roberts 1992, Kiley-Worthington in prep.).

One of the areas that is not necessarily neglected in theory when teaching student teachers (but, alas, is often neglected in practice) is the integration of the horses with the land, and how this should be managed. Grazing grass exclusively with horses (and curiously those who have horses, and certainly riding schools, rarely have any other animals other than the odd pet, such as dog, peacock or cat) results in a reduction of the grass growth and substantial changes in the species composition of the sward over a period of years. In order to keep the grass growing well and evenly to feed the horses, rather than just acting as a run out area, the grass needs proper management. This is not the place to discuss this at length which has been done elsewhere, (see Kiley-Worthington 1987 chapter 8). The management of the land the horses live on is of considerable relevance to the equines' welfare. With appropriate management, not only will the equines have more grass and herbs to eat (their natural diet which can have dramatic beneficial effects on their physical and psychological health) but the owner can then save money by buying less food, the equine can be kept in environments that are more ecologically sound (see chapter 20), and even small patches of ground can be used to benefit both the equines and humans.

Another important concern for the management of land by equine owners is concerned with aesthetics. Throughout Europe, and even in the United States and Australia there are growing populations of people living on the edge of cities who have horses. This has developed to such an extent that, nowadays, outside most major towns there is an area of land denoted 'horse culture' where equines live in various shacks, sheds, behind hedges, and graze between tin cans, plastic bags, brightly painted bits of wood, oil drums and other odds and ends, which are often used as jumps. Such areas show the typical results of continuous unmanaged grazing by equines, the debarking of trees, destroying of hedgerows, with frequent fences breaking up the landscape often in bad state of repair and tied up with baler twine, collapsed gates, muck heaps and the general debris of modern human urban–rural existence. Such areas are generally viewed as unaesthetically pleasing and they can also have unacceptable environmental effects, such as run off from chemicals used, and muck heaps contaminating the local water ways, deforestation, the introduction of pests, smells, nuisance to others and reduction in species diversity.

Just as important aesthetically and in terms of environmental impact is the construction of large buildings in the suburbs or countryside for riding schools, the building of stables, and the effects on the landscape and environment of the 'industrialisation' of horse-keeping is becoming an important planning issue. The point relevant to the equines' welfare, is, are such changes necessary? The provision of stabling, indoor schools and landscape changes in order to 'improve' the equines' welfare are often given as important arguments to support the planning applications. This cannot be taken as necessarily true or even likely, thus, in future, other arguments need to be made for their development.

There are many areas for review, change and development in the teaching of people about riding and equines. It is a challenging and exciting area which, because of the need for change and the effect on future generations of humans, is *central* for the future development of equine welfare. A serious rethink, review, questioning of current practices, and trial of others is clearly indicated for riding schools and human teaching establishments . . . if equine welfare is to be a serious consideration.

18

Working equines around the world

So far we have concentrated on the ethics and welfare of keeping equines mainly in 'developed', high consuming countries where most people assume that there is likely to be less suffering and cruelty than in countries where equines are still working for their living by being the energy supply, by providing one of the main methods of transport for humans and their goods, and helping with food production and agriculture and consequently ensuring the survival of human populations.

Some of the animal welfare lobbies are keen to try to reduce the number of equines kept in this way on grounds that this type of use (particularly by poor people) is the main area of suffering for equines in the world. In the West and North we may be somewhat ignorant of what the real state of play is on the use of equines in developing countries, and be predisposed by the charities' publicity and tear-jerking pictures, to assume that the people are less likely to care for or about their equines, primarily because (1) They are poor and caring for equines (or children for that matter) requires money, (2) Their cultures are different and they care less for animals generally than we in the West. Equines in developing countries, it is believed, are beasts of burden who are unloved, over-worked, underfed, whose feet are not looked after and who are diseased. They are 'better off dead' is often used as a derogatory phrase for others' care of equines. (3) Many poor people are considered 'backward', and 'ignorant' about how equines should be kept and cared for. Even if they are taught the way that it is done in the 'developed' world (which itself is certainly open to question as we have already discussed), they will not do the necessary things because they are poor.

Riding in Kenya's Athi River valley. Although horses and donkeys are used in the tourist industry, in many countries their main role is still that of providing equine power for millions of people.

Donkey and horse single furrow ploughs being sold at a market in Morocco. Why do not more people in Europe use horses to look after their land?

In this chapter we will examine whether these suppositions are in fact generally correct, or simply used to raise money to try to 'better the role of working equines', or replace them by other forms of transport and draught power.

In the last five years there have been several International conferences on Draught Animals and now Working Equines (Edinburgh 1990, Fielding and Pearson 1991, Rabat 1994). These have to a large extent been sponsored by equine welfare charities, but there have been a variety of speakers reporting on the research they have been doing, from the equine's role in pastoral societies, to their possible increase in use, and introduction into different countries to help the poorer rural communities instead of inappropriate engine power. There is also research continuing on equine energy output and the physiology of their energy production, desired nutrition, and design of appropriate harness and implements for them, using updated design ideas and local materials.

The first thing to understand is that the use of horse or more particularly donkey power in many countries in Africa, Asia and South America is not a quaint old custom for tourists, but is the mainstay of many millions of peoples' lives. They could not function in the way they presently do without them. It is estimated that there are over three million working equines in the world. This is by no means a small number, in fact there are probably more working equines today than competitive and companion equines.

So *are* all these equines worse off than the competitive horse in the North in a top stable yard? If so how are we going to judge this? We have already drawn up guidelines by which we can judge the suitability of the husbandry system and the work performed by the equines (part I and chapters 19 and 20). How do these working equines figure in the 'welfare stakes' on the roads of Rajasthan, Rabat, Malawi or Mexico? To date no one has surveyed the occurrence of prolonged suffering and distress as a percentage of particular populations as we have done for horses in top competing, teaching and racing yards; however it is clear that there are welfare problems with many of these equines.

One of the major problems which has been identified by the Donkey Sanctuaries' researchers is something remarkably simple. The majority of working donkeys in the populations that have been looked at in Africa and Mexico have had disease, malnutrition and been suffering because of heavy worm infections. Cure the worms, provide wormers and teach their owners to use them, and the donkeys' health dramatically improves. Other diseases occur of course locally, but malnutrition and the occurrence of other diseases including infections is dramatically reduced simply by deworming.

What about overwork? Are these animals generally overworked and underfed, and starving? Of course there are animals who are and owners who exploit their animals to the limit, as elsewhere, including in the North, but again this does not seem to be such a major problem as one is led to believe, although there could be more information on this. Many working equines in these countries work very hard long days, but do more in fact die, and is their life expectancy in reality any less than in, for example, top competing and racing yards? We don't know the answer to these questions.

What about the generally accepted idea that the different human cultures who keep working equines do not care for them as we in the northern latitudes care about our equines, and may often exploit them ruthlessly, have little understanding of them, and affection towards them? Again evidence for this is by no means convincing. If one is spending all day, every day working with a donkey, a mule, a horse or pony, it is very difficult not to have some emotional contact and even grow quite fond of the animal, particularly if only by his work is one going to survive. It may be hard for human and equine, but it is not necessarily clear that the equines are usually exploited by the people who rely on them to live and function. Again we need some surveys to see if the situation is much worse from the equines' point of view than it is in the consumer societies.

One interesting success story emerges from the East – that of the Cairo Brooke Hospital for Animals who offered a prize to the fittest and best-turned out horse and barouche on the streets of Cairo. To begin with, this was little known about and there was a slow start to the annual competition. Now, however, some years on, this prize is very strongly competed for; imagination, ingenuity in design, and decoration, not to mention careful husbandry of the horse have led to a spectacular improvement in the condition and health of the horses, and the turn-out. Another success is the presence in Rabat market in Morocco of the 'Societé pour le Protection des Animals d'Afrique du Nord' dispensary. By no means all

Donkeys on a rubbish dump.

Giving guidance and help to equine owners concerning the welfare of their donkeys is often all that is needed. In Lamu, the Donkey Sanctuary runs a low-cost help centre (pictured here). As a result, we hardly saw a donkey in Lamu that was undernourished or overworked.

Donkeys in Lamu, an island off the Kenya coast, carrying sand from the beach back to the town for building. Notice how, even while being loaded, they are standing loose and quiet with no bridles or other restraints.

Directing a donkey with minimal harness in Kenya. The home-made collar is simple, effective, and does not rub. However, the donkey should have a pad to carry some of the weight on its back because it is pulling a 2-wheeled vehicle.

*Three donkeys pulling a barrel of water on a 2-wheeled vehicle.
Again, the minimal harness would be adequate for a 4-wheeled
vehicle which takes the weight, but there should be a pad to support
the weight of a 2-wheeled vehicle. The Kenya Society for the
Prevention of Cruelty to Animals is active in this area, and the
people are learning humane methods.*

*In Lamu, donkeys are the only transport. When not
working, they wander around among the people. They clear
up much of the waste which otherwise would be a problem.
This one is eating the discarded top of a pineapple.*

A Moroccan boy looks with longing (or disdain?) at the car whizzing past on the main road as he rides home on his donkey with its load. Note, there is no need for bridles; both donkey and boy know what they are doing and where they are going, and could go many places in this rugged mountainous terrain where the cars cannot.

Morocco market. An Arab horse with light breast-plate harness canters along with a load, while a donkey (left) is ridden with no tack other than a halter.

the horses and donkeys there could have been said to be suffering from neglect, malnutrition or disease. There is indeed evidence for physical disease and distress in some of these animals in any country which one visits, but this is by no means a usual occurrence in most. What about behavioural distress which is clearly a major problem with equines in the Northern countries? What about behavioural restraint; do the developing countries have more examples of this too? The answer is that they usually have fewer. The animals are restrained behaviourally to a degree, sometimes by tethering (not always well done) and being in stalls, but large numbers wander around freely. The restriction of sex and interferences with breeding by manipulations and drugs is minimal or absent, the animals are more often than not allowed access to form their own social groups and not kept in single stables. They appear to be behaviourally better off generally than the top competitive horses in the developed countries. Yes, they work, and work hard some of the time but that does not necessarily mean that they are *so* overworked and underfed that they are incapable of behaving in inappropriate ways. In Rabat market last year we saw stallions parked next to mares in the car park, left while their owners went to trade, quietly standing next to each other, and they were not starving or exhausted, just relaxed and well-adjusted. This does not and could not happen at present at any driving event in Europe, except perhaps at a gypsy fair.

I remember seeing a young boy standing in the cart of a rather pretty Arab horse who was trotting along the road in a relaxed way with no bridle or reins. No one was worried or distressed, and the horse judged the width of the oncoming cars and lorries, avoiding them – clearly experienced at this type of decision-making cognitive task. How many Arabs, or even small ponies or donkeys, could do this in Europe, even off the road? I have yet to see one animal able to be driven this way. The expectations of the humans of their equines' behaviour are different and perhaps greater from time to time than those in Europe and the US.

There is much more we need to know about the working equines in these countries, and equally certain that we have much to learn from the equines and their owners and workers just as much as they may have things to learn, particularly about physical disease, and work control, from our culture.

(Above) A British Council project in Malawi, teaching people to use draught animals for rural transport and farm work.

(Opposite above) A 2-wheeled cart designed for a donkey at the Agricultural Engineering department of the University of Zimbabwe. This cart will only be appropriate for donkeys if they carry the weight of the shafts on their backs with a pad. It has been developed from an ox wagon.

(Opposite below) Morocco market. The transport waits patiently in lines for their owners to return. There is little to worry about from the welfare point of view, thanks to the World Society for the Protection of Animals, who have an adviser at this market.

One is left with the serious impression from visiting various third-world countries and looking at projects there that more cultural exchange concerning equine use, behaviour and welfare could be nothing but a good thing for all concerned. It would not be a bad idea for some of these wealthy equine welfare organisations to take a group of top competing and teaching people from Europe or America to see what *they* could learn from the peasant and his horse or donkey . . . if we are interested in the welfare of equines and not just in putting across *our* own particular cultural position and beliefs.

Improvements are needed everywhere in catering for the physical, emotional and intellectual needs of equines. It is rather doubtful that on balance the working equine of the poor of the world has by any means the worst deal. There is a growing 'aid industry' beginning to teach and give advice on 'sustainable' projects appropriate to low-tech draught animal use. I have been involved with some of these and although there is much to be said in favour of them as a benefit to the poorer communities and that they are not necessarily 'bad news' for the animals, there is often (as with most animal husbandry schemes) some confusion or lack of thought about the *equines'* needs, since the main aim of the aid industry is to benefit *people*.

It is important that equine and people welfare develops in tandem, if they are *both* sentient beings, and perhaps there are chances here and there that some of the developments in the husbandry, use and teaching of equines in 'developed' countries which are not to the benefit of the equine could be avoided. Also, steps forward could be taken by *combining* the more thoughtful and beneficial techniques from all cultures rather than perpetuating the North's arrogant beliefs that it has the last word in the understanding of correct equine welfare and husbandry. This applies equally to the cognitive training of animals for draught work, as well as recreation and competition (Randle 1994).

Part 4

Possible ways forward

19

Towards equine/human symbiosis

We have looked at many of the ways in which equines are kept and used today and at current establishment practices and beliefs. We have discussed our understanding of equines, and what we know about their cognitive abilities. This has, I suspect, raised more questions than it has answered, but it is much easier to be critical and derogatory than constructive – so, if we have decided that keeping, using, competing with and teaching equines is morally and ethically acceptable, *provided it does not cause suffering*, then how can it best be done?

This chapter outlines the criteria which it would be necessary to fulfil to be able to justify our equine/human relationships. That they *can* generally be fulfilled the majority of the time we have shown on our own experimental/working stud and farm over the last twenty years. There are, I admit, some problems in fulfilling one or two of the criteria – but there are very considerable benefits in many unexpected ways.

The methods which we have used are not impossible 'pie in the sky' for donkey, mule, shetland, zebra, thoroughbred or shire – or any other breed of equine for that matter. Our recommended methods do need thought, planning and motivation to put into effect, but if we are seriously interested in equine welfare they must be our guidelines. Of course, much remains to be done, in particular a study of where exactly the boundaries are to be drawn, but what we do know is that current practices are *not good enough* for a great number of equines, if we are seriously concerned with their welfare, and that *we can take the first steps to improving them*.

Ethologically sound environments for equines

We have some idea how to assess and measure when we have got it wrong from the horse's point of view, that is when he is suffering and there is evidence of prolonged behavioural distress or physiological stress; we also have some indications of when he is happy and feeling pleasure. How are we to know how to design the environment correctly in order that he will not be distressed and will have pleasure? Clearly, as we have seen, we have not yet managed to achieve this with current established methods of horse husbandry, even at the top end of the market with the most expensive horses kept in what is considered 'the best possible way'. From the horses' point of view at least, it would seem that improvements must be made.

There are guidelines which can be used to design environments for our equines which will ensure their physical and behavioural well-being. In the first place, this involves understanding a little about evolutionary theory which maintains that the species (or individual) has over millions of years come to be the way it is because that has been the most successful way for that species. There have been genetic changes (mutations) in the animal (or human) which have resulted either in an improvement in the survival and reproductive ability of the animal or a failure in this. Those changes that have been favourable and ensured that the individual left offspring (who may also carry this gene) have survived and consequently been selected for over many millions of years. These genetic changes are certainly involved with the body. In the case of the horse the best-known example is the evolution of the foot from 3-toe to a single toe with longer legs, resulting in a specialised ability for movement and running far and at speed.

It is not, however, only morphological changes which have occurred in this way, but everything about the animal has had the benefit of evolutionary selection: his body, his habitat, his social life, his needs and desires and his mind. Therefore, in order to maximise the chances of success in the horse's ability to survive, breed, live long and adapt, it is sensible to try to

*A purebred Arab mare and stallion standing quietly
in harness before harrowing a field.*

Harrowing and getting fit at the same time.

*Goodwood House, where 20 plus horses are stabled, using a tractor
and harrow to level the school.*

design the environment to a considerable extent around those conditions with which he has evolved to cope. We do have a fairly accurate knowledge now of what these are, partly because of the fossil record, and partly because of studies of wild and feral equines.

One of the stumbling blocks that is often encountered is the argument that equines have been changed so dramatically by domestication that evolutionary considerations no longer apply: that the equine is genetically so different, his appearance, his behaviour, his social life, his habitat choice, his desires and needs and his cognition have changed beyond all recognition from those of his wild ancestors.

It is true to say that domestication, with artificial selection for particular characteristics, has resulted in substantial genetic changes in terms of very obvious things like size, speed of growth and colour of many domesticated animals. In addition we have developed different 'breeds' which certainly have morphological differences which are genetic. Because some equines, the thoroughbred horse for example, are taller and can run faster than the *Equus caballus* of the Asian plains, his wild ancestor, are we correct in assuming that he is genetically likely to choose a different habitat from an open plain, that he is genetically not social (because he has been kept in single stables for 4,000 years), that his genetic behavioural tendencies will be quite different from those of his ancestors: how he communicates, breeds, moves around, what he eats and so on?

There is one sure way of finding out, and that is to look at feral horses who have been domesticated for thousands of years then gone wild. How do they behave? What social system and habitat do they choose? In this way we can assess if there are significant genetic differences from their wild ancestors. We do still have some wild equines around; the zebras, some wild asses and now some genetically wild *Equus caballus*: Przevalsky's horse which has been re-established in Russia to live wild in its original habitat; another population has recently been established in France. There have been many studies on feral horses in Britain, in the United States and in Australia, and there is a considerable amount of information on the wild equines (e.g. zebras) too. The interesting thing is that as far as fundamental behavioural tendencies go, they vary very little. Of course they have different lifetime experiences and because horses are very able learners and cognitively complex, they are able to adapt during their lifetime to an enormous number of different types of environments and experiences, yet they do not appear to have changed genetically from their wild counterparts as regards behaviour (see Kiley-Worthington 1987 for summary of evidence).

Since this is the case the argument concerning the domestic equines' genetic difference in behaviour from his wild ancestors is not convincing. Fundamental behaviours, such as social living, sex, maternal behaviour, communication, feed habits and so on have changed very little – when the equine is given an option. Therefore as a first step it is useful to use the feral equines' behavioural needs as a model for the design of the optimal horse environment. In this way we can work with the way that horses have evolved to live, rather than try to change it. We do now have much information which can help us to draw up a list of guidelines for the optimal equine environment: 'ethologically sound environment'.

(1) *The equines should show no behavioural distress or evidence for prolonged physiological stress.* This means that there should be no stereotypies, no high levels of aggression, no excessive excitement and worry, no frequent diseases including lameness: no need for surgery to enable the animal to live in those conditions, and no persistent need of drugs.

(2) *The equine should be able to associate in the appropriate stable group size and structure.* Equines are social animals, and if we are to ensure their well-being, then we should ensure that they live in social groups of similar size and structure where possible to those that they have evolved to be successful in. Equines live in matriarchal family groups and have very strong long-term relationships between generations (mother to daughter in particular), as well as forming strong bonds within their peer groups or with other familiar equines (see Kiley-Worthington 1987).

The basic structure of their herds is the mother–daughter relationship but there may also be several mothers who have been together since birth or for a long time, with their daughters. Some of these may be grown up and have foals too. When supplies (of food for example) are short in feral equines, they will tend to disperse into smaller groups based on family relationships; when there is plenty, they will often congregate together in larger herds, several families together. The mares will live together and, given a choice, with a stallion. They are intolerant of strangers, mares or stallions, who might want to join with them, and will make life unpleasant for them if they can, but they tend to be more tolerant of young pre-pubertal males or females (even strange ones), who join them provided they are *not* fully attracting the stallion's attention – that is if an unknown filly joins when in season, she is not accepted into the group easily.

Male equines – stallions – are fundamental chauvinists: the adult males will not tolerate other adult males near the females they are with, and will do their utmost to get ride of them by chasing them, fighting and harassing them without cease until the other male either fights or goes away. The resident stallion will also chase both fillies and colts who are coming up to puberty and try to get rid of both although once the females become fully in season, his attitude changes, and he may try to court them. This behaviour interestingly appears in part to be an incest taboo. On our experimental stud we have now had four stallions who have behaved very unsocially towards both their sons and daughters once they are pubertal. We need more information on this. Most studies of feral horses have not continued long enough to trace the behaviour of the second generation fully.

The extra stallions tend to associate in bachelor groups. Here the males move around trying to obtain a harem by replacing a resident stallion, or find one or two mares or fillies without a stallion and stay with them. Some males will stay in the bachelor group for years, and it may be that some never manage to breed; we don't know enough about bachelor groups since in many feral populations, the young males not required for breeding are often removed or castrated. We do know that males are extremely interested in each other (just like male humans). They monitor each other's behaviour constantly and spend a large amount of time watching and interacting with each other, particularly playing rough 'horse play' games. Provided there are no mares near or in sight it is possible to keep groups of stallions together without serious fighting; in other words create a 'bachelor group'. It is easier to ensure the success of such a group if most of the stallions are young (1–5 years old). However unless

*A group of bachelor horses. The colt in the middle has its tail
withdrawn, indicating submission.*

The stallion on the left defaecates, watched by the mare.

Both turn to smell it.

*The stallion grazes and the interested mare is very aware of him –
note left ear position.*

*The stallion approaches to smell the mare's vulva. She stops, tail
wags, and pays attention to him – notice the ears.*

the stallions have had previous experience running with other horse groups (which is rare with domestic horses these days) the group will take some time to establish, as each horse must learn equine manners and how to relate to one another, the individual differences, and personalities and thus how to cope socially. We have had such bachelor groups running together on three occasions, varying in number from two to five stallions.

The normal grouping of horse society is one stallion with from two to around ten mares, depending on the resources of the area and the number of other competing stallions. There is much socialising in the groups, and this is by no means all aggressive. In fact the majority of the interactions between horses in such groups are affiliative: to cement bonds rather than to try to break them and split the group. The general idea that there is a 'boss' and a dominance hierarchy is also incorrect. Individuals have roles and these change with the situation; they show a large amount of individual differences: personality differences, and their relationships between each other are extremely complex. The more we study them the more we find! It is however quite easy, by ensuring that there are scarce resources and/or crowded conditions, to create situations where a type of 'dominance hierarchy' does emerge. This 'dominance hierarchy' however is generally the result of difficult conditions. It is *not* the way equines normally organise themselves. High levels of aggression and/or the need for appeasement and other behaviours which disperse the group are not the norm. If there is much aggression, then the conditions are not right for the horses. We must think about what we may have got wrong and put it right (see Kiley-Worthington 1987 for further details of the social organisations of horse society).

As we have already mentioned, equines are remarkably adaptable, and they are capable of living by themselves if they have to. But even equines who have been brought up alone, after weaning at least, will seek out and try to stay with other equines, even if their presence is not desired by the others, who may show this in no uncertain terms. Lifetime experiences can mould an individual's social desires to a point, but horses still remain social and prefer equine to non-equine company (unless they were brought up from birth by another species when they may have become 'mal-imprinted').

The sensible thing, therefore, as far as designing the best environment for them is to keep them in groups; but in groups where they can interact as they wish and develop their complex social life. Ideally, the groups should remain stable but if some horses leave and others come, the horses themselves must be allowed to integrate with the new members. The best way of doing this is to allow them plenty of space so that the strangers, unwelcome to start with, can initially withdraw and gradually integrate themselves as the existing group allows.

Once the group is integrated, however, equines do not necessarily need more space per individual than they do when kept in single stables. In the winter (or dry season in the tropics) they can have access to yards to escape bad weather, and reduce the over-use of grass.

The ideal group could be a group of from two to ten mares with a stallion and their foals, and youngsters, who remain with the group until the stallion starts to try to kick the 'youth' out. In this group all can have sex, be maternal and enjoy an integrated equine 'social world' with different ages and sexes. In this type of group relationships can be extremely mellow and relaxed, although there may well be the odd mare who is so in love with the stallion that she won't leave him alone!

One way of not having all the mares pregnant most of the time yet allowing them to have sex and associate with a stallion as they would in feral groups is to run a vasectomised stallion with them. This also allows, of course, more males to remain stallions – not be castrated. This is something we have been experimenting with at our farm over the last six years. One of the interesting consequences is that the mares appear to encourage sex and copulation from the stallion, and in some cases this has continued through the year. Interestingly enough it looks as if the mares are happy to have sex with him when they have been separated and returned and even when, according to their cycling they should not be in season. Whether they are having sex at other times than just when in season remains to be confirmed, but what is very clear is that sex is frequent and appears to be extremely important to both the stallion and the mares. After all why should it not be as important to them as it is to humans? Perhaps more so, if they are such emotional creatures.

Extra males can be left in bachelor groups even when entire but there are some problems here. For example the males must be young when they enter the group, and there must not be any females around or serious fighting between the stallions will result.

(3) *The equines should be in an appropriate physical habitat.* Equines evolved in the plains of central Europe and Africa as far as we can tell, and they have all the characteristics of being particularly well adapted to a plains environment. Their escape from predators is to run, not to stand and fight, and they are good at it. They have good, long sight, are suspicious of shadows and dark places, and unfamiliar things. They are primarily grass eaters and can graze very close and have evolved to cope with a high-fibre diet; they move considerable distances each day (30–40km) and can cover up to 80 km per day if they need to. They have very good eyesight and communicate primarily by vision (although other senses are also important); which is a sensible strategy in open plains. They have home ranges of which they learn the topography and features and they become extremely adept at finding their way around, avoiding the windy spots, picking the best grazing areas and so on as the seasons progress. All of these characteristics and skills are very suitable for an open plains life.

Therefore the type of environment they are likely to feel most 'at home' in is one where there is open space and views, where they can move freely at all times, where they have access to high-fibre food at all times, where they can run to escape if they need to, or to play or just for fun, where they can have sufficient changes in topography, weather, ecology, and challenges (equivalent of avoiding predators) to ensure they have enough to do and 'think about' – that is avoid 'boredom' – where they can make decisions themselves: to go into a building to avoid the blizzard, or to stand outside in it. They are competent decision makers otherwise they would not still be around for us to worry about – but would be extinct. It is therefore not helpful to equines to overprotect them, and take away all freedom of choice – 'for their good' as is so often stated – for example to shut them in or out, deck them with 'anti-fly' drapes, rugs, bandages and so on.

Many of these priorities can be achieved in the husbandry of our equines. There are some simple improvements that can be made easily when it is realised how important the environment is for the health and happiness of equines. For example, building a barn to house equines facing a white stone wall with no view is likely to be much less easy for them to adapt to than if the barn is placed so they have an open view and can move out into a field as they wish (even a small one) and have plenty of things to do, including work of one sort or another.

Keeping horses in single cages in enclosed barns (chapters 1 and 2), one of the modern developments in horse husbandry, may be of benefit to the grooms – as they do not get wet while moving between stables – but the enclosure, the restricted views, lack of possibilities for movement, inappropriate and restricted foods given, are as alien to the equine's natural habitat as it is possible to construct. However clean and sterilised it may be, it will be as bad or worse for the equine as the dingy, wet, isolated, mucky old stables such modern structures replace. In the latter at least the equine could look out. Yet it is the latter that is reported to the welfare organisations, the former applauded by the reporters!

(4) *The equine should be able to perform all the behaviour in his repertoire that does not cause suffering to others.* We cannot draw distinctions on what is more or less important for the equine to perform but this inevitably changes with time. For example, food can be considered an essential, whereas sex is considered a 'luxury'. But when the horse is not hungry, then sex may become very important – an essential. To give him the benefit of the doubt, we must assume that all his behaviour has a functional importance and therefore is important for him to perform – if we are really interested in his well-being. We therefore need to structure the environment so that behavioural restrictions are reduced.

(5) *The animal's* telos *must be catered for.* The *telos* of the animal/equine is the word used by Aristotle to describe the 'horseness of the horse' . . . he must be allowed to be a horse. But the question is, what does this mean? Are we right in the assumptions we have made about what it is to be a horse? What do we know now about this which might make us review our preconceived notions of what will benefit our equine?

In the first place, to understand what it is to be 'an equine', we must understand what he perceives, what he sees, smells, hears, tastes and feels. Is he like you or me? The first problem here is do you and I do this in the same way? We don't of course, we perceive things slightly differently because our eyes are slightly different, and we interpret what we see differently depending on our past experiences, our upbringing, our culture and so on. So it is more difficult to say anything meaningful about how an equine might do it. What we can do at least, is find out what his eyes, ears, nose, taste and tactile receptors can pick up. These are not *all* that different from ours but there are some important differences which have been discussed elsewhere (e.g. Kiley-Worthington 1987, Fraser 1968).

How the equine interprets the messages from his receptors is even more problematic. The best we can do at the moment is to look at the potential of his brain, its size, volume and structure, to tell us what might be possible. We can also examine *what* he can learn, how he communicates and how sophisticated this is (see chapter 8); whether there are any indicators that he is conscious of himself, or others' minds, whether he can think, plan, use symbols and so on, has needs and desires, makes decisions (chapter 7).

Is he all that different from we humans when it comes to cognitive skills? It is true he cannot design and send a man to the moon, but are we correct in assuming that all these other attributes are unique to man? These are the fundamental questions facing animal welfare today. If we wish to design the environment to fulfil his physical and social needs – and even we know a little about his emotional needs – we can do this. We just don't know enough about his 'cognitive skills' and their emotional interrelations. If they prove to be much more similar to humans than we previously thought, then indeed we will have to review our ideas and particularly our 'beliefs of convenience'. We will have to go further towards including equines in the 'bill of rights', . . . if we are seriously interested in equine welfare. We may decide not to be of course, if it were to mean giving similar consideration to equines as we do to humans.

This is an area where more research is needed. The truth, ironically, is that we know more about the cognitive skills and 'mind' of dolphins and apes than we do about the mind of the equine (see Bryne 1995, Shusterman 1988) even though they have lives in close association with humans for some 5,000 years and even though each horse lover may have their own opinions.

(6) *The equine is not only a representative of a species, he is also an individual, and his past experience and its effect on how to design the environment must be catered for.* To what extent can he adapt to quite different conditions as the result of his life-time experiences? It is clear that equines are very adaptable and can manage to do this to a considerable degree, but there are limits. For example, horses or donkeys that have been kept isolated since birth, thrust out with a group of their own kind may be highly traumatised but they should not have been raised in isolation.

Surely, the experiences during an equine's lifetime must be taken into account in designing the way he is kept and what he does, but that does not mean that we should not be able to design better environments in the next generation. For example, stereotypies (crib-biting, weaving, wind-sucking etc.) generalise and occur in a whole variety of situations once they are established. By changing the environment for that horse (usually by reducing his behavioural restrictions and giving him more of the options as shown above) when he is under 5-6 years old we may manage to eliminate the stereotypy completely. Most importantly though, there is *no reason why we should have any stereotypies in the next generation . . . we know enough about them to wipe them out in horses, if we want to, but it will mean changing our husbandry systems.*

Take another example: a pathologically disturbed stallion who has never, or rarely been allowed to court and copulate naturally with mares will act differently towards the mares when allowed to run with them. He may be extremely aggressive and may not be able to read normal equine messages accurately. If he is suddenly released with mares, both he and the mares may be badly injured. However, with careful educating, the majority of stallions and mares can relearn their approach to sex and develop courtship and mutual relationships. The important thing is *to be aware of the past experience of the animal, and re-educate and redesign the environment as appropriate.* In the next generation again *if we want to*, we can design horse breeding to allow the horses proper equine upbringing in groups, run stallions with mares, reduce drug use and veterinary manipulations, allow stallions and mares to court and mate as they have evolved to do.

Or should we continue to control and over-protect as in modern breeding procedures, even where the animal suffers as a result (much more frequently than just as a result of an accident)? The modern way is also expensive (although it does create jobs) and as we have seen, less efficient.

If then we re-design the equine's environment in the above-mentioned ways, and ensure that when we have done so we have got it right, and the equine shows no evidence of prolonged distress as a result of our management, then can we continue to work, ride, and use equines in the many ways we do with a clear conscience? Can we defend our right to do so; or are the 'animal liberationists' justified when they argue for no use of animals at all?

Provided that the work and play we do with our equines does not cause prolonged suffering, as we have defined it, and shows evidence of the equine and the human experiencing pleasure, then we can. We must ensure that we have fulfilled the equines, various needs, and thus will have acknowledged that they have certain rights. We do after all, all live on the earth, and all have evolved to do so, not in species isolation, but rather with a network of inter-relationships with each other and other species.

If humans are not to interact, live with, have to do intimately with other animals at all as some would argue (because they say, inevitably humans will change the world for the animal, and inevitably cause suffering), then there would be a state of *animal apartheid*. Animals, if they continue to exist at all, will become confined to 'animalistans' where humans go only occasionally and then behave in very particular ways. Such a development is taking place in some parts of the world, depending on local positions on conservation. Some Nature Reserves or National Parks practise a similar philosophy by disallowing a great many human activities and enjoyment (e.g. camping, swimming, riding, walking the dog, etc.). These reserves have of course important functions. However this does not mean that animals should not be elsewhere; that the whole of the rest of the world is to be reserved for humans: 'anthropocentricistans' it might be called! Surely animals and humans should interact, perhaps not everywhere, but at least in much of the world. Provided they are satisfying the criteria for 'ecologically sound' environments, why should the animals (or humans) not be there doing whatever it is they want to do, provided they are not causing suffering to others?

A better approach, more in line with the way much of the world actually works, would be to work out systems of living together to our mutual advantage: *symbiotically*, rather than *parasitically*.

Apart from this being the way evolution prepared us and all other species to live, there is another reason why it is important not only to preserve the species-interaction but to cultivate it and improve it. This is that life can be enriched for both participants, both human and equine (or other animal) as a result of exposure to each other and interacting together, working, playing, living together, provided it is done appropriately. If this is the case, then as most of us who have had to do with equines will know (and this is one of the main reasons why we have to do with them and keep them), by becoming more familiar with equines, our own lives can become enriched in many ways. It may be that as a result of our contact and interaction we pick up different approaches to the world, different possible solutions to problems, different ways of looking at things, and of assessing them. These can be exciting, enlightening, sometimes terrifying, but whatever else they are, they are enriching and give one glimpses of different worlds. An analogy can be made between getting to know and understand another human culture; it is exciting, stimulating, sometimes infuriating; but we go away enriched, with a greater understanding of other approaches to life which we can, if we wish, adopt into our own lives.

If one talks to anyone who has spent much of their life with other animals, particularly those who have studied them in depth, many will tell you stories of how this association has helped them with their life: their emotional, intellectual, social, or cognitive life. Think of how equines have helped you and your life. The important glimpse through this still opaque window to knowledge of equines, for me, is their enormous, quick ability to pick up signals of others' emotional states and act on them; the subtlety of their signals; their speed of learning; their profound aesthetic sense and style; their awareness of where they are and the whole world around them. They must find us humans very crass much of the time!

At the same time what do they, the equines, pick up from you and me? How, if at all are their lives enriched by us? One thing perhaps is the extra stimulation they receive from learning to co-operate with us in their training, by doing various different things, going different places, and by their willing participation they do appear to enjoy some of these experiences, if not all of the time. They continue energetically to take part in the activities we do with them, and, if they seriously don't want to participate, they always have the option not to and there is little one can do to make them without causing them considerable distress.

One example of an equine's participating in life to the full is a mare called Shiraz (whom we bred and is now twenty-five); she is still producing foals every now and then, teaching, working on the land, taking part in displays and shows and so on. Some ten years ago she was the heaviest horse we had and we were running a teaching and long-distance riding centre in the Hebrides. She used to have the heaviest people, and one day when a particularly large journalist got on, she lay down. I thought she must be ill, and the client had to get off and watch while I kept an eye on her. She stood very relaxed by the side of the school. She did not appear to be ill, so I changed riders around, and a light girl got on her. She lay down again. In these circumstances, where she was doing a lot of teaching (around two hours a day on average) it seemed reasonable to consider that if she had really had enough of giving lessons to lie down, whatever the weight of the rider, then we really ought to allow her a break, a holiday. For the rest of the season she did no more teaching, the following year she had a foal, and she has been teaching ever since, without lying down, but we are careful not to do more than around two lessons a week. There are plenty of other things she can do (working in the garden and on the farm, delivering and collecting shopping, fun rides and displays and so on).

Just as with humans, it is important to be reasonably sensitive to the animal's likes and dislikes; to try to motivate him/her and make life and work as pleasant as possible. Some will enjoy and excel at some things, some at others. They may have to do some of each (from time to time most of us have to do the washing-up, make the beds, clean the house – but not one person every day if they don't want to or dislike it). It is a question of working out how to ensure the work is done and that both human and equines are benefiting; a *symbiotic* relationship, not exploitative of either the equine or the human.

20

Equine environmental ethics

We have so far been considering the welfare of the individual, what to ponder, and how to measure when we have got it right or wrong for that individual. However, the world is not composed of individuals who are isolated from the environment; they are products of the environment and have effects on it, whether they be humans, horses, or Hondas. Thus, if we are seriously interested in the individual, inevitably we must be interested in the impact that individual has on the environment in order to ensure he and his offspring will be able to be supported within it. It is not only in others' interests but also in the individual's interests to consider the impact he and his activities have on the environment: the equine environmental impact and where the limits are to be placed: equine environmental ethics becomes a crucial part of equine welfare.

The study of ecology is primarily the study of the interrelations of species, how they support each other, fit together and develop an integrated living system which is always changing and dynamic, but can continue to sustain life. In order to do this the effect of each on the other is studied and understood so we can predict effects and problems and act accordingly. You, the horse owner interested primarily in your horse and hopefully getting on well with him, may feel that this is of little relevance to you and him; I shall try and convince you otherwise. For example, if there is a local outcry about the nuisance of all the horses on the roads, how it slows the traffic and is likely to cause accidents, how are you going to counteract this? It will certainly affect your and your horse's welfare if you can no longer use the piece of road outside your paddock which connects to the only two bridle paths in the neighbourhood. Perhaps the local village committee have voted to try and stop the spread of what has become known as 'horsiculture' on the outside of your city by vetoing planning applications for stables or sheds to be constructed; or, maybe they are closing the bridle path cum foot-path to horses because a child has been stepped on by a horse, and the ramblers do not want to walk through mud.

At another level, supposing there is no longer any soya bean meal available because Brazil has stopped exporting it to feed animals in Europe and is concentrating on growing food to feed its own population? This would dramatically affect the price of compounded foods for your horse: and you can no longer afford it. What can you do?

Another example, supposing they have banned hunting in the Dartmoor National Park where you live, not because of the problems of animal welfare, but just because of the traffic jams and accidents the horse boxes and hunt supporters have caused. Or say, 'The European Horse Society' have brought in a legislation to make it compulsory that everyone who owns or keeps a horse has to have a licence or the horse will be removed and euthanased, but there are only a limited number of licences to be distributed in each neighbourhood . . . you have not been given one.

Or, you are a Mexican peasant and rely on your donkey to cultivate the land for your food and the small income you have, but the local committee have decided to ban the grazing of donkeys on the village common and the rubbish heap where your donkey has gained most of his food, because a group of United States environmental activists and public health visitors have visited and told the village elders that they would have a prize (which will improve their image and create further investment and jobs in the locality) if they did this and allowed the wild flowers to flower on the common . . .

None of these are idle or far-fetched examples that will not happen. They have happened, or very similar events have happened, in various parts of the world already. To be angry, to resort to violence, or even just to accept these legislations and changes without examination, debate and an effort at understanding will achieve little or nothing for either yourself or your horse. The first step is to be aware of the environmental effects that you and your horse create and how this may affect other people and animals is increasingly important, and a responsibility of every human today as the problems become increasingly acute. It is becoming more and more necessary to work out ways of keeping your donkey or horse while not adversely affecting others of any species anywhere, not just in your immediate neighbourhood. If in the future we want to continue to be free to have our equines and do what we and they like we must consider all the effects that it will have on the environment.

At the moment, there is still remarkably little legislation concerning the environmental impact of keeping other species, but as the human and horse population rises and consumerism increases, inevitably there will be more and more conflicts of interest. These can be understood and catered for, but again it needs much rethinking in terms of management and often attitudes.

For the environment of our equines to be ecologically acceptable, we must not only think of the effect on other people or animals locally, but also the global implications (in the above example, where does the food come from that you feed your horse, and what are the environmental implications of its production?). Where do the materials for building the stables come from, and what is the environmental effect of their production and transportation? What about all the energy used in the maintainance of your horse, the electric equipment: water heaters, clippers, vacuums etc., the tractors levelling the school, and making the hay (if you make any). Can we go on using energy at an ever increasing level indefinitely without affecting many aspects of the environment? The horsebox that is used to take your horse to an event, the roads, and fuel it uses and the materials it has used in its construction, all have to be produced somewhere.

The particular irony when thinking about horses and their environmental impact is that they were originally kept in order to do all these sorts of jobs, for their energy and strength! There is nothing more absurd than being stuck in the traffic jam being created by horseboxes attending an endurance riding competition, and here there is a fleet of cars as well that are compulsory if a horse is to compete! The horses come to ride 50 miles or so, but are often driven 200 to 300 miles! What about being jammed behind an enormous vehicle taking horses to a 'horse-ploughing competition' or 'driving event'? Here the motorised vehicle carries the vehicle and the 'engine' to pull it which the roads were made for in the first place! This is not to say that we should not transport equines around, but it is necessary to consider the impact and try to reduce it in one way or another. For example, you can ride or drive your horse to some of the events that are near. You can share your box/trailer with others (something many horse owners rich enough to have such a conveyance are remarkably loathe to do!) and don't take unnecessary vehicles.

The keeping of your horse or donkey in the way that you do must not endanger the survival of other species in the habitat by, for example, transferring disease, or creating a nuisance of one sort of another, not only by blocking the roads, but also by polluting rivers with the run off from the muck heap, the smells and flies perhaps near a large centre of humans. They must not chase cows or kill lambs who are in the same fields, or denude the grassland. None of this means that horses should not be kept in any environment, it just means that the consequences on the environment and others must be considered and catered for, so the horses outside the housing estate, instead of being bearers of disease, flies, and smells to the inhabitants become a source of delight and pleasure, enriching the lives of the inhabitants.

There are ways in which this can be done. Firstly we need to think of how to integrate horses with agriculture. At present they are a blot on the fields of most farmers because (1) most horse owners do not look after their grass appropriately, and when grazed exclusively by horses there are problems, and (2) farmers and horse-keepers believe that there is nothing that can be done about this. Equines inevitably reduce the production of their fields, they say, and in addition they cannot mix with other stock. This is untrue, horses can and do mix well with all other stock provided this is done sensibly and the animals are not pathological as a result of confinement or isolation. In the wild, grazing species are often to be found together and gain in various ways from this association.

If the equine owner has some land, then the easiest way to try to develop environmentally sound environments for your equines is as far as possible to develop a *self-sustaining system*. This is where you buy in very little, and keep the nutrients recycling so that the land can grow more again. Recycling the muck (instead of selling it off) will grow more grass and some of this can be cut for hay or horshage for the winter or dry season. The horse can help with all these tasks too, so instead of going to competitions all the time, or using time to 'get him fit' and then rushing off to work to earn money to pay a contractor to move the muck, to buy and bring the hay from miles away, you can do it yourself with him, working together in such a way (e.g. taking the muck out and harrowing it around the field, making the hay and bringing it in from the field) is fun and also educational for horse and human, whatever breed. You learn much more about him, and how to educate him to put up with strange and different things, which pays off when you are out and about doing other things.

The advice given to horse owners about their grassland is often to pick up all the muck (usually with a tractor collecting them all, and hours of work!) because of the worms. If the animals are being wormed regularly, then all this does is take away the nutrients from the grass so less grows next year; there is no evidence that horses living on such pasture need worming less. You can put on fertiliser, but this has disadvantages, it is expensive, it is soluble and quickly runs off and away, often polluting water ways, it does not give humus to the soil to encourage the decomposers, and kills off the clover which is palatable to horses, fixes nitrogen and increases growth. So the system with inappropriate management, becomes more and more reliant on fertiliser, or it becomes less and less productive. The management of grass organically is reasonably well worked out now, and it works for horses, as well as other livestock (see Kiley-Worthington 1993, and Soil Association Organic Standards).

It is important to think where the food you buy comes from and how it is produced, not only from the point of view of the health of your horse, but also the health of others and the whole environment. Horses fed on organically produced food and fodder will have much less unacceptable environmental impact than those not.

One of the most important aspects of reducing the negative impact of equines in the community is to encourage their positive integration with other humans. Efforts can be made to exploit the cultural interest in horses. They are part of our cultural heritage; count, for example the number of advertisements you see using horses as a symbol of beauty, freedom and strength, or as forepieces or covers of books (see Animal Liberation, Singer 1976, see also Barclay 1980, for further discussion of the horse in human culture).

By encouraging others to have to do with the equines that may live near them, and have some enriching experiences from them, a step towards inter-specific toleration and even enjoyment can be made. In fact riding schools on the edge of cities often do this anyway by providing some work to do for school children and young adults to allow them to be in and around the stables. More could be done here, and new ideas and practices need to be developed (see chapter 17).

Another area that stable owners, like farmers, are often rather blind to is the aesthetic considerations of the design and building of their stables and indoor schools. The problem here seems often to arise from the cultural belief that a 'good stable' is one which shows the dominant hand of man everywhere. No plant must grow where it has not been planted and organised by humans, every fence must be straight, and often dominate the landscape by being painted white, the buildings must be large, and obvious so that they can be seen from miles around, with high clock towers often with no function other than bearing the clock, with white painted paddock railings, large walls, and so on. Often such premises can be easily designed to fit better into the landscape without changing their function: for example the planting of trees around, creepers up walls and on roofs, allowing rough areas and not mowing every blade of grass. There are many debates around the subject of urban and rural architecture, but it is very important at least to consider the aesthetics of what you are doing, whether you have your pony in someone's allotment, your race horse is in Newmarket or you own several thousands of acres on which your hunters are kept. It is not money, it is motivation and thought that make the world go round, and can improve things.

Finally, when thinking about the wild equines, there are environmental, as well as ethological (behavioural) concerns about when and where they should be captured, transported and kept in captivity. Again there is no reason why this should not be to the advantage of both the individual and the world as a whole, but the questions must be clearly thought out and the answers defended properly.

If these criteria are seriously considered, discussed and thought about by each individual, then we should be able to keep and enjoy our horses unrestricted: keeping them as a symbol of freedom, and beauty for the future. If we don't, legislation will catch up on us all and restrict our contact and life with horses more and more (e.g. you must not ride your horse in this and that place, you must wear particular clothes, you must not graze your horse here and there, you must not live with your horse ...). There are many areas in which improvements must be made both by the horse owners, and those who are not. The continual existence and expansion of bridleways is one area that is being worked on hard by a dedicated minority to allow safe riding off the ever increasing traffic-ridden roads. One linking system that would cost very little, and could be invaluable in the future is to encourage councils to have a bridle, cum foot, cum cycle path fenced off along the edge of new major roads, including motor ways. This would link bridle/foot and cycle routes countrywide, and would enable many more people to enjoy the glorious living world away from the cities, and consequently help conserve it all.

Working together with different groups of people with different interests is by no means difficult. I remember when the gypsies, the motor bikers and we, the horse riders, amicably shared an old quarry in the chalk in Sussex ... until the local prim councillors decided they did not like gypsies and motor bikes and dug ditches across the access. Why? No one else wanted to use it. Could we not be slightly less convinced of our own worth and a little more tolerant in the future?

21

The individual horse owner today

We have dealt with many of the arguments concerning the welfare of equines in relation to the different ways in which they live, with and without humans. But the question remains, how can anyone who is involved with equines cater better for the equines' needs in the real world in which we live? The stud owner, the race-horse trainer, the riding-stable proprieter, the single-horse owner, the peasant who relies on his donkey to help him grow his food, the wildlife manager who has to cope with problems of one sort and another with the zebras in the park for which he is responsible, and many others, will consider, having read this book, that all of this is all very well, but how can it apply in the *real world*? How can the individual alone even approach these ways of ensuring the 'happy life' of the equine?

I am very well aware that it can all look too 'airy fairy', too extreme, too idealistic to be possible. I don't think this is in fact the case. It is possible to follow methods I have outlined relatively easily and cheaply. We, at our farm, have managed to achieve most of them for all our competition, breeding and working horses. It is also possible for zoos, wildlife sanctuaries and circuses to achieve these aims, if they wish, and there are different examples gradually emerging how this can be done. Finally, it is possible in developing countries.

Difficulties may arise where you have to keep your horse in someone else's stables who has different ideas, or you may be controlled by people sending their horses to you to train or race, and the owners want things to be the same way as always. Most commonly, however, you will be a student or a working pupil, as I was, who has nothing to lose and has not yet been filled up with the cultural beliefs concerning equine husbandry and training and, if you are intelligent, you may start to question and argue with: How can it improve here, in this stable, with this manager? How can we start?

To help in this quest, this final chapter outlines some steps, which are not too difficult to begin with, and which will indeed improve the equines' environments a little at least. Then perhaps when you have seen that it is possible and has many advantages, both from the equines' and the humans' point of view, you will be able to see how, and take the next step and, thus, perhaps, finally most of us will be able to achieve the aims outlined, and consequently will be living symbiotically with our equines, to our mutual benefit. This may in turn become the current dogma; so eventually this too will need questioning and revising, thinking about and assessing . . . if we are seriously interested in our equines' welfare. We are still a long way off, but here are some helpful steps along this road, starting with the amateur horse owner, and progressing to the various professionals who are involved with horses.

The single horse/pony owner

In the so-called 'developed' countries, the single equine owner is certainly in the majority. Often such a person does not own land, or stables, she or he may live a very urban life in a city and either the equine will be kept in the city in a livery stable of some sort, or will be used (partly at least) as a reason for the owner, who earns his/her living in the city, to get out of it, and visit the country and ride his/her horse. Such a person is of course reliant on the manager and grooms where her horse is kept to ensure the well being of her horse. She may not even see him every day. What can she do about improving her equine's life? Firstly before she sends her horse to a stable to live, she must visit many and assess them. Even if the people are nice, are the equines happy?

There are a series of questions which can be asked of the staff, and observations that do not require a great deal of skill which can be made by the potential customer. It is important that the equine owner does not become so embroiled in the human environment in the stable, its order and organisation and its technical facilities that she places them at a higher priority than those of the equine. This is very easy to do, and since the stables want the custom, they will be as charming as can be, and display their technical wares to great effect. The important concerns for the equine owner interested in ensuring an improved environment for her horse are as follows:

(1) Will the staff discuss the issues of welfare and traditional practices with you? Or are they convinced they are doing the best they can, and are right, quote a few famous names of winning riders of one sort or another to convince you how 'right' they are? If you see a horse eating wood, biting his box, weaving, crib-biting, or being aggressive and you ask them about him, do they say 'yes, he is much better since he has been here, but he has done it all his life, and it is nothing to do with us'? or do they discuss how, why when and although he may have done this before he came to them, the progress and the possible approaches to reducing or preventing such behaviour?

(2) For how long are the animals confined to their stables? Can they be out for even a few hours each day in a group, in a field or even in a yard or the indoor school or some other small enclosure? Do they have many subdivisions of their land and have rules about how one horse cannot go with another, how mares must be separate from geldings and so on? If they do, what justification do they have for these 'rules'? Are they not making more problems for themselves? Discuss this with them.

(3) Do the stables have solid partitions between the horses, or can they touch each other over a bar (the best arrangement), or over half a partition? Do they have top stable doors, and if they do do they shut them any time, and why? Do they have anti-weaving bars over the stable doors; if so ask them why. This is a good indicator of a 'modern' high-tech, high-income, low-thought type of stable.

(4) How long have the other livery horses been at the stables? If there is a quick turn over, you can be fairly sure that all is not well for the horses or the people are difficult to get on with. This does not lead to happy humans or horses.

(5) Is there a view from the stable, or can the horse only look out on to a yard that is not going to be busy all the time,

or even worse around an enclosed large and expensive barn where he is shut in a cage? The better the view, the better the situation. A view of a road, or the approach lane is preferable. Even better is the long-range view of hills, woodland, water, to add interest to the environment. Exposure to the changing light, the weather, any action around the yard is better than just a view of the horses opposite in an enclosed encampment.

(6) What are the horses fed? Do they have *ad lib* access to hay/horshage or straw, some high-fibre diet? If not why not? Just because they eat too much will not make a satisfactory argument. How much concentrate food are they fed and how is this worked out in relation to the work they do? Be very careful about yards that feed very fancy foods with high supplement levels; they are more likely to have feeding problems than those who feed nothing but hay/horshage and grass.

(7) Do the horses have some exercise out of the stable every day, even though the owner may not be able to be there? If so how long, how fast, what sort, who rides, and so on.

(8) Make sure you meet the groom who will be responsible for your horse and see how she handles the other horses, what sort of background she has, and what her interests really are. Is she going to be able to develop a good emotional relationship with your horse (as she is the one who will probably see most of him), or is it just a job? Are you happy about how she handles the other horses, and if not can you discuss this with her, and will she be likely to help you and your horse and listen to your ideas and discuss them?

(9) What efforts are the stables making to improve the environment for their horses? If they have any young horses or foals, are they isolating them, and training them with 'discipline and dominance', or are they trying to think about how to make things better for the next generation, and raising the foals with other horses as well as their mothers, keeping the young horses occupied and socially and physically involved so that they, at least, will be able to be easily kept in groups rather than single stables when they are mature? Could they do more in this direction and if you discuss this, what response do you get?

If they mention the horses are 'just too valuable to take risks with', I would not send my horse there, it means they do not, and do not want to think about welfare problems.

(10) Where is the food produced that is fed to the horses? What about the material used for the buildings, the fences, and all the equipment they have; would the horses be better off having more time learning and working and the staff spending less time on general housekeeping including mucking out and sweeping all the time?

(11) Do they have a tractor and harrows to flatten the school, or are they thinking about using at least one of the horses for this? If not why not? Do they do any other different and interesting things with their horses, for example liberty, harness work and driving, camps, or long holidays with their horses and clients in beautiful places; do they have good maps of bridleways and access nearby indicating that riding out and about is encouraged?

(12) Make sure you look at every aspect of the stables. Who is the farrier, and how does he work, how does he handle the horses, has he ever used a twitch? The same with the veterinarian; is he an up-market vet with every conceivable piece of equipment or not? How does he handle the horses, and what is the history of illness and lameness in the stables? How old are the horses, are there any who are over twenty and still working? Longevity can be an important indicator of past welfare, for both humans and horses.

(13) How are the horses bedded and, if daily mucked out, how much straw is used; could they be kept on deep litter beds more comfortably, which would reduce labour and dust? Are they rugged all the time in the winter, and clipped? Is this really necessary, or is it just to keep the horses clean? If so is it desirable?

(14) Think of your visit to the stable as if it were a potential school for your child. Would you be happy with all aspects, and particularly will your horse be happy with all aspects? Unlike your child, you cannot ask him, but you can make a fair number of important assessments.

The important thing to bear in mind is not to be diverted by the impressive rosettes on the wall, the enormous new indoor school, the special equipment for soaking the hay, the whiteness of the fences and the geraniums in straight lines around the immaculately swept yard. If you are interested in the welfare of your horse, those that may cater best for his emotional physical and cognitive needs, and cause fewer environmental problems may well be the old timber stables on Mr Smith's farm, which at least will have an equal chance of competing with the 'high tech professional competitive yard'.

In the market place it is important to realise that the single horse owner who will have to keep her horse at a livery stable can have very considerable effects on change, just by not accepting the conditions as they are, and taking her horse and her money elsewhere.

It is also important not to be diverted from looking at all these things because there is a famous horse, rider, or teacher there. Many famous riders and teachers have not considered these factors carefully but just believe they know it because they have been successful at teaching riding or winning rosettes. The famous horse may have a different story to tell.

The owner of several horses

The horse owner who has a few horses of her own to ride and compete has to think also of improvements that can be made in all aspects of the horses' life, and these same considerations can be made initially. It is important to consider seriously whether or not your top competing horse should really not be able to run around in the fields with others at least part of the time, and of course, the more he can do this, the less chance there is of serious injury to him, as he will be less excited and more socially integrated. Another useful way of looking at it, is that 'there is very rarely any such thing as an accident' when it comes to horses or riding. If the horse shies and is hit by a car, it is the fault of whoever is in charge of the horse and rider . . . it should have been realised that this might happen and therefore they would not have been in that place at that time.

This does not mean that no risk should ever be taken, as of course this would destroy much of the point of riding and competing, but it does mean that one has to think very carefully about what the risks might be and whether or not they should be taken, and if so how to minimise them by training horse and riders appropriately. It also means that there is no way that whoever is in the decision-making position can slough off the consequences 'Oh, it was just an unfortunate accident'; no it was not, it was bad management, 'I should have known this might happen in that situation, and either decided to take the risk, or change the chances.' But this is hard; it is much easier to blame the horse, the rider, the weather, the day, the driver, the world. This is important because it makes the horse owner consider cause and effect and not just blame the horse's past experience, or his sex, his breed, and so on if, for example he is kicked by another. In consequence, it ensures that one has to think about how to integrate and allow the equines to perform more of their behaviour that does not cause suffering to others. It can reduce over-protection and consequently reduce risk in the future and allow the equines to develop and use their innate adaptability. This results in an easier, cheaper, worry-free life for humans and horses. Where there is a will, there is a way to improve the equines' environment. . . But there has to be the will.

The stud owner

Stud owners can consider and change many of the criteria given above, if they are interested. By definition they have stallions and mares and breed. Although the older stallions who have never been allowed to run with mares or other horses since weaning may have become pathological and not be able easily to integrate in equine social groups, this is not the case for the next generation of youngsters if they are raised properly. It is vital, if things are to change in the area of breeding – and this is one of the most questionable practices in modern horse husbandry – that the young stallions become behaviourally normal horses. They do not have to be turned into abnormal over-excited psychopaths because of their experiences of isolation, forbidden to run with the mares for fear of injury to both. If the breeding stallions are to be properly tested in performance then they must be ridden and work in one way or another. In addition this helps them become more adaptable, be handled more and generally require much less fuss and fear.

They can get used to being out in fields with mares, being in yards with them, and also leaving them and being alone for some periods without problems, if they are properly brought up and handled. It is the stud owner's duty if he is going to breed equines to ensure that he/she knows how to do this and is confident and happy with it. It is not acceptable to keep stallions of any breed isolated in stables or single small paddocks, nor to 'rape' mares with physical and pharmacological restraints.

If the stud owner believes for *whatever reason* that he cannot do this with the next generation of his mares and stallions, then he should give it up and go and become a shop keeper or a train driver. There are however, many preconceived notions to be dropped, and much learning to be done about handling and how to raise animals so that natural breeding becomes economically possible.

The race-horse trainer

The trainer has even more pressure put on him, often by his clients (whom he charges a great deal), to 'over protect' the horses in his care. Again, it is quite possible to introduce many small improvements in racing stables. People will say that the animals must not be in a field as they will rush around and may break a leg out there just galloping around. The reason why they might break or strain a leg galloping around in a field is because they have never learnt how to gallop about a field safely, when to slow up, how to turn safely, and so on, which feral horses for example gradually become more and more skilled at as they mature. It is like assuming that a child even of several years old who has been kept in almost a strait jacket and never been allowed to learn all the complex movements required to feed himself, when given food for the first time, will manage to get most of it in his mouth. He will not; it will be splattered everywhere, the spoon dropped and food all over his face and in his eyes. It requires a whole host of complex neuro-muscular interactions to coordinate complex movements, which take time to learn, whether it be manipulating four legs at speed on rough ground while galloping around fields avoiding hedges, fences and other horses, or manipulating a spoon and attempting to put food in your mouth. Going out for a gallop on a prepared surface carrying a weight once a day is not likely to ensure these skills are well learnt, and injury avoided. The race horse needs to learn these skills, and for them to become automatic responses, so that he will be able to go to more races, last longer and even cope in races with difficult unforeseen situations.

The farrier

A farrier not only needs to be able to shoe a horse well, and keep up to date on the new ideas and trends, and look at the mechanics of the foot, but he also and most importantly needs to be able to handle horses well, and not teach them that the farrier is someone to be anxious about. It is curious how little time, if any, is spent in the training of farriers on teaching about handling and how to do it well. Again, it is just meant to be something you 'pick up' and you are either good at or bad at. The result of this is that the horse is normally blamed for not behaving well with the farrier when it is the result of bad past or present experiences. It should not be necessary for a farrier who knows his job to use a twitch. The time and appropriate skills must be spent on ensuring that the horse is not difficult. It is surprising how many problems farriers have with horses, and how frequently a twitch is used by some farriers. When we lent our 25-year-old Welsh Mountain pony to a riding school, we discovered later that the farrier who came there would only shoe her using a twitch! She had been shod before by us for twenty years without any problem and was 12.2hh!

The veterinarian

Sometimes the veterinarian can also have problems with handling animals. Again, it is not in the interests of the horse's welfare for the veterinarian to rely on pharmacological or physical restraint. If she or he takes the time and is prepared to learn, there is no need for the horse to become suspicious of the veterinarian as soon as he walks into the yard. It often happens, but proper handling (which cannot be taught in a couple of afternoons in veterinary school!) can make a very important improvement to the vet's abilities. The veterinarian and the farrier should understand all aspects of their job; some do of course, but the handling of the animals is an aspect that received too little attention in the training of both veterinarians and farriers at present.

The veterinarian is looked to for advice on almost anything to do with animals, and consequently he can have a large amount of power and much influence on the changes to improve the husbandry of equines at least. Consequently it is extremely important that the veterinary fraternity begin to consider these serious concerns with horse management, read, think and keep up-to-date with the thinking on animal welfare issues and developments in husbandry.

One very important aspect which needs to be understood are signs of distress in stabled horses, and pointing out to the clients what these are and how they can be reduced. Another seriously important aspect is horse breeding and the involvement of the veterinary profession with the highly debatable aspects of horse welfare. There is no doubt that if the veterinary profession were to back up and advise on the types of improvements suggested here, many horse owners would make changes.

The working donkey owner

Owners in developing countries can have the opposite problem. Far from over-protecting and structuring their animals' lives too much, they are more likely to have insufficient food, materials and too much work for their donkeys. Unfortunately, those trying to help from organisations from the West may be giving advice which makes things impossible for the owner to keep a donkey. Although the advisers from the West are becoming more aware of the limits of what they can suggest should be done (how can you feed your donkey 2 lbs of hard food a day when you do not even have enough for your family?), nevertheless they are often too entrenched into their way of doing things to be able to help very much in very poor societies. For example, the advice for the donkey owner to build a separate stable for his donkey and concrete the floor is far too expensive a proposition and also generally quite unnecessary. The supplying of elaborate harness as a pattern to be followed is also unrealistic, and again unnecessary; a simpler harness made cheaply with local materials and skills can often be better.

The concerned donkey owner will make every effort to feed his animal enough, not to over-work him and try and have disease treated but even here there are often ideas that can be useful about how better to do this cheaply and fit the donkeys into the societies and environments in which they have to live.

Wildlife, circuses, zoos

Finally, the circus or zoo owner and wildlife manager may have some equines of one sort or another: Przevalski horses, onagers, wild asses, or zebras. The circus owner can follow the improvements suggested in the list, and he should be able to keep his equines (originally domestic or wild) as species groups. The central key for these institutions is that they must bear in mind, as must all who have horses, how to design the environment better so that the animal can perform all the behaviour in his repertoire, which does not cause suffering to others, and how to keep him so that he is in an environment which is ecologically acceptable.

Here again, handling of the captive animals is crucial in order to treat them for disease or routine care – such as feet trimming – without trauma or the risks of drug immobilisers. It is surprising how few zoos are able to trim their captive-born zebras' feet. This is largely because there is rarely anyone in zoos who is experienced or trained at handling, which is neither taught nor studied.

The wildlife manager has extra problems involved with over-stocking, what to do with the extra animals, should they be killed for meat (a frequently suggested solution, because it can feed people and raise money for conservation). There is considerable outrage in the United States for example concerning the killing of feral horses whose increasing population is threatening other species and changing the conservation areas in which they live.

If horses should not be killed for meat, what about zebras? They are also equines and we have evidence to suggest that they are as cognitively advanced as horses. But if populations are not going to be 'culled' as it is politely put, is there an alternative? There are many current debates on these issues, but we will have to leave it here. The important thing is to point out that if one is interested in equine welfare, and working out successful solutions, approaching the subject either with preconceived notions (whether they come from personally held opinions and emotive ideas, or a dogma of any type that has been learnt) is not an adequate approach and is highly unlikely to solve these complex issues in rational ways that will allow present and future generations to benefit.

I have suggested some approaches that might be useful in thinking and discussing these issues, and have discussed many current practices which seriously need reassessing from the horse's point of view. However, although there are some general rules concerning our approach to this subject, which I have also pointed out, nevertheless, assessments of the 'right' thing to do will vary depending on individual circumstances. The important thing is that these are thought about and discussed and if there is a conflict of interests between humans and equines, this should be assessed and considered rather than falling back on traditional ideas and practices, including assuming humans' interests will always trump those of equines.

Select bibliography

Note: there are many more scientific publications to which I am indebted. These are just a selection for the interested reader.

Adams, E. M. (1960) *Ethical naturalism and the modern world view*, Chapel Hill, University of N. Carolina Press

Aristotle 320BC, *Basic works*, ed. R. McKeon, Random House NY

Attfield, R. (1983) *The ethics of environmental concern*, Blackwell, Oxford

Barclay H. (1980) *The role of the horse in man's culture*, J. A. Allen, London

Barry E., Landjerit, P. and Walter, R. (1991) Shock and vibration during the hoof impact on different track surfaces, *Equine Exercise Physiology*, 3, 97–106.

Brambell report on the welfare of intensively farmed livestock (1965) HMSO, London

Bristol, J. (1982) Breeding behaviour of a stallion at pasture with twenty mares in synchronised oestrus, *J. Reprod. Fert.*, Suppl. 32, 71–7

Bryne, R. (1995) *The thinking ape*, Oxford University Press.

Burger, U. (1986) *The way to perfect horsemanship*, J. A. Allen, London

Candland, D. K. (1993) *Feral children and clever animals*, Oxford University Press

Capra, F. (1982) *The turning point. Science, society, and the rising culture*, Flamingo Press, London

Chambers (1993) Recognition of pain and distress in horses, British Veterinary Roadshow, *Pain in practice*, BVA, Plymouth Medical Centre

Clarke, S. (1978) The rights of wild things, *Inquiry* 22, 1–2, 171–88

Darwin, C. (1859) *The origin of species*, reprinted 1950 Watts and Co., London

(1868) *The emotions in men and animals*, Watts and Co., London.

Decarpentry, General (1971) *Academic equitation*, J. A. Allen, London

Dent, A. and Goodall, D. M. (1962 and 1988) *A history of British native ponies*, J. A. Allen, London

Descartes (1596–1650) The principles of philosophy in F. Alquie (ed.), *Oeuvres philosophiques de Descartes*, Paris, Liarnier Frères, 1973

309

DeGrazia D. (1996) Taking animals seriously, *Mental life and mental status*, Cambridge University Press.

Dickinson, A. (1980) *Contemporary animal learning theory*, Cambridge University Press

Duncan, P. (1980) Time budgets of Camargue horses, *Behav.*, 72, 26–47

EEC Recommendations, Farm Animal Welfare, 1992

Fielding, D. and R. A. Pearson (1991) *Donkeys, mules and horses in tropical agricultural development*, CTVM, University of Edinburgh

Fillis, J. (1902) *Breaking and riding*, reprinted J. A. Allen, 1969, London

Fiske, J. C. (1979) *How horses learn*, Stephen Green, Vermont

Fraser, A. F. (1968) *Reproductive behaviour in ungulates*, Academic Press, London

(1992) *Horse behaviour*, C.A.B. Wallington, UK

Frey, R. G. (1983) *Rights, killing and suffering*, Blackwell, Oxford

Gallup, C. G., Boren, J. C., Gregg, J. G. and Wallnau, L. B. (1977) A mirror for the mind of man, or will the chimpanzee create an identity crisis for *Homo sapiens? J. Human Evol.*, 6, 311

Gardner, K. A. and B. (1969) Teaching sign language to a chimpanzee, *Science* 165, 664–72

Griffin, D. R. (1992) *Animal minds*, University of Chicago Press, Chicago

Harrison, R. (1964) *Animal machines*, Stuart, London

Hartley Edwards, E. (1963) *Saddlery*, J. A. Allen, London

Hayes, H. (1968) (6th edn) *Stable management and exercise*, J. A. Allen, London

Heird, J. C., Cokey, C. E. and Cogan, D. C. (1986) Repeatability and comparison of two maze tests to measure learning ability in horses, *Applied Animal Behav. Sci.*, 16, 103–19

Herrenstein, R., Loveland, D. and Cable, P. (1976) *Natural concepts in pigeons. J. Expt. Psychol. Animal Behaviour, Proceedings*, 2, 285–302

Hickman, J. (1977) *Farriery*, J. A. Allen, London

Hockett, C. F. (1958) *A course in modern linguistics*, MacMillan, New York

Humphrey, N. (1984) *Consciousness regained*, Oxford University Press

Hutt, C. and Hutt, S. J. (1965) The effects of environmental complexity on stereotype behaviour of children, *Animal Behaviour*, 13, 1–4

Huxley, J. (1969) *Proc. Royal Society on Ritualisation*

Iggo (1984) *Pain in animals*, University Federation of Animal Welfare, Potters Bar

Jolly, A. (1966) Lemur social behaviour and primate intelligence, *Science*, 153 (3735), 501–6

Kant, Immanuel (1963) 'Duties to animals and spirits', *Lectures on Ethics*, trans. Infield Harper and Row, NY

Kaselle, M. and P. Hannay (1995) *Touching horses*, J. A. Allen, London

Kellog, N. A. and L. A. (1993) *The ape and the child*, McGraw Hill, New York

Kennedy, J. S. (1992) *The new anthropomorphism*, Cambridge University Press

Kiley-Worthington, M. (1977) *The behavioural problems of farm animals*, Oriel Press, Stockton

(1983) Stereotypes in horses, *Equine Practice* 5, 34–40

(1987) *The behaviour of horses in relation to management and training*, J. A. Allen, London

(1990a) Preventative equine psychology, *J. Equine Medicine*, 10, 15–25

(1990b) *Animals in circuses and zoos. Chiron's world?* Little Eco-Farm Publ. Basildon

(1993) *Eco-agriculture, food first farming*, Souvenir Press, London

(in prep.) Competition and cooperation in horse society

Kiley-Worthington, M. and Randle, H. (in prep). Learning and teaching in four species of higher mammals; and language comprehension

(1996) Handling animals, Eco Research and Education Centre, Occasional publ. 12a and b

Kline, P. (1991) *Intelligence. The psychometic view*, Routledge, London

Lawrence, M. (1980) *Flyers and stayers*, Harrap, Boston

Lea, S. E. G. and M. Kiley-Worthington (1996) Can animals think? In *Unsolved mysteries of the mind*, ed. V. Bruce, chap.7

Leahy, M. P. T. (1991) *Against liberation. Putting animals in perspective*, Routledge

Leakey, R. E. (1993) Elephants today and tomorrow, *Wildlife conservation.*

Lorenz, K. (1975) *Year of the Greylag Goose*. Eyre Mathews, London

MacDonald, D. W. and P. J. Johnson (1996) The impact of sport hunting: a case study', in *The exploitation of mammals*, ed. V. J. Taylor and N. Dunstone, Chapman Hall, London, pp. 160–207

MacPhail, E. M. (1987) The comparative psychology of intelligence, *Brain and Behav. Sci.*, 10, 4

MAFF (1990) Codes of practice for dairy cattle, pigs and hens, HMSO, London

Mason, G. J. (1979) 'Beast and man' stereotypies, a critical review, *Animal Behaviour*, 41, 1015–37

Masson, J. and S. M. McCarthy (1994) *When elephants weep. The emotional lives of animals*, Jonathan Cape, London

McGreevy P. O. (1994) Management factors associated with stereotypie and redirected behaviour in the thoroughbred horse, *Equivet.*

Midgley, M. (1979) *Beast and man*, Methuen University Paperback

(1983) *Animals and why they matter*, University Press Georgia, Athens

(1992) *Science as salvation – a modern myth and its meaning*, Routledge

Miller, R.W. (1989) Imprint training in the newborn foal, *Large Animal Veterinarian*, 44.4.21

(1975) *Western horse behaviour and training*, Dolphin Books, Montana

Morel, Mina and C. G. Davis (1993) *Equine reproductive physiology, breeding and stud management*, Farming Press Books, Ipswich

Moss, C. (1988) *Elephant memories*, Elm Tree, London

Nagel, T. (1974) What is it like to be a bat? *Philosophical Review*, 83, 2–14

Pearce, J. 1987 *Introduction to animal cognition*, Hove, UK

Pearce, Persson, Lindholm and Jeffcott (1991) *Equine exercise physiology*, 3, ICEEP Pubs. Davis Calif.

Povenelli D. J., Nelson, K. E. and Boysen, S. T. (1990) *Inferences about guessing and knowing by chimpanzees*, J. Comparative Psychology, 109, 203–10

Premack, D. (1986) *Gavagai*, MIT, Mass.

Price, H. and Fisher, R. (1989) *Shoeing for performance*, Crowood Press, Marlborough

Proceedings of the Conference on Working Equines, Rabat, Morocco, 1994

Randle, H. (1994) *Adoption and personality in cattle*, PhD thesis, Exeter

Rendle, C.C. (1994) Improved harness and implement design for draught equines, International Symposium for Working Equines

Reagan, T. (1982) *All that dwell therein*, University of California Press, Berkeley, Calif.

Rees, L. (1984) *The horse's mind*, Jonathan Cape

Roberts, Monty (1992) *The man who listens to horses*, Hutchinson, London

Robinson, H. E. (1987) (ed.), *Current therapy in equine medicine*, W. P. Saunders, Philadelphia

Rollin, B. E. (1981) *Animal rights and human morality*, Buffalo NY, Prometheus

  (1989) *The unheaded cry. Animal consciousness; animal pain and science*, Oxford University Press

Rossdale, P. D. (1983) *The horse from conception to maturity*, J. A. Allen, London

  (1989) Study of wastage among racehorses, 1982–7, *Vet. Rec.*, 116, 66–9

Sainsbury, D. W. B. (1984) *Horse management*, ed. J. Hickman, Academic Press

Salt, H. S. (1980) *Animal's rights considered in relation to social progress*, Centaur Press Ltd

Selye, H. (1950) *The physiology and pathology of stress*, Acta Inc. New York

Sewell, A. (1877) *Black Beauty*

Shustermann, R. J. (1988) Animal language research: Marine mammals re-enter the controversy, *Intelligence and evolutionary biology*, ed. H. J. Jerison and I. Jerison, New York: Springer

Singer, P. (1976) *Animal Liberation*, J. Cape, London

Skinner, B. F. (1938) *The Behaviour of Organisms*, New York, Appleton-Century

Spooner, G. (1979) *The handbook of showing,*. J. A. Allen, London

Stamp-Dawkins, M. (1980) *Animal suffering. The science of animal welfare*, Chapman and Hall

  (1988) Behavioural deprivation. A central problem in animal welfare, *Applied Animal Behaviour Science*, 20, 200–25

Swift, S. 1985 *Centred riding*, The Kingwood Press

Svendsen, D. (1986) (ed). *The professional handbook of the donkey*, The Donkey Sanctuary, Sidmouth, Devon

Tellington Jones, L. (1992) *The Tellington touch*, Cloudcraft Books

Tembrock, G. (1968) Communication in land mammals, *Animal communication*, ed. Sebeok, T. A., University of Indiana Press, Indiana

Thorpe, W. H. (1956) *Learning and instinct in animals*, Methuen, London

University Federation of Animal Welfare (1990) *Animal training*, Potters Bar

Voltaire (1974) *Dictionnaire philosophique*

Wanless, M. (1987) *Ride with your mind*, Methuen, London

Welsh, B. L. (1964) Psychological response to the mean level of environmental stimulation – a theory of environmental integration, *Medical aspects of stress in a military climate*, US Govt Print, Washington

Welsh, D. A. (1973) *The life of Sable Islands wild horses*, PhD thesis, Dalhousie, USA

Whitmore, S. (1990) Athletic horse training, *Animal training* (UFAW), Potters Bar

Wildlife Conservation (1993) *Appointment at the end of the world. African elephants*

Wittgenstein, L. (1953) *Philosophical investigations*, Basil Blackwell

Wright, M. (1983) *The thinking horseman*. Wright Armidale

(1989) *The Jeffrey method of horse handling*, Wright, Armidale

Xenophon (350BC) *The art of horsemanship* (trans. M. H. Morgan, 1969), J. A. Allen, London

Index